Viking-Age War Fleets

Morten Ravn

Viking-Age War Fleets

Shipbuilding, resource management
and maritime warfare in 11th-century Denmark

Roskilde 2016

Morten Ravn
Viking-Age War Fleets
Shipbuilding, resource management and maritime warfare in 11ᵗʰ-century Denmark

This book is Volume 4 in the series *Maritime Culture of the North*
Externally peer-reviewed

Published by the Viking Ship Museum in Roskilde

Series editor: Morten Ravn
Book design and DTP: Carl-H.K. Zakrisson & Tod Alan Spoerl
Picture editor: Narayana Press
Translation: James Manley

Print by Clausen Grafisk, Odense
Printed on acid-free paper

ISSN 1904-3139
ISBN 978-87-85180-72-8

Published with support from:
Dronning Margrethes & Prins Henriks Fond
Frimodt-Heineke Fonden
Konsul George Jorck og Hustru Emma Jorck's Fond
Landsdommer V. Gieses legat

Viking Ship Museum books can be ordered online via:
www.vikingshipmuseum.dk or www.oxbowbooks.com

Front cover: Five Skuldelev reconstructions under sail. From left to right: *Helge Ask* (Skuldelev 5 reconstruction), *Roar Ege* (Skuldelev 3 reconstruction), *The Sea Stallion from Glendalough* (Skuldelev 2 reconstruction), *Ottar* (Skuldelev 1 reconstruction) & *Kraka Fyr* (Skuldelev 6 reconstruction). Photo: Erwan Crouan, Viking Ship Museum in Roskilde.

Contents

Preface • 9

I. INTRODUCTION • 11

Realms of Danish kings in the 11th century • 11
Ship finds • 13
Definitions • 14
   Specialised ship types • 15

II. SHIPBUILDING • 17

Experimental archaeology • 17
Concepts and methods • 20
Shipbuilding technology and regionally delimited shipbuilding practices • 21
From appropriate resource to ship component • 24
Wooden parts • 25
   Felling, clearing and cutting • 26
   Cleaving, dressing and transport • 26
   Building site • 28
   Building sequence • 29
   Maintenance • 31
Tar and paint • 31
   Wood tar production • 32
Iron parts • 35
   Charcoal • 35
   Smelting • 36
   Cleaning • 37
   Forging • 37
Sails • 42
   Sails made of wool • 42
   Quality • 44
   Spinning • 45
   The warp-weighted loom • 45

Sewing sails · 46

Coating · 47

Sails made of linen · 47

Farming · 47

Preparation · 48

Rigging · 48

Ropes of lime bast · 50

Ropes of skin, hide and hair · 50

Making withies · 53

Caulking · 53

Caulking materials · 53

III. RESOURCES · 55

Tree species used in late Viking-Age shipbuilding, and their qualities · 55

Alder · 55

Ash · 55

Beech · 56

Hazel · 56

Maple · 56

Oak · 56

Pine · 57

Woods used for treenails · 57

Woods used for wedges · 59

Qualities of raw materials · 59

Resources required for shipbuilding · 62

Natural resources · 62

Small cargo ship · 63

Medium-sized cargo ship · 64

Large cargo ship · 66

Medium-sized personnel carrier · 68

Large personnel carrier · 70

Human resources · 71

Small cargo ship · 72

Medium-sized cargo ship · 73

Large cargo ship · 74

Medium-sized personnel carrier · 75

Large personnel carrier · 76

Building and maintaining war fleets · 78

IV. WOODLAND MANAGEMENT · 85

The woodlands of late Viking-Age Denmark · 85
Woodland composition and structure · 88
Dominant tree species · 90
Areas with appropriate wood resources for shipbuilding · 91
Shipbuilding sites · 91
Snekke place-names and areas with appropriate wood resources · 93
Regulated woodland management · 97

V. MARITIME WARFARE · 99

Fleet size · 100
 Operating fleets · 100
Fleet composition · 101
 The fleet from Fribrødre Å · 102
 Written evidence of ship types involved in military operations · 102
The ships at sea · 104
Ship and crew · 107
Amphibious warfare · 109
Battles at sea · 110
Logistical aspects · 113

VI. CONCLUSIONS · 115

Summary · 118

Resumé på dansk · 121

Terminology · 124

References · 133

Catalogue: 11th-century ship finds in Danish waters · 146

Appendix 1: Analyses of 11th-century ship finds in Danish waters · 152

Appendix 2: Speed analysis of the Skuldelev 5 reconstruction *Helge Ask* · 161

This book is dedicated to my friends and teachers
Anton Englert and Morten Gøthche

Preface

During the work on this book several individuals and institutions have provided considerable help and support. The book is a revised version of my PhD dissertation, which was funded by the Faculty of the Humanities at Copenhagen University. Throughout the PhD process I had expert guidance from my main supervisor Henriette Lyngstrøm, for which I am grateful. In addition I thank my secondary supervisors, Anton Englert and Carsten Jahnke, for their great help and support. The constructive criticism from the critical opponents to the dissertation, Kristina Winther-Jacobsen, Lars Jørgensen and Björn Varenius, have been of great importance in ensuring that the path from dissertation to book has succeeded.

For more than 30 years the Viking Ship Museum in Roskilde has conducted experimental archaeological research projects, resulting in an immense amount of empirical data and much new insight into and understanding of maritime aspects of the societies of the North in the past. I am deeply grateful for being granted access to this unique empirical data and for the numerous inspiring discussions with the researchers at the Viking Ship Museum.

It has been important to the genesis of the book to be able to discuss theses and issues in various research networks, for which I thank members of the following networks: Baltic Maritime Archaeological PhD Research Network, Faro-Arm Rhino Archaeology Users Group, Forskningsforum på Vikingeskibsmuseet i Roskilde, Kontaktudvalget for maritim historie- og samfundsforskning, Dansk Militærhistorisk Kommission, Forbundet Kysten, Maritimhistorisk fagforum, Middelaldercirklen ved Københavns Universitet, Smedens Rum, Strukturel dialektik og Vikingetid på SAXO på Københavns Universitet.

Good advice has come from David Bloch, Stefan Brink, Ole Crumlin-Pedersen († 2011), Michael Gelting, Kjeld Hillingsø, Poul Holm, Thomas Højrup, Birgitta Hårdh, Kristina Jennbert, Gunnar Lind, Johannes Møllgaard, Niels Lund, Peter Friis Møller, Olaf Olsen († 2015), Bodil Petersson and Anders Ödman.

I further thank the following professional colleagues for generously sharing their knowledge: Erik Andersen, Vibeke Bischoff, Niels Bonde, Aoife Daly, Peder Dam, Tinna Damgård-Sørensen, Bo Fritzbøger, Jon Godal, Morten Gøthche, Ivan Conrad Hansen, Thomas Heebøl-Holm, Eldar Heide, Anette Hjelm Petersen, Jeppe E. Høst, Morten Johansen, Ole T. Kastholm, Jakob Kieffer-Olsen, Claus Malmros, Niels A. Møller, Nigel Nayling, Tom Nicolajsen, Hans P.J. Nielsen, Søren Nielsen, Anna Nørgård, Terje Planke, Jørgen Poulsen, Lasse Sonne, Eva Andersson Strand, Gry Søbye, Anne C. Sørensen, Tríona Sørensen, Jacob Tullberg and Astrid Tummuscheit.

I thank Rikke Johansen, Werner Karrasch and Lis Pinholt for assistance with the choice of illustrations. Patiently and carefully James Manley has translated the manuscript of the book from Danish into English. However, any linguistic errors and shortcomings are exclusively my own responsibility.

This publication would not have been possible without the generous financial support of the foundations and grants *Dronning Margrethes & Prins Henriks Fond, Frimodt-Heineke Fonden, Konsul George Jorck og Hustru Emma Jorck's Fond* and *Landsdommer V. Gieses legat.*

Finally, the support of my family has been of great importance to the writing of this book.

Morten Ravn
Roskilde, June 2016

I. Introduction

The great importance of the ship to the Scandinavian society of the Viking Age has been pointed out by many researchers. The ship was a symbol of status and was given as a gift among the most powerful men in society.[1] At an ideological level the many ship-settings as well as ship and boat burials suggest that the ship also played an important role in the religion and cosmology of the era;[2] and finally the ship was a precondition for the extensive sea transport of the time, including military transport, which is the subject of this book.

The ship is the central requirement for maritime warfare. For that reason an analysis of the processes related to the building of ships has been chosen as the point of departure for this investigation of the war fleets in 11th-century Denmark. Many people and crafts were involved in the building of the ships, and it is therefore necessary to analyse a wide range of craft knowledge and skills, and how manpower and production were maintained and developed further. For such analyses it is not sufficient to use traditional archaeological and written sources. Instead, the starting point is experimental archaeology. With this we can argue plausibly how much raw material and how much manpower had to be procured to build and maintain the war fleets, and on this basis subsequently discuss how magnates and kings managed the appropriate resources for shipbuilding. Finally the widely varied operational war fleets of the 11th century and maritime warfare of the time are analysed, which will lead to the book's concluding synthesis of central features of the war fleets in Late Viking-Age Denmark.

Realms of Danish kings in the 11th century

In the Old English version of *Orosius* there are two travel accounts by seafarers: Ohthere[3] and Wulfstan.[4] Each describes in its own unique way political, ideological and economic aspects of the Scandinavian societies at the end of the 9th century, as well as the seamanship of the time. In these accounts we read that the Danish, Norwegian and Swedish territories[5] were defined, separate geographical entities,[6] which makes it likely that Denmark, Norway and Sweden were also viewed as three different, separate territories a good 100 years later – that is, in the 11th century.[7]

The western Baltic created a boundary that was both political and cultural, as is evident from the written sources, the place-names and the archaeological material.[8] Another boundary was defined by the Great Belt, where in the Early Viking Age there were considerable differences in building customs and the choice of pottery types in western and eastern Denmark respectively. In the later part of the Viking Age, the differences in construction customs were less marked, but the differences in the choice of pottery types still applied.[9] In this connection it should be remarked that in the Old English version of *Orosius* there is a distinction between North Danes and South Danes, more or less matching the boundary suggested by the archaeological material.[10] Other archaeological finds and the inscriptions on the rune stones show on the other hand that in the Viking Age West and East Denmark were closely connected, so much so that they can be viewed as parts of the same kingdom.[11] The archaeological material from the southwestern

1. Bill *et al.* 1997: 65.
2. Schjødt 1995: 20–24; Wamers 1995: 156–158; Sørensen 2001: 118–120; Bill & Daly 2012: 818–822.
3. Ohthere, see Bately 2007: 40–50.
4. Wulfstan, see Bately 2009: 14–28.
5. Land areas that were defined on the basis of the dominant population group's ethnicity, see Lund 1991.
6. Bately 2007: 40–50; Bately 2009: 14–28.
7. Bolton 2009: 241–288.
8. Sindbæk 2008: 68.
9. Stilke 2001: 34; Sindbæk 2008: 69.
10. Bately 2007: 43.
11. Sindbæk 2008: 69.

part of Jutland shows clear relations with the Frisian area, which may explain why in the High Middle Ages Saxo Grammaticus[12] called the western part of South Jutland 'Little Frisia'.[13]

The Danish kingdom of the 11th century is described by some researchers as comprising Jutland, Funen and the adjoining islands, Zealand and its adjoining islands, Bornholm as well as Scania, Halland and Blekinge,[14] while other researchers do not count Bornholm and Blekinge as part of the realms of the Danish kings until some way into the 12th century.[15]

Furthermore, Charlotte Fabech, Frederik Svanberg and Søren M. Sindbæk have argued that eastern Scania was only gradually, during the course of the 11th century, integrated into the Danish kingdom, which may mean that the area only became part of the realms of the Danish kings in the 12th century.[16] Finally, Timothy Bolton has argued that only parts of western Scania – centred around Lund – were under the control of the Danish kings in the 11th and 12th centuries.[17]

Halland's connection with the Danish realms in the 11th century is also controversial. Are the indications of a different political, ideological and economic structure evidence that the actors in Halland organised themselves in a fundamentally different way – independently of the interventions of a Danish king?[18] As for ritual practices Halland was more closely linked with Vendsyssel in northern Jutland. In these respects Vendsyssel and Halland have more in common with each other than both areas have with their respective landward neighbours. However, Søren Sindbæk interprets these shared ritual traditions across the water as ideological links and therefore does not necessarily see the resemblances as an expression of political ties between the two areas.[19] In the part of Ohthere's account that deals with his voyage from Kaupang[20] to Hedeby[21] the land on the port side is described as part of Denmark.[22] Ohthere was probably referring to what is now Halland and the northwestern part of Scania.[23] If this area was part of the territory of the Danish king

late in the 9th century, it is possible that it was similarly part of the realms of the Danish king in the 11th century. However, it is also possible that the land areas that were viewed as subject to the Danish king late in the 9th century were not necessarily so in the 11th century. The determining factors for the extent of the territories of the Viking Age kings were the king's relationship with the magnates and the domains of the magnates themselves.[24] If the king could achieve a relationship of mutual recognition with many magnates, the geographical extent and resource area of the realm was large. If on the other hand only a few magnates recognised a king, the geographical extent and resource area of the territory were smaller.

The relationship of Viken[25] and Bohuslän[26] with the realms of the Danish kings is the subject of ongoing discussion.[27] On the basis of the existing source material it is likely that Harald Bluetooth and perhaps also other Danish kings of the 9th and 10th centuries enjoyed periodical sovereignty over the Viken area, while the rest of what was viewed as Norway at the end of the 10th century was periodically under the sovereignty of Harald Bluetooth, but ruled by the Norwegian Earls of Lade.[28] In this connection it can be mentioned that the large Jelling Stone does not claim that Harald won *all of* Norway – perhaps it was only the Viken area?[29]

The relations between the powerful men of Bohuslän and the Danish kings and magnates were probably close late in the 9th century,[30] and these links seem to have continued during the next two centuries.[31] From Bohuslän, large parts of the sea and land traffic in the north-south direction could be controlled, so the area was of great importance to the Scandinavian powers of the Viking Age.[32] Over the course of the 11th century, the area was alternately under the supremacy of Danish or Norwegian kings, but in practice was ruled by the magnates of the area.[33]

Judging from the written sources of the Viking Age which mention Denmark, Norway and Sweden, it is thus highly likely that in the

12. Saxo Grammaticus: Preface [Friis-Jensen & Zeeberg 2005: 79].
13. *Fresia minor.*
14. Christensen 1938: 2; Randsborg 1980: 2–3; Stenholm 1986: 25–35; Ingesman 1999: 13–14.
15. Roesdahl 1999: 20; Brink 2007; Lihammer 2007: 122–125 & 261–263; Sindbæk 2008: 75; Gelting 2012: 107; Ingvardsson 2013.
16. Fabech 1993: 222; Svanberg 2003: 148; Sindbæk 2008: 72.
17. Bolton 2009: 229–240.
18. Nicklasson 2001: 161–166; Lihammer 2007: 236–237.
19. Sindbæk 2008: 74.
20. *Sciringes healh.*
21. *Æt Hæpum.*
22. *On þæt bæcbord Denamearc.*
23. Brink 2007: 71.
24. Steuer 2006; Gelting 2007: 77.
25. In present-day Norway.
26. In present-day Sweden.
27. Forseth 2003: 66; Brink 2007: 71; Skre 2007: 468–469; Bill & Daly 2012: 818–822; Pedersen 2014.
28. Ladejarlene, see Bill & Daly 2012: 818–822; Roesdahl *et al.* 2014: 461.
29. Lecture, 8 November 2012 by Professor Michael H. Gelting at Aberdeen University, Centre for Scandinavian Studies.
30. Brink 2007: 71.
31. Forseth 2003: 66.
32. Sigurðsson 2003: 21–22 & 25–26.
33. Howard 2003: 8; Sigurðsson 2003: 7–9, 18–19 & 25–26.

Fig. 1. The primary geographical area of investigation. Map: The author, Viking Ship Museum in Roskilde.

34. Pedersen 2014: 316.
35. Jensen 2004: 244–250.
36. Lecture, 8 November 2012 by Professor Michael H. Gelting at Aberdeen University, Centre for Scandinavian Studies.
37. See chapter III.

cally demarcated kingdom. Secondly, the Danevirke may have functioned as a customs boundary in relation to the regional or supra-regional transport of goods.[36] A combination of these possibilities is equally likely.

To sum up, the primary geographical area of investigation in this book is hereby defined as Jutland down to the Danevirke and Hedeby/Haithabu, Funen and its adjacent islands, Zealand and its related islands, as well as western Scania and Halland (fig. 1). These areas are considered more or less constant regions within the various realms of the 11th-century Danish kings, and as the demarcated area also gave ship construction a generally uniform resource basis,[37] the area of investigation as defined above is thus considered appropriate. Ship finds in the waters between and around the regions mentioned are also considered part of the book's primary empirical material (fig. 1).

However, the recognition of the geographical extent of the Danish realm was determined by the King's dynamic relations with magnates, and the fact that scholarship today cannot unambiguously establish the boundaries of the realm means that the area investigated may be expanded or contracted if this is deemed relevant.

Ship finds

59 ship finds, distributed over eight sites, are analysed. One of the ship finds, the Äskekärr 1 ship, was found outside the area of investigation, but the ship has been tree-ring determined to have been built with timber from trees felled in the vicinity of the Götä river valley, which means that the ship may have been built inside the book's primary area of investigation. The Äskekärr 1 ship has therefore also been included as part of the empirical material of the investigation (fig. 2). Reference may be made to appendix 1 for a detailed analysis of the datings and provenances of the ship finds, their dimensions and ship types, as well as the hydrostatic data and propulsion methods of the ships.

11th century, Viken and Bohuslän were mainly viewed as part of the domains of the Norwegian kings. Since this book deals with the Danish kingdom in the 11th century, Viken and Bohuslän fall outside the primary area of investigation. However, since both Viken and Bohuslän were intermittently part of the Danish kings' domains in the period under investigation,[34] the general discussions will consider these areas where appropriate.

Towards the south, the Danevirke and the semicircular ramparts of Haithabu/Hedeby are often perceived as defining a boundary between the Danish kingdom, the Holy Roman Empire and the Slavic societies.[35] However, it is doubtful whether the geographical placing of these rampart systems reflects true territorial borders in the 11th century. Firstly, it is probable that, as mentioned above, the determining factor for the realms of the Late Viking Age was the King's relations with the magnates and their domains, rather than a territorial, more stati-

Fig. 2. The sites with analysed ship finds. Map: The author, Viking Ship Museum in Roskilde.

Definitions

The vessel type designations used require some explanation. The vessel types have been separated out by virtue of their constructional dimensions and details, as well as their primary suitability for transport. For the latter to make sense we must assume that the design of the vessels was related to their function, and that this form-function relationship can be interpreted and understood by researchers today.

Another matter that should be clarified is the dimensions associated with the choices of terms. A boat designates a vessel that is less than

10 m long, while a small ship is defined as between 10 and 14 m long; a medium-sized ship as 14–20 m long, and finally a large ship as over 20 m long (fig. 3). It is in this context less important whether the vessel is a cargo ship or a personnel carrier.

Length (in metres)	Type
< 10	Boat
10-14	Small ship
14-20	Medium-sized ship
> 20	Large ship

Fig. 3. Designations based on vessel length. Partly based on Klassen 2010: 65. Table: The author, Viking Ship Museum in Roskilde.

I. Introduction

Fig. 4. Artist's impression of a large personnel carrier and a large cargo ship. The design of the personnel carrier made it suitable for fast transport of a large crew. Likewise, the design of the cargo ship made it suitable for carrying large volumes of cargo. Drawing: Sune Villum-Nielsen.

38. Logboats, expandend boats and different plank-built boats and ships.
39. Exemplified by the Klåstad ship and the Äskekärr 1 ship.
40. Englert 2015: 58–60.
41. Sørensen 2001: 55–56.
42. Crumlin-Pedersen 2010: 82–83.
43. Andersen & Andersen [1989] 2007: 353.
44. Englert 2000; Crumlin-Pedersen & Olsen 2002: 306–330; Crumlin-Pedersen 2010: 107–112.
45. Crumlin-Pedersen & Olsen 2002: 306–330; Englert 2004: 111–119; Andersen & Andersen [1989] 2007: 353; Bill 2010: 22–25.
46. Englert 2015: 51–54.
47. Englert 2004: 113.
48. Crumlin-Pedersen 1999a: 11–20; Sørensen 2001: 55–56; Crumlin-Pedersen & Olsen 2002: 306–330; Andersen & Andersen [1989] 2007: 354; Bill 2010: 22–25; Crumlin-Pedersen 2010: 71–94.
49. Crumlin-Pedersen 1999a: 11–20; Crumlin-Pedersen & Olsen 2002: 306–330.
50. Jesch 2001: 122–123.
51. *Herskip.*
52. *Kaupskip*
53. Mentioned in the Norse literature of the High Middle Ages and the Anglo-Saxon Chronicle.

Specialised ship types

The vessel finds of the late Viking Age demonstrate that different vessel types were built by the boatbuilders of the time.[38] Within the various vessel types, there is also evidence of a specialisation in terms of there design. Ships were built to transport either a cargo or a crew (fig. 4). The specialised cargo ship was introduced, judging from the ship finds,[39] around the year 1000,[40] while the long, narrow ship that was particularly suited to the transportation of a large crew was gradually developed throughout the 10th century[41] only to be specialised further in the proceeding century.[42]

Trading ships[43] and cargo ships[44] are both used in the research literature to designate the shorter and broader ships (fig. 4). This ship type has been defined by maritime archaeology researchers as less than five times as long as it is wide and primarily or exclusively propelled by sails. In addition, the ship type is so designed that relatively large volumes of cargo can be transported.[45]

With the designation trading ship the vessel type is ascribed a function that is presumably only situationally determined. However, the cargo that was carried on board the ship type did not necessarily have any relation to trade. Therefore, cargo ship is a more unproblematic designation. This refers exclusively to what is indicated by the design of the ship – that is, it was especially suitable for transporting a cargo. As such, cargo ship is used in the following as a designation for the vessel type (fig. 5).

With the specialised cargo ships it became possible to transport large volumes of goods, and if the great hold capacity of the cargo ships was used rationally, the sea transport of one's own or others' trading goods would probably have been a particularly lucrative occupation.[46] The cargo ships could moreover be used to transport large amounts of military equipment and supplies,[47] which would probably have made the logistical challenges on longer raids and wars of conquest more manageable.

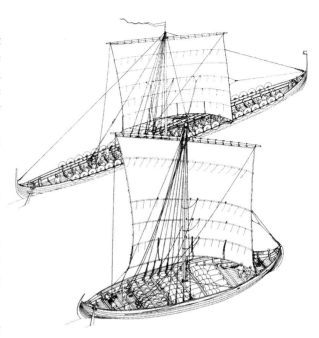

In the published literature, the long, narrow ships (fig. 4) are designated warships, personnel carriers and longships.[48] Today, the ship type are characterised as at least five times longer than they are broad, and propelled by both oars and sails. There was room for many rowers on board, and the shallow draught of the ships (fig. 4) and the hull form made it possible to run the ships aground in shallow water or on a beach and land one's crew.[49]

When the designation warship is used, it is assumed that the long, narrow ships were mainly used in warfare, which is contestable, since their use as civil transport vessels for a magnate or a king and his retinue is also likely. In the latter function, the long, narrow ships should be viewed more as prestige ships which played a considerable role in the domains of the itinerant kings and magnates.

On rune stones and in skaldic poetry, the designations warship and trading ship do not often appear. In the few cases where they do it is always function-related. The function of the ships is for example described[50] in terms of being a warship[51] or a trading ship.[52] This means that neither warship nor trading ship was a

	Cargo ship	*Personnel carrier*
Especially suited for transport of	Cargo	Personnel
Morphological description	Less than five times as long as the maximum beam of the vessel	More than five times as long as the maximum beam of the vessel

Fig. 5. Designations based on the transport suitability of the vessel. Table: The author, Viking Ship Museum in Roskilde.

term reserved for specific vessel types in the Late Viking Age and the High Middle Ages, but were concepts used to describe their situational-functional use.

A longship may on the one hand mean an historically[53] known ship type, while on the other, a construction made by maritime archaeological researchers with a view to analysing constructional and technical details. In its present-day meaning, the longship is defined in terms of the relationship between the length and width of the vessel. A particular value[54] defines whether a ship find is to be designated as a longship or as something else.[55] The problem with the designation longship is that it should

be explicit whether one is referring to the historical or present-day usage of the term.[56]

The designation personnel carrier is defined by current scholarship and refers to the primary transport suitability of the ship type – that is, for the transportation of a crew.[57] This designation is not unproblematic either, since goods and other cargo may also be transported in the long, narrow vessels. However, it is clear that a large crew is a precondition of the functionality of the ship, and the vessel type's design – long, narrow and without a cargo hold – also indicates that the ship was primarily built to carry people rather than cargo. To sum up, personnel carrier is viewed as the most suitable designation and is used in the following as a present-day name for the vessel type (fig. 5).

54. At least five times longer than the width.
55. Jesch 2001: 122–123; Crumlin-Pedersen 2010: 90–91.
56. Ravn 2015a.
57. Crumlin-Pedersen 1999a: 11–20.

II. Shipbuilding

1. Crumlin-Pedersen &
Olsen 2002: 134.
2. Sands 1997; Høgseth 2013.
3. Crumlin-Pedersen &
Olsen 2002: 97–304.

Fig. 6. The ship finds whose construction or repair area is probably within the investigated area. Based on data from the catalogue and the analysis in appendix 1. Table: The author, Viking Ship Museum in Roskilde.

This chapter exclusively analyses the ship finds which, based on tree-ring or building technological analysis, can be determined as having been built or repaired within the primary area of investigation (fig. 6). It should be noted that tree-ring based determinations of provenance suggest an area within which the tree resources used were felled. This means that the area for the construction and repair of a boat or ship can only be suggested if one can assume that the wood resources used were felled in the same area the vessel was built or repaired in.[1]

Experimental archaeology

In order to examine the techniques, methods and conceptual understanding that the construction of a Viking-Age boat or ship involved, the preserved vessel parts must be documented in detail. Traces of the use of tools and construction-related markings may suggest the techniques that were used during the building process,[2] while other traces suggest how and in what order the various vessel parts were positioned and installed in the vessel.[3] Futhermore,

Vessel finds	Construction area	Repair area
Fotevik 1	Building technique and applied tree species make it probable that the ship was built in southern Scandinavia	
Fotevik 2	Building technique and applied tree species make it probable that the ship was built in southern Scandinavia	
Fotevik 3	Building technique and applied tree species make it probable that the ship was built in southern Scandinavia	
Fotevik 4	Building technique and applied tree species make it probable that the ship was built in southern Scandinavia	
Fotevik 5	Building technique and applied tree species make it probable that the ship was built in southern Scandinavia	
Fribrødre Å	Timbers most likely from both Denmark, Scania, Schleswig-Holstein, the southern Baltic Sea region, the southern and western regions of Norway and the western Sweden	
Hedeby 1	Dendro: Schleswig-Holstein	
Hedeby 2	Dendro: Schleswig-Holstein (not the pine planking)	
Hedeby 3	Dendro: Schleswig-Holstein	
Roskilde 3	Dendro: Jutland or Schleswig-Holstein	
Skuldelev 1		Dendro: Second phase: Eastern Denmark, Scania, Småland or West Gothland (Västergötland)
Skuldelev 3	Dendro: Western Denmark	
Skuldelev 5	Dendro: Jutland, Schleswig-Holstein or Scania	
Äskekärr 1	Dendro: Göta Älv valley	

experimental archaeological analyses – aimed at reconstructing the shipbuilding process – can indicate both technical and methodological choices. Reconstructing the building sequence also makes it possible to elucidate the conceptual understanding behind the building of the boat or ship.[4]

The first experiments with making and using reconstructed archaeological objects as an analogy to a body of archaeological material go back to the 19th century. Experiments with flint-knapping were predominant,[5] while analogies to the production of other prehistoric artefacts were sought by way of ethnographic studies. From the end of the 1870s until the beginning of the 1880s, Niels Frederik Bernhard Sehested[6] conducted a number of experiments with the production and use of polished flint axes. After Sehested's death his accounts of the experiments were published.[7] His experiments are mentioned, for example, in the publication by Henrik Olaus Zinck,[8] *Nordisk Arkæologi, Stenalderstudier II*.[9] Zinck's reference to Sehested's[10] and his own[11] flint-knapping experiments are evidence that the experimental approach to the understanding of the societies of the past was accepted as a scientific method at the end of the 19th and the beginning of the 20th century. Another example of this is Sophus Müller's theoretical and methodological reflections on the use of analogies in archaeological research.[12]

In the course of the first half of the 20th century, the professional archaeological recognition of the experimental approach as a suitable analogical method of acquiring scientific knowledge declined.[13] It is notable that the corn-harvesting experiments conducted in the 1930s with reconstructed flint and bronze sickles, Jens Kusk Jensen's downscaled prehistoric and historic ship-find reconstruction models in the 1930s, and the Draved experiments in the 1950s, which tried to conduct slash-and-burn agriculture with reconstructed Neolithic tools, techniques and methods, did not involve the participation of archaeologists.[14]

A more amenable attitude to the experimental methods can be observed in connection

Fig. 7. Experimental iron extraction conducted at A/S Varde Staalværk in 1963. Left: Olfert Voss and right: Robert Thomsen. Photo: The Robert Thomsen Archive at Varde Museum.

with the processual currents in archaeology from the 1960s onwards. The positivist scientific ideal on which processual archaeology was based aspired to stringency and logical inferences were made on the basis of direct sensory data.[15] Processual archaeology wanted to include human action in archaeological research so that the field would not be restricted to just investigating cultures and typology.[16] The role of the actor and the processual action connected with production became focus areas in archaeological research, but it was still the registration of metric and morphological data that was the point of departure for the analyses.[17] In connection with the increased focus on the role of the actor in production, and on production in general, there arose a gradual recognition that the experimental approach offered potential for new knowledge. From the 1960s on, professional archaeologists became participants in experiments. The collaboration between the archaeologist Olfert Voss and the civil engineer Robert Thomsen, which was begun as early as the start of the 1960s, is an example of one such interdisciplinary collaboration (fig. 7).[18] Through the 1970s and onward, experimental archaeology was developed methodologically and theoretically with a starting point in the scientific ideals of processual archaeology.[19]

4. Ravn *et al.* 2011: 233.
5. Johnson 1978: 337–359.
6. Lived 1813–1882.
7. Sehested 1884.
8. Lived 1833–1902.
9. Zinck 1893: 70.
10. Zinck 1893: 70.
11. Zinck 1893: 68.
12. Müller 1884: 183–203.
13. Rasmussen 2007: 13.
14. Steensberg 1979; Thirslund & Poulsen 1986: 108–113; Rasmussen 2007: 13.
15. Flor 2005: 62–63.
16. Binford 1962.
17. Hill & Gunn 1977.
18. Lyngstrøm 2012.
19. Reynolds 1977; Coles 1979.

Controlled approach	Contextual approach
Seek to isolate as many variables as possible	Does not intend to isolate as many variable as possible
Provides measurable and repeatable results	Provides arguments and inspiration
Can make a particular hypothesis probable or dismiss a particular hypothesis	Can evaluate relevance

20. Olsen 1997: 59–67.
21. Brattli & Johnsen 1991; Beck 2004; Beck 2011; Sørensen 2015; Damgård-Sørensen in prep.; Ravn 2016.
22. Rasmussen 2001: 6.
23. Beck 2011: 187.
24. Archaeological, written and ethnological as well as results gained from scientific analyses and other cultural and sociological research.

Fig. 9. The model illustrates how the interpretation of the find and its context interacts with the archaeological experiments. At the same time, the model shows the dynamic character of the experimental archaeological process. After Bischoff et al. 2014.

During the 1970s and early 1980s, processual archaeology was criticised for focusing all too one-sidedly on gathering and registering sensory data, and especially for claiming that analyses of this material could lead to objective statements about social and cultural history. The umbrella term 'post-processual archaeology' is often used of the various archaeological currents that criticise processual archaeology's positivist-inspired theory formation and method.[20] However, this criticism of post-processualism was not incorporated in experimental archaeological theory formation until later.

Throughout the 1990s and on into the new millennium, archaeological experiments were increasingly criticised for taking too one-sided a point of departure in scientific experimental set-ups, with a view to verifying or falsifying hypotheses. In this criticism there is no dismissal of the stringent, systematic collection of sensory data and attempts to apply scientific methods as a path towards new knowledge of the societies of the past, but there is a clear tendency in favour of one's own experiences and reflections in connection with the conduct of the experiments – an understanding with the situation of the humans of the past – also to be acknowledged as a method of gaining scientific knowledge.[21]

In an article from 2001, Marianne Rasmussen describes archaeological experiments as being fundamentally based on two different approaches: a controlled approach and a contextual approach (fig. 8).[22] However, it must be pointed out that no archaeological experiment is solely rooted in either of the posited approaches. The individual experiment involve both approaches, but often with one as the predominant.

Whether an experiment seeks to procure measurable results or to obtain arguments and inspiration, its starting point should be the archaeological material. The relationship between the find and the experiment must be dialectical.[23]

In a dialectical approach, experimental archaeology is viewed as a method producing results – both measurable data and arguments and inspiration – that can be used to interpret the source material anew, and, during the actual experiment, the reflective practice must engage in constant dialogue with the other sources[24] of historical knowledge. Furthermore, the experimental archaeological process is dynamic and continuous (fig. 9).

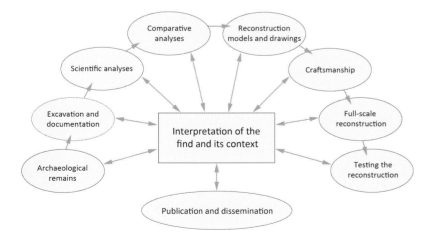

Process and methods of experimental archaeology applied at the Viking Ship Museum in Roskilde

Concepts and methods

The Viking-Age boat and ship finds and the iconographic and written sources show that the plank-built vessels were constructed in the understanding that the shell, not the skeleton, was the starting point for the design and the final hull form.[25] This practice prevailed more or less throughout the northeastern Atlantic area, the North Sea area, the inner Danish waters and large parts of the Baltic area.[26]

There is nothing to suggest that the boatbuilders of the 11th century used drawings or templates to shape and monitor a construction.[27] Some archaeological finds show that models of stem sections and ships may have served as first attempts to visualise the desired form of the finished product. Such a visualisation might have been created for those involved in the construction work,[28] for the building client or for potential new clients.[29] However, the majority of these boat and ship models were probably used as toys.[30]

It would have been necessary to envisage the fundamental form of the finished vessel as early as the laying of the keel and the raising of after and fore stems. Markings on the keel and stem parts[31] indicate that efforts were made to establish the placing of some of the floor timbers early in the construction. However, it is equally clear that the final positioning of the floor timbers did not always follow these initial markings.[32] On several planks from Roskilde 3, lines that presumably mark where the frame parts were to be laid in the ship can be observed. Other lines should probably be interpreted as markings of the intended length of the scarfs.[33]

One fundamental feature of the shipbuilding of the 11th century was that the various components of the vessel were made in a process where the basic product was tested and modified until the desired form had been achieved.[34] However, alongside the stepwise, dynamic production of the hull form, it was necessary for the boatbuilders to have a basic idea of the design of the craft, and of the dimensions and forms that the raw materials were to have. In support of the latter claim, it should be mentioned that several fully-cut stems dated to the Viking Age and the High Middle Ages have been found in northern European bogs. None of the stems have holes for, or imprints of rivets, spikes or roves, which shows that the stems had not been used.[35] It thus seems probable that the stems had been laid out for leaching.[36] The stems had been prepared with mating surfaces to the hood-ends of the planking and scarfs for a keel or stem timber, which makes it likely that the basic design behind the vessels for which the stems were intended was known before the stems were laid out for leaching.

Several researchers have proposed that a measuring system based on circles related to the keel length and a measuring unit of ca 30 cm[37] was used in connection with the building of Skuldelev 3 and perhaps also other boats and ships built in the Viking Age and High Middle Ages.[38] However, a measuring system based on a unit of ca 30 cm has not been proven likely in connection with the construction of other 11th-century ship finds. It thus seems more probable that a variety of measuring systems, rather than a single one, were used in connection with shipbuilding, and that the basic features of the measuring systems were the use of relative dimensions,[39] allowances for the character and properties of the raw materials, as well as an understanding of the vessel as a whole.[40] Such a shipbuilding practice produced guidelines and rules of thumb[41] which were, however, constantly negotiable, because the conceptual understanding of the design of the vessels was concerned with the run of the strakes which were gradually formed. The discrepancy between the Skuldelev 3 stem's mating surfaces and the actual number of strakes in the ship supports this interpretation.

Similarly important in connection with the understanding of the 11th-century construction concept was the intended ship ideal – the cognitive understanding of what a ship was. Both personnel carriers and cargo ships were built as light, elegant ships with a wealth of technical details and decoration. During the course

25. Hasslöf 1966.
26. Christensen 1996b; Crumlin-Pedersen & Olsen 2002: 131–132, 179–180, 227–238, 273–274 & 299.
27. Christensen 1995: 127; Crumlin-Pedersen 1997b: 177–195; Vadstrup 1997b: 84.
28. The community of practice.
29. Christensen 1985: 157; Crumlin-Pedersen 1997b: 172.
30. Ravn 2012a; Ravn 2012b.
31. Small holes or scratches.
32. Crumlin-Pedersen 1997b: 87.
33. Bill 2006b: 10.
34. See chapter II, section: Wooden parts; Vadstrup 1997b.
35. Shetelig 1929: 41–43; Crumlin-Pedersen 1986: 142–143; McGrail 1987: 101 & 124–125.
36. Crumlin-Pedersen 1986: 142–143; Crumlin-Pedersen & Olsen 2002: 231–232.
37. One foot.
38. Crumlin-Pedersen 1986: 143–145 & Crumlin-Pedersen & Olsen 2002: 235–238 Godal 1990: 56–80; Christensen 1995: 127; Andersen 1997c: 31; Vadstrup 1997b: 84–85.
39. Compared with the proportions of the other vessel parts.
40. Area of use and primary function.
41. Crumlin-Pedersen 2004: 50.

42. Bill 1997: 144 & 160–161;
Englert 2000: 49–52 & 143–145;
Crumlin-Pedersen 2004: 47–50.
43. Crumlin-Pedersen 1981; Bill *et
al.* 1998; Englert 2000: 124–131;
Crumlin-Pedersen 2004: 47;
Klassen 2010: 207–210.
44. Christensen 1995: 123;
Crumlin-Pedersen 1997b:
197–198.
45. Crumlin-Pedersen 2004: 43.
46. Bill *et al.* 1997: 108;
Crumlin-Pedersen 1997b:
196–202; Indruszewski 2004:
217–240; Klassen 2010: 207–213.

of the 12th century, a gradual change began in shipbuilding, where the light, elegant ship design of the Viking Age was rejected in favour of a wish to increase the volume of cargo on board, and to build vessels using raw materials that could not earlier be used for shipbuilding. Large cargo ships with closely spaced floor timbers, greater thickness in the planks and long scarfs with lips, show – along with the abandonment of *bitis*, larger dimensions in the transverse beams, and, in the course of the 13th century, also protruding beams – that cargo capacity rather than ship design became the primary status-giving factor.[42]

Shipbuilding technology and regionally delimited shipbuilding practices

The identifying characteristics of what in archaeology is called the *Nordic clinker tradition* in the Viking Age are: 1) a shell-based construction concept where the ideal vessel is a light and elegant ship with a wealth of technical details and decoration; 2) evenly curving sheer lines; 3) raised stems; 4) a frame system that also includes *bitis*; 5) a mast placed in a longitudinal, centre-line timber of the vessel, a keelson; 6) cleft planks with 7) mouldings on many of the vessel components; 8) the use of rivets with mainly round shanks and roves to hold the overlapping planks of strakes together; 9) short scarfs with no lip; and 10) the use of animal hair as a primary caulking material.[43]

This shipbuilding technology was used over an area consisting of Denmark, Sweden, Norway, parts of Finland, the part of England mainly populated by Anglo-Saxons, and the Norse settlement areas in the North Atlantic, as well as in Scotland, Ireland and Iceland.[44] Moreover, almost identical techniques and methods were used by the West Slavic societies along the coast of the Baltic, and a few isolated examples can even be found in the Iberian Peninsula.[45]

The vessel parts from the Fribrødre Å site occupy a special position in the discussion of building traditions (fig. 10). At the site, features characteristic of the Nordic clinker tradition were found, mixed with features characteristic of what maritime archaeology researchers have defined as the *Slavic shipbuilding tradition*. The characteristics of the latter tradition are described as 1) moss as caulking material; 2) closely set treenails and wedges to hold the overlapping planks of the strakes together; 3) no mouldings on the vessel components; 4) thick strakes; and 5) the positioning of the mast in an element in the vessel.[46]

Fig. 10. Aerial photograph of part of the excavation field at Fribrødre Å from the autumn of 1983. Photo: Lars Kann Rasmussen, Viking Ship Museum in Roskilde.

This mixture of the characteristic features of the two main building traditions is not unique to Fribrødre Å. Hedeby 2's planks are held together by rivets and roves as well as treenails and wedges. Hedeby 2 may have been made by boatbuilders with a practice that was technically not so 'traditional'. Such a production history would make the vessel difficult to place in a present-day attempt to categorise building traditions. Skuldelev 1's planks are joined with rivets and roves, while planks in the 11th and 12th strakes are held together with treenails and wedges (fig. 11).[47] In addition, several vessel finds from southern Denmark, northern Germany and the southwestern Baltic area show that Nordic and Slavic techniques and methods were used together to build one and the same vessel.[48] One may thus ask whether the building traditions defined by research stand in the way of understanding the 11th-century shipbuilding communities and their activities. Practice and tradition are both dynamic factors,[49] and perhaps the shipbuilding of the Viking Age was more locally or regionally rooted than the general divisions of the shipbuilding traditions directly suggest?

The very fact that the resource basis differed within the large sphere covered by the Nordic clinker tradition was of direct importance for the way the vessel parts were made and the dimensions the individual components could be given. In southern Scandinavia, it was possible to fell oak in suitable dimensions for shipbuilding, and cultural and functional choices made oak the primary wood resource used for shipbuilding. The properties that the ships of the time had to have required long, thin, light and strong planks, and to achieve this oak was mainly radially cleft. Farther north in western and central Norway, it was possible to fell pine in dimensions suitable for shipbuilding, and for both cultural and functional reasons, it was pine that was chosen as the primary wood resource for shipbuilding in these areas. To obtain the dimensions and properties required for planks, tangential splitting was used. The resource basis thus interacts with the technical

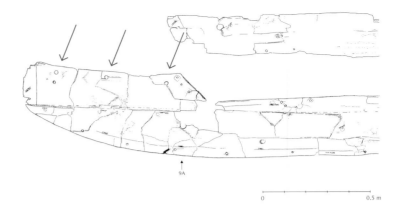

and methodological choices as well as the conceptual approach, and, in the end, also with the finished product.

As an example of a local or regional practice within the present primary geographical area of study, one can mention the resemblances[50] between the hull structure and technical solutions of the Skuldelev 3 and 5 ships.[51] Structural similarities[52] can also be seen between the ship finds from Fotevik.[53] It appears likely that the structurally identical vessels were constructed by boatbuilders with a local or regional practice, which is expressed in the chosen methods and techniques.

Since the provenance of Skuldelev 3's wooden raw materials has been determined as the western part of Denmark and that of Skuldelev 5 as Jutland, Schleswig-Holstein or Scania, it is possible that the local or regional design and building practice for these ships is to be found in the western or southwestern part of 11th-century Denmark. The provenance of the Fotevik ships has not been determined by tree-ring analysis, but the raw materials used as well as the building technique and method make it seem likely that the ships were built in southern Scandinavia.

The regional practices indicate that shipbuilding was decentrally organised, but at the same time the basic conceptual, methodological and technical principles appear to be highly uniform – which makes it probable that at least one of the participants in the shipbuilding had a wide knowledge of the skills and practice re-

Fig. 11. Skuldelev 1. The aft end of strake 11B. The three red arrows mark holes with a diameter of ca 2 cm. Evidence of the use of small treenails locked with wedges as fastenings between the 11th and 12th strakes. Drawing: Viggo Kjær Larsen, Viking Ship Museum in Roskilde.

47. Crumlin-Pedersen & Olsen 2002: 105.
48. Klassen 2010: 207–208.
49. Ravn 2015b.
50. For example, the termination of the *biti* knees against the thwart stringer, the joint between the top stringer and the thwart knees, and the placing and form of the top stringer.
51. Crumlin-Pedersen & Olsen 2002: 255.
52. For example, the cross-section of the frame ribs is trapezoid.
53. Crumlin-Pedersen 1984: 49–50.

quired, and that this knowledge and practice were based on a conservative tradition. As expressed by Ole Crumlin-Pedersen: "Shipbuilding of the past, therefore, must always be studied in the light of the interaction between tradition and innovation".[54] However, instead of viewing innovation and tradition as contradictions, I argue that innovation is a vital part of a tradition.[55] In the following, this dialectic will be analysed and discussed.

In an article from 1995, Arne Emil Christensen describes two different types of boatbuilders. In the areas where there were plenty of suitable resources for shipbuilding, the boatbuilders travelled around to whoever ordered the building of a boat. The client secured the raw materials necessary for the shipbuilding, and these were often procured in the client's own forest. The client often participated in the building as an assistant and provided board and lodging during the work. The other type of boatbuilder had his own workshop and procured the necessary raw materials himself. The finished boats were sold on a market or were ordered in advance. In some areas close to the sea and with plenty of resources for shipbuilding, building boats was part of the occupation of almost every household in a village.[56]

Both types of boatbuilder still plied their trade in Norway in the 20th century, and the basic organisation of the work can possibly be traced all the way back to the Middle Ages. Christensen deals with this in depth and compares the different working conditions for the two types of boatbuilder to Robert Kloster's account of the *village artisan and artisan village* of historical times, inasmuch as the village artisans were good at many different trades, while production in an artisan village was far more specialised and products were manufactured in relatively large series.[57] Christensen further mentions that the itinerant boatbuilders could have a personal style, while the boats of the artisan villages were often highly uniform – they were 'type-approved'.[58]

As described above, it is likely that the plank-built vessels of the 11th century were made using guidelines based on relative measuring systems and rules of thumb, but at the same time the vessels of the time were all built as one-offs. Several of the vessel finds exhibit resemblances in technical solutions and morphological details, which have been referred to above as examples of 'regional practices'. They could also be regarded as personal styles. It therefore seems likely that the shipbuilding of the 11th century should be viewed organisationally as based especially on skilled boat- and shipbuilding craftsmen who, either for payment or as part of the obligations of the time entailed by the relationship between ruler and subject,[59] were responsible for the supervision and to some extent the actual construction of the vessel ordered by the client.[60]

In this context, the client would have been a magnate or the king, and would have organised the procurement of raw materials and the necessary extra manpower. The client had to plan for and obtain several of the necessary raw materials, long before the actual construction was started, which probably meant that all year round – in certain periods – several of the client's subjects would be working to ensure that the proper resources were present and to produce the necessary raw materials and basic products. In his PhD dissertation, Jan Bill has noted the same tendency and explains it by arguing that even the smaller plank-built vessels were owned by magnates, but that it was the farmers who built and crewed the vessels. Not until the later part of the Middle Ages did the farmers begin independently to build and use plank-built vessels.[61]

The organisational model outlined here also meant that the magnate's raw material reserves could be exploited in the best way possible. Specialists and the other manpower could be moved to a place with suitable resources, which meant that large amounts of the raw materials and basic products only had to be transported over short distances. When the raw materials were no longer available in an area, the subsequent shipbuilding activities could be moved to another place. In this way, shipbuilding was

54. Crumlin-Pedersen 2004: 50.
55. Ravn 2015b.
56. Christensen 1995: 124–125.
57. Kloster 1972: 126–143.
58. Christensen 1995: 124–125.
59. Hybel and Poulsen 2007: 299–300.
60. Crumlin-Pedersen 1996a: 17.
61. Bill 1997: 159–161.

decentralised, and this made it easier to procure the raw materials that were most difficult to transport.

As long as guidelines for the work had been established, the progress of the work could be monitored, and much of the shipbuilding could be carried out by a non-specialised workforce. The participants in the many different practices prior to, during and after the actual construction would have entered into complex relations with one another and the traditions of their community.[62] It was the collectivities themselves who constituted and developed their knowledge and skills, which meant that learning would have been an important part of their practice.[63] The ship finds testify to a fundamentally uniform conceptual understanding, methodological approach and – broadly speaking – technical execution, which suggests that the shipbuilding collectivities of the 11th century were particularly effective at sustaining their traditions, skills and knowledge. Perhaps the successful spread of uniform skills in an otherwise decentralised active practice was due to the fact that the craftsmen with particular building skills who supervised the building of both small and large plank-built vessels were part of a community[64] with a long-standing tradition of ship- and boatbuilding. The regional differences can then be explained in terms of the areas where the various communities worked.

The craftsmen with special shipbuilding knowledge did not work exclusively with ship- and boatbuilding. The saga of Saint Olav mentions the boatbuilders Torstein Knarresmed, who besides functioning as a 'stem-smith'[65] was also a merchant,[66] and Torberg Skavhogg, who is called a stem-smith in connection with the construction of *Ormen Lange*, has to abandon the construction work and go to his farm. Skavhogg was thus also involved in other practices than shipbuilding.[67] Both these stem-smiths belonged to the free men of the society, but as Arne Emil Christensen points out, we cannot preclude the possibility that unfree men too, for example slaves, worked as specialised boatbuilders – perhaps even as stem-smith.[68]

From appropriate resource to ship component

Production takes place in an interaction between raw material(s) and producer(s).[69] The relationship is conditioned by technological, economic, ideological and political factors, and the actual making of the product is processual and consists of several operational phases.[70] Technological and cognitive aspects are both active in connection with production. Human thinking is thus a foundation stone of production. There are intentions behind the technological choices, and these intentions are governed by knowledge and skills as well as the conceptual approach and the raw materials available or chosen. The character of the raw material – its physical properties – interacts with the producer's intention and the technological and methodological choices.

It is important to understand production as a totality of many different, interdependent factors. However, the complexity of a production process requires subdivision of these factors when it is analysed. The *chaîne opératoire* analysis relates to the above-mentioned dialectic by structurally setting up a stepwise analysis of production, and also by viewing production as a relationship between technique, method and intention.[71] This analytical method will therefore be used as a starting point for the following systematic analysis of the building of the ships that were used for warfare, which requires a brief presentation of *chaîne opératoire* analysis.

The epistemological foundation of *chaîne opératoire* analysis has been ascribed to André Leroi-Gourhan, who, as a structuralist, wanted to challenge the scientific understanding of typology that prevailed during the 1960s. Leroi-Gourhan introduced the concept of the *chaîne opératoire* and emphasised that a tool only became a tool in connection with its production and use, and that the producer's mental and motoric abilities were therefore an important part of the character of the tool.[72]

Pierre Lemonnier added three fundamental factors to *chaîne opératoire* analysis: that the

62. Reference may be made to Lave & Wenger 1991 and Wenger 1998 for a general introduction to the subject.
63. For a general introduction to the subject see Wendrich (ed.) 2012. For a study of learning in maritime communities of practice in the Viking Age, see Ravn 2012b.
64. Perhaps a family or lineage.
65. A term for craftsmen particularly skilled in shipbuilding and with a leading role in shipbuilding.
66. Snorri Sturluson's *Heimskringla, Olav Tryggvason's saga* [Hødnebø & Magerøy (eds.) 1979b: 101–103].
67. Snorri Sturluson's *Heimskringla, Olav Tryggvason's saga* [Hødnebø & Magerøy (eds.) 1979a: 186–187].
68. Christensen 1995: 126–127. See also Brink 2012.
69. Leroi-Gourhan 1965: 132.
70. Pelegrin 1990: 116.
71. Lemonnier 1980: 1; Valentin Eriksen 2000: 75–80.
72. Leroi-Gourhan 1965: 35.

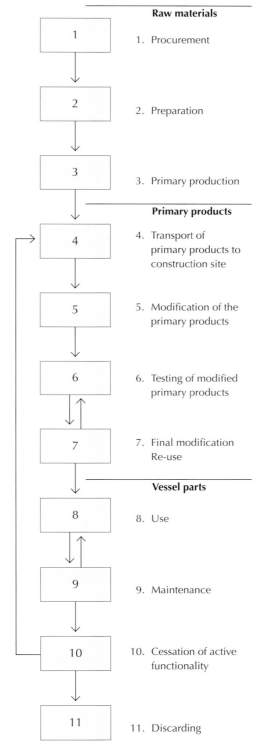

73. Lemonnier 1980: 1–9.
74. Pelegrin 1990: 118.
75. Valentin Eriksen 2000: 80–82.
76. Jørgensen, L. 2008; Christensen 1993; Schmidt 1993; Larsen (ed.) 1994.
77. Schou Jørgensen 1997.
78. Hellmuth Andersen 1998.
79. Crumlin-Pedersen 1997b; Crumlin-Pedersen & Olsen 2002; Bonde & Stylegar 2011.

Fig. 12. The general processes in connection with shipbuilding. After the procurement of the raw materials, shipbuilding continues. The raw materials are converted into primary products which then become parts of a vessel. The transformations are rarely a one-way process. A vessel component may be re-used, but will always be modified: a nail hole is pegged, an oar hole is closed, floor timbers are adjusted, the rivet or spike is re-forged, etc., before becoming a part in another vessel. Drawing: The author, Viking Ship Museum in Roskilde.

Raw materials

1. Procurement
2. Preparation
3. Primary production

Primary products

4. Transport of primary products to construction site
5. Modification of the primary products
6. Testing of modified primary products
7. Final modification Re-use

Vessel parts

8. Use
9. Maintenance
10. Cessation of active functionality
11. Discarding

actions in connection with production are determined by technical processes, the objects used and the underlying knowledge.[73]

In the 1980s, Jacques Pelegrin expanded the understanding of the underlying knowledge to consist of both knowledge and skills. Knowledge was defined as the experience-based awareness of the expected course of action and the mental understanding of form and material, while skills were divided into a mental side and a motoric side. Mental skills were described as the ability to envisage the desired result and the actions that were necessary to achieve this result, while the motoric skills were characterised as the ability to carry out the necessary actions in practice.[74]

The analytical method consists of five fundamental sequential phases:[75] the procurement of raw materials, production, use, maintenance and discard, which in the face of empirical data, are often expanded with more phases (fig. 12).

In the following paragraphs, the processes in connection with the manufacture of the various vessel components will be investigated. Both the production of the wooden and iron components of the hull, and of tar and charcoal as well as sails, rigging and caulking material, will all be analysed.

Wooden parts

The ships of the Viking Age were all built of wood, and in general wood was one of the most important resources in the construction work of the time. Wood was used as a raw material in connection with more or less all production. Archaeological finds show that several of the craftsmen of the time had extensive knowledge of the different suitabilities of the wood resources, and not least that the craftsmen were able to translate this knowledge into practice in the form of impressively large construction works such as the building of houses and halls,[76] bridges[77] and defensive works[78] as well as what were presumably the most high-technological constructions of the time: the biggest cargo and personnel carriers.[79]

Felling, clearing and cutting

In wooden shipbuilding practice of the 19th and 20th centuries, the winter is often described as the most suitable time for felling trees. The reason given for this is that the sap has not yet risen in the trees. Sap-filled trees will warp during drying and may also continue to warp after the raw materials have been made into ship components and installed in the ship, which in the worst case may twist the hull out of shape.[80] In connection with this, Søren Vadstrup points out that in the case of oak, the starch is not converted over the course of the winter, and that the turgor pressure in oak is therefore not strikingly less in winter than at other times of the year.[81]

It should further be mentioned that a written source from 11th-century England, *Rectitudines singularum personarum*, speaks of May, June and July as months when trees can be felled, but does not say whether these months were the generally preferred ones for the felling of trees, nor which tree species were felled, or their size.[82] Finally, the same written source says that timber and other wood is split in the winter during severe frost.[83] In more recent times, it has also been recommended that tree roots and small logs should be split in the frozen state.[84]

Another factor of relevance was the transport of raw materials out of the forest. In the winter, snowfall may have facilitated transport by sledge, and the deciduous trees would have shed their leaves, which makes both felling and transport easier.[85] Perhaps it was also easier to assess the suitability of a deciduous tree as raw material when it had no leaves on it?

The suitability of a tree for shipbuilding must be understood in relation to the building of a specific vessel. The people who had selected the suitable trees would have searched for particular qualities, properties, shapes and dimensions, and would do so in relation to particular vessel components for one or perhaps two or three vessels. The selection of suitable resources has in several cases turned out to be problematic in connection with the building of recon-

structions of Viking Age ships. A highly suitable tree may be impossible or difficult to use because of twisted growth, hidden dead branches, knots or rot.[86] This raises certain questions: could the individuals in the collectivities that were involved in selecting and felling trees in the Viking Age determine the suitability of a tree more accurately than it is done today, or was an unsuitable felled tree simply used for something other than shipbuilding? According to written sources from the Early Middle Ages in Ireland, specialised craftsmen were in some cases involved in wood preparation activities such as felling, cutting, dressing and transport,[87] but whether something similar was the case in Denmark is unknown.

After a suitable tree has been selected, the raw materials can be procured in several ways. The wood can be felled and cut for certain curved resources in the treetop. Suitable curved branches can be lopped off, and finally the tree can be dug out and cut up with its roots – in a process called clearing. The process can provide pieces of root and trunk that can be used as raw material in connection with the making of knees, floor timbers and futtocks as well as other curved vessel components.

The advantage of both lopping and clearing is that the crooked timbers can be procured more non-intrusively than when a tree is felled in the normal way where the tree crown can be severely damaged.[88]

Cleaving, dressing and transport

With the raw material lying on the forest floor, the tree was presumably examined for features[89] that made the wood less usable or directly unsuited for making the vessel components for which it was intended. Further treatment of the raw material probably took place at the site where it had been felled. First, the branches would be lopped off the trunk, or the twigs would be lopped off the branches. Afterwards, the log would either be transported out of the forest or cleft and dressed at the felling site. In the research literature, the latter is described as the case,[90] but it should be noted that the

80. Frost 1985: 2.
81. Vadstrup 1997a: 39.
82. *Rectitudines singularum personarum* [Lund 2015a].
83. *Rectitudines singularum personarum* [Lund 2015a].
84. Ihlen 1932: 8.
85. Suenson 1922: 17; Ihlen 1932:8.
86. Vadstrup 1997a: 38–39; Poulsen 2005: 81; Damgård-Sørensen *et al.* 2004: 26 & 45–47.
87. O'Sullivan 1994: 679.
88. Crumlin-Pedersen 1997b: 180; Vadstrup 1997a: 39–40.
89. For example lightning damage and knots.
90. Crumlin-Pedersen 1997b: 179–184; Vadstrup 1997a: 40; Damgård-Sørensen *et al.* 2004: 16–17.

91. Frost 1985: 3.
92. Crumlin-Pedersen 1997b: 180; Daly 2007: 187–202 & 236–238.
93. Crumlin-Pedersen 1997b: 180–181.
94. Christensen 1995: 125; Crumlin-Pedersen 1997b: 181.
95. Daly 2007: 187–202 & 236–238; Hybel & Poulsen 2007: 18–23; Jahnke 2015.
96. In wood.
97. Stefánsson 1997: 41; Sigurðsson 2005: 187.
98. Haarnagel 1979; Jessen 2015: 203.
99. [M 328, 327, 234] & [M 64, 65, 66].
100. Crumlin-Pedersen & Olsen 2002: 67 & 203–207.

Fig. 13. An ash log, cleft into halves, providing material for two tangentially-oriented planks. The outlines of these planks are marked in black on the log. Photos: Werner Karrasch, Viking Ship Museum in Roskilde.

transport of raw materials in log or branch form may be advantageous, since this solution makes the raw materials less susceptible to damage during transportation.[91]

Archaeological experiments have made it clear how problematic it could be to transport unprocessed raw materials from felling site to building site, which has led to the rational supposition that logs were cleft or otherwise processed before they were transported from the felling site to the building site. The raw materials for the crooked timbers were probably also dressed before transport to the building site.[92] However, neither the raw materials for planks, inboard timbers nor other vessel parts could be cut to their final form before the vessel parts had been assessed, adapted, tested and adapted again at the building site.[93]

Most of the raw materials for shipbuilding were, therefore, probably felled near the building site, but we cannot preclude the possibility that raw materials were also obtained farther away, and that long-distance transport of raw materials was therefore necessary.[94] Dendrochronological analyses and written sources suggest that timber was an important commodity in northern Europe from the middle of the 13th century onwards, and that the timber was transported across long distances.[95] In addition, the widespread church and house building[96] on Iceland around the year 1000 indicates that extensive sea transport of timber was necessary, as Iceland's limited tree resources at that

time could not provide the raw materials required.[97] Finally, the archaeological traces of wooden buildings in the treeless northwestern German marsh areas show that timber must have been transported there in considerably quantities.[98] It therefore seems likely that wooden raw materials and timber were transported before any evidence of this appeared in the written sources, but the extent of southern Scandinavian timber transport in the late part of the Viking Age cannot be specified in more detail on the basis of the present sources.

Knowledge of the techniques used for cleaving logs into smaller, more workable basic products is fundamental to the understanding of the construction of the 11th-century Scandinavian boats and ships (figs. 13 & 14). Cleft planks have greater strength and more stability than planks that have been sawn from a log.

This strength and stability was essential so that the boatbuilders of the Viking Age could use the thin planks and relatively short scarfs without lips (fig. 15). The importance of the strong planks was further reinforced in the cases where the planks were long and relatively broad.

It seems reasonable to assume that several components of the same vessel were made from the same tree. Two tangentially cleft oak planks from Skuldelev 3[99] have the same average growth-ring breadth and plank width, as well as a length of about 7 m[100], which suggests that they were made from the same log. Another

example is the three radially cleft oak planks[101] from Skuldelev 1, whose growth-ring widths and synchronisation values[102] match so well that it is highly likely that they were cleft from the same log.[103]

However, far more components in the individual ship finds were presumably made from the same tree. The problem is that demonstrating this takes even more detailed documentation of the specific ship components than has been possible in the present analysis – we lack

the necessary information and it will require extensive growth-ring analyses to remedy this lacuna.

Building site

The most important things in connection with the establishment of a building site were room to build, access to suitable resources and a good place to launch the finished vessel. A flat surface was necessary to lay the keel, as well as enough room around the laid keel to continue with the building process. At the building site, space would also have been needed for rough- and fine-dressing, and room for primary products. If the building lasted a long time, a living area with related furnishings would also have been necessary. The size and the furnishings of the building site and accommodation area would have depended on the size and extent of the construction. A log boat could be built more or less anywhere without a pre-established infrastructure, but we must expect the building of a large cargo ship or personal carrier to have required considerably more organisation and infrastructure establishment.[104] The absence of traces of living quarters at the Fribrødre Å site is therefore remarkable.[105] The shipbuilding-related activities at the site have been interpreted as extensive – new ships were probably not built, but several hundred boats and ships were repaired and fitted out over short periods of activity – and this must have involved many

Fig. 14. An oak log cleft into halves, quarters, eighths and a few sixteenths, providing material for many radially-oriented planks. Photos: Werner Karrasch, Viking Ship Museum in Roskilde.

Fig. 15. Top: The scarf type used in the Viking Age and the early part of the High Middle Ages, which was short and terminated smoothly. Bottom: The scarf type used in the course of the High Middle Ages, which was longer and terminated with an edge called a lip. Drawing: Morten Gøthche, Viking Ship Museum in Roskilde.

101. [P 190, P 182, P 179 & P 181], [P 262 & P 253] & [P 217].
102. Also called T-values.
103. Crumlin-Pedersen & Olsen 2002: 65–66 & 136.
104. Crumlin-Pederssen 1997b: 177–179.
105. Klassen 2010: 293–302.

craftsmen and workers.[106] Finds of meat skewers, spoons, bowls and cups of wood suggest that those who participated in the shipbuilding-related activities ate and drank in close proximity to the working area, but traces[107] of a true settlement area are absent.[108] Perhaps boatbuilders and workers lived in tents, which do not necessarily leave clear archaeological traces.[109] The military context within which the Fribrødre Å site should probably be viewed[110] may possibly support this interpretation. In that case, a camp would have been established in the area around Fribrødre Å. Alternatively, it is possible that the living area has not yet been found and excavated. Only a small part of the activity area has been excavated and the activity area itself is located in a river valley surrounded by hills.[111] Perhaps the living area is to be found at the top of these hills? Perhaps on the west side of Fribrødre Å in the area between Nørre and Sønder Snekkebjerg, where there is a farm today?

That building sites could also be established in urban surroundings is a reasonable assumption, but to date, no archaeological excavations have been able to prove this empirically. However, it is likely that boats and ships were to some extent fitted out and repaired in the Hedeby harbour area.[112]

After transport to the building site, the rough-dressed raw materials were probably processed into primary products that were either used directly or stored in water. Water storage has two purposes: on the one hand to keep the primary products wet, on the other to initiate a leaching process that can limit shrinkage, warping and cracking in the vessel parts caused by drying-out. Several archaeological finds make it seem likely that water storage and leaching were used in the Viking Age and the High Middle Ages.[113] At the site Eskelund near Viby, south west of Aarhus, excavations have unearthed chips and preliminary work for vessel parts – primary products – that were sunk in shallow water and weighed down with stones. The activities have been interpreted as having a long chronological time span from

ca 797 until 1266, but it is not clear whether there were shipbuilding-related activities throughout the period.[114] At Poole in Dorset, England, excavations have suggested a similar storage of primary products for shipbuilding. The shipbuilding site[115] was not fully excavated, but the documented artefact material consists of 61 vessel parts. There were no planks, but primary products for keels, floor timbers, knees and stems were all present. The vessel parts were sunk in groups based on their form and function in a vessel.[116]

The archaeological traces of shipbuilding activities are usually limited primarily to chips from drilling, cutting and chopping, and worn-down, laid-aside or lost tools, as well as broken or lost treenails of wood or rivets of iron. It is therefore difficult to recognise a site where shipbuilding or shipbuilding-related activities took place.[117] Thus, perhaps only a small fraction of the operational shipbuilding sites from the 11th century are known archaeologically today.

Building sequence

After the establishment of a suitable building site and the procurement of the necessary raw materials, the keel was laid.[118] Once the keel was laid, the after and fore stems were raised. Often the after and fore stems consisted of several parts,[119] which were nailed, spiked and riveted together, partly to one another, partly to the keel.

The written sources of the High Middle Ages speak of the man charged with the responsibility for the erection of the stem[120] as a man of high social standing with great craftsmanship skills.[121] Experimental archaeological ship reconstruction projects demonstrate that the forming of the stems in particular is of importance to the general appearance and sailing properties of the vessel.[122] It can therefore come as no surprise that the boatbuilder with this responsibility was regarded as someone special.

After the stems were raised, the building of the vessel's plank shell was begun (fig. 16). The planks of the first strake were held together with the keel by spikes or rivets and roves. If the

106. Klassen 2010: 353–354.
107. For example post-holes.
108. Klassen 2010: 261–267 & 293–302.
109. Klassen 2010: 293–302.
110. Klassen 2010: 343–351.
111. Skamby Madsen 2010.
112. Crumlin-Pedersen 1997b: 177–179; Kalmring 2010: 365–367.
113. Crumlin-Pedersen 1986: 142–143; Vadstrup 1997a: 36; Vadstrup 1997b: 91–92; Nielsen 2011: 68.
114. Skamby Madsen & Vinner 2005: 94–95.
115. Dated to the 15th century.
116. Hutchinson 1994: 24–26.
117. Lundström 1981: 74–81; Crumlin-Pedersen 1997b: 177.
118. Vadstrup 1997b: 80–81.
119. The so-called 'lot' and actual stem parts.
120. A *stafnasmiðr* (lit. stem-smith)
121. Snorri Sturlusson's *Heimskringla, Olav Tryggvasons saga* [Hødnebø & Magerøy (eds.) 1979a: 186]; *Gulatingslovi*, XIII, chapter 12, section 306 [Robberstad 1952: 276–277].
122. Vadstrup 1997b: 85; Damgård-Sørensen et al. 2004: 25.

keel was 'winged', rivets and roves were used, while the first strake planks were spiked to the keel if it had rabbeting. The winged keel[123] from the Fribrødre Å site shows, however, that the first strake planks could also be held together with the keel using small treenails and wedges.[124] Towards the ends of the vessel, the planks were always spiked together with the keel.

As mentioned above, the scarfs between the planks in the individual strake were mainly made short and without a lip (fig. 15). It should however be mentioned that two planks[125] from Skuldelev 3, both in the second strake to starboard, have scarfs with lips,[126] which is the earliest example of scarfs with lips in southern Scandinavia. The planks from the analysed ship finds show that the short scarfs were generally sealed with inlaid caulking material and fixed together with rivets and roves.

The planks of the next strake were positioned so as to overlap the planks of the first strake. The planks were tried out and the 'land' between the planking of the two strakes was trimmed with a plane or adze until the desired positioning had been achieved.[127] During trimming it would have been necessary to fix the new planks temporarily, which may have been done with strut sticks[128] and planking clamps.[129] Planking clamps are known from archaeological excavations in Tårnby on Amager[130] and in Gdansk in Poland.[131]

When both lands were trimmed to size, the land was lined with inlaid caulking material, and afterwards holes were drilled through the land on both planks at the same time.[132] In these holes were placed either rivets that were fixed to roves, or small treenails that were split with a wedge, which locked the treenails in position.

Only when the plank shell up to the turn of the bilge had been fixed were the floor timbers installed (fig. 16). The primary products for the floor timbers were tested and inserted several times, until they were satisfactorily fitted inside the plank shell. After this, holes were drilled through both the floor timbers and the plank shell, and planks and floor timbers were subse-

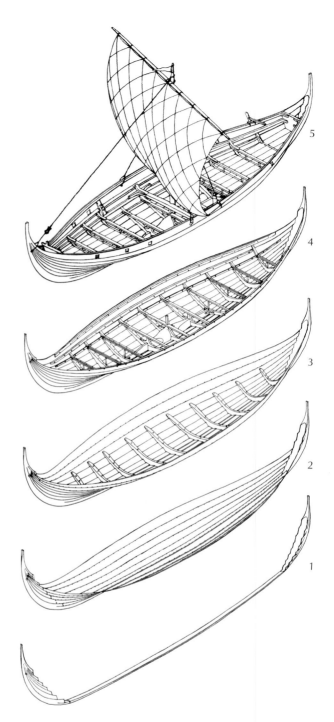

Fig. 16. Building sequence for Skuldelev 3. Irrespective of size and type the plank-built vessels of the Late Viking Age were in principle built in the sequence shown here. After the stems had been raised the construction of the plank shell of the vessel began (1-2). Only when the plank shell up to the turn of the bilge had been installed, were the floor timbers laid in and the setting-up of the plank shell continued (3). Before the bitis were laid in, the keelson was placed and supported with knees (4). Then the last frame parts, planks and longitudinal reinforcements were installed in the vessel, and the vessel was fitted out with sails and rigging as well as other equipment (5). After Crumlin-Pedersen & Olsen 2002: 235, fig. 47.

123. KE I.
124. Klassen 2010: 390.
125. M 283 & M 284.
126. Crumlin-Pedersen & Olsen 2002: 204.
127. Vadstrup 1997b: 98–100.
128. Skorestokke.
129. Damgård-Sørensen et al. 2004: 28–31.
130. Myrhøj 2005.
131. Christensen 1985: 177, fig. 13–10.
132. Vadstrup 1997b: 100; Damgård-Sørensen et al. 2004: 28.
133. Vadstrup 1997b: 105.
134. Vadstrup 1997b: 110; Damgård-Sørensen et al. 2004: 34–37.
135. Vadstrup 1997b: 112–125; Damgård-Sørensen et al. 2004: 37–39.
136. Hedeby 1, Roskilde 6 and Skuldelev 2.
137. Vadstrup 1997b: 112–116.
138. Vadstrup 1997b: 116–128; Damgård-Sørensen et al. 2004: 39.
139. Vadstrup 1997b: 128–139; Andersen 1997a; Andersen 1997b: Damgård-Sørensen et al. 2004: 39–41.
140. Hägg 1984: 15; Crumlin-Pedersen 1997b: 146–147; Kalmring 2010: 417.

quently held together with treenails. In some cases, spikes were used instead of treenails. In most cases, the floor timbers were not held tight against all the planks they extended over, which may have been because the floor timbers had to follow the movements of the plank shell and should not make the shell too rigid.[133] The treenails were hammered in from the outside and split with a wedge on the inside.[134]

With all the floor timbers installed in the vessel, the erection of the plank shell continued (fig. 16). Probably one or two strakes were installed before it was again reinforced with stringers, beams and knees.[135] The largest of the personnel carriers[136] and the medium-sized cargo ship Roskilde 3 also had side frames.

Before the *bitis* were installed, the keelson was positioned and supported with knees. The knees were fixed partly to the keelson, partly to the planks and the floor timbers. Spikes and treenails were used to hold the vessel parts together. After this, the last frame parts were laid in the vessel in a process consisting of trial installations and adjustments.[137] Finally, the last planks were laid in the ship and the shell was strengthened with more frame parts and longitudinal reinforcements (fig. 16).[138] The various parts of the internal elements were fixed partly to one another, partly to the plank shell, and it was primarily treenails and secondarily spikes as well as rivets and roves that were used for this.

The vessel was then equipped with rudder, mast, sail and standing and running rigging, oars, anchor and other equipment, depending on the use of the vessel.[139]

Maintenance

Continuous maintenance of wooden ships is necessary (fig. 17). Hull, rigging, sails and other equipment must be treated regularly with tar and other products. Interesting in this context are the many finds of tar brushes in the harbour of Hedeby. A whole 93 tar brushes were found during the excavations in 1979–1980. The find-site of the tar brushes indicates that vessels were tarred while they were moored at jetties and the large platforms at the end of the jetties.[140] Replacements of damaged vessel components and the drawing-up of repair lists and repair slips would have been necessary. The analysed ship finds demonstrate several examples of replacements of damaged vessel parts.[141]

Tar and paint

Surface treatment of the ships' hulls is mentioned in both skaldic poems and the later saga texts. The skaldic poems describe coal-black, dark blue and red ship hulls,[142] and the *Saga of Erik the Red* speaks of a special surface treatment with seal tar[143] as protection of the outside of the ship's bottom planking against shipworm.[144] Analyses of plank and treenail scrapings and caulking material further suggest that the vessels of the Late Viking Age were surface-treated,[145] and many ships with painted hulls can be seen on the Bayeux Tapestry.[146]

Several of the 11th-century ship finds were smeared with a mixture of wood tar, yellow ochre and presumably also a binder consisting

Fig. 17. *The processes in connection with the production of vessel components in wood. Table: The author, Viking Ship Museum in Roskilde.*

General processes	Procurement	Preparation	Primary production	Modification, testing and modification	Use and maintenance
Processes in connection with the production of vessel parts in wood	Trees felled, lopped or cleared.	Rough dressing of the log and transport of raw materials to the building site.	The log or branch is cut to a provisional form and either used directly or put in water with a view to storage and leaching.	The form of the vessel part is tested and modified until the desired form is achieved. The vessel part is placed in the vessel.	Ongoing maintenance and replacement of vessel parts.

Ship finds	Sample Numbers	Results	References
Fotevik 4	4K	Traces of yellow ochre	Jespersen 1986: 141
Hedeby 1		Traces of yellow ochre	Crumlin-Pedersen 1997b: 86
Skuldelev 1	2	Treenail: Tar (birch bark and pine)	Jespersen 1986: 141
Skuldelev 2	30	Plank: Tar (pine)	Jespersen 1986: 187
Skuldelev 2	33	Caulking material: A fatty substance (maybe seal blubber?), and yellow ochre	Jespersen 1986: 187
Skuldelev 2	34	Caulking material: Tar (probably from pine)	Jespersen 1986: 187
Skuldelev 2	35	Treenail: Yellow ochre	Jespersen 1986: 188
Skuldelev 2	39	Caulking material: Tar (birch bark and pine)	Jespersen 1986: 188
Skuldelev 2	44	Plank: Yellow ochre	Jespersen 1986: 189
Skuldelev 5	1K	Caulking material: Yellow ochre	Jespersen 1986: 189
Skuldelev 5	3K	Caulking material: Tar (pine)	Jespersen 1986: 189

Fig. 18. Traces of surface treatment. Table: The author, Viking Ship Museum in Roskilde.

of a fatty substance such as linseed oil or tallow (figs. 18 & 21).[147] Besides yellow ochre, other pigments were made, either by burning or heating plants, animals and minerals.[148] Most colours could be made locally, while a few pigments were imported.[149]

Laura White's new analyses of three Norwegian ship finds,[150] like Kirsten Jespersen's analyses from 1986[151], show traces of pine wood and birch bark.[152] The presence of birch bark has been tentatively explained as the result of lining the bottom of the tar-burning stacks with birch bark, a practice that is known from ethnological studies of wood tar production in Sweden and Finland. The birch-bark molecules thus appear to have been a result of this lining.[153] Another explanation may be that tar made from birch bark was mixed with pine tar, which is mentioned as a common practice in Poland in historical times.[154]

The chemical content of the above-mentioned product *seltjöru* (seal tar), which was used to treat the outside of the bottom of the ship's hull, is not known. It is possible that seal blubber was the fatty substance in the tar, and that this is where the tar got its name. Perhaps

the unidentified[155] grease in specimen 33 (fig. 18) from Skuldelev 2 was extracted from seal blubber?

However, the most frequently used binder was probably linseed oil, which is made by cold-pressing linseed (i.e. flax seed) or by heating linseed and later pressing it. Both the cold-pressed and hot-pressed oil must be cleaned afterwards.[156] Another binder used was tallow or leaf fat – that is fat from an ox, a horse or a sheep.[157]

Wood tar production

In several experiments with tar-burning in small stacks, the Zealand based, Aggebo and Eskilstrup Charcoal-Burners' Guilds have contributed to the understanding of historical tar production,[158] while ethnological studies, primarily among tar-burners of recent times in Finland, have contributed to the understanding of burning in large stacks.[159]

Local and regional customs have an influence on the construction and use of the tar-burning complexes, but at the same time it is clear that a number of fundamental factors across time and space also apply, and it is these that will be described in the following.

141. See appendix 1.
142. Jesch 2001: 144.
143. *Seltjöru* – see *Eiríks saga rauða*, chapter 13. Accessible online at http://heimskringla.no/wiki/Eir%C3%ADks_saga_rau%C3%B0a. The content of the website was used on 6 August 2013.
144. *Sjómaðkr*, see *Eiríks saga rauða*, chapter 13. Accessible online at http://heimskringla.no/wiki/Eir%C3%ADks_saga_rau%C3%B0a. The content of the website was used on 6 August 2013.
145. Bischoff & Jensen 2001: 239–241.
146. Rud 2008: 89–99.
147. Jespersen 1986: 5 & 141–191.
148. Fentz 1999: 159.
149. Bischoff & Jensen 2001: 239–241; Bill *et al.* 2007: 27.
150. Dated to the 13th–17th century AD, see White 2012.
151. Jespersen 1986.
152. White 2012.
153. White 2012.
154. Surminski 1997: 120.
155. Linseed oil could be precluded.
156. Møller Hansen & Høier 2000: 72.
157. Andersen 1997b: 212 & 216–217.
158. See for example the unpublished report from 2014 from the Viking Ship Guild Sif Ege about the tar stack at Aggebo Hegn. The report can be read in the library of the Viking Ship Museum in Roskilde.
159. Surminski 1997; Nielsen, S. 2002; Glastrup 2010.

160. Forest fire, lightning strikes and bark damage.
161. Nielsen, S. 2002: 3.
162. 40–60 years old.
163. Nielsen, S. 2002: 3.
164. Hoff 1997: 283.
165. Hoff 1997: 284.
166. Hoff 1997: 286.
167. Ihlen 1932: 3; Jespersen 1986: 123–124; Egenberg 1997: 143.
168. Surminski 1997: 117; Glastrup 2010: 152.
169. Nielsen, S. 2002: 3–4.
170. Hjulström *et al.* 2006.
171. Ihlen 1932: Fig. 13; Nielsen, S. 2002: 4.
172. Often made of cleft and partly hollowed-out birch.
173. In Norway called a *roe*; see Ihlen 1932.
174. In Norway called a *rende*; see Ihlen 1932.
175. Egenberg 1997: 142.
176. Mainly of pine.

A high content of resin in the raw materials used is of great importance for the quality of the tar and the amount that can be extracted. Damaged trees[160] produce more resin, which can give a greater yield.[161] Studies of tar production in recent times in the Nordic countries have shown that pine trees[162] have been debarked to the height that a man could reach. Only a small strip was spared, ensuring the tree did not die. The next year, the debarking continued farther up the trunk, but still with the life-giving strip of bark. After a period of around three-to-four years the bark strip too was removed, and after the tree had died, it was felled. Through this treatment, the tree trunk had produced a thick layer of resin, which made the tree especially well suited for tar production.[163] In this respect it is interesting that the regional laws of the High Middle Ages speak in detail of legal matters connected with the debarking of trees. It is emphasised that the debarking of a living tree in another man's woods could be punished as theft, which meant that the culprit could be condemned to death.[164] The bark of the trees was used as animal fodder and in special cases also as human food,[165] and for the tanning of skins.[166] An-

other possibility is that the trees were debarked with a view to tar production and that this production was so extensive that debarking had to be regulated by law.

The ethnological studies and written sources show that tar-burning stacks were made both in funnel form and bowl form, and either dug into a hillside (fig. 19),[167] or dug down into the soil as a pit (fig. 19).[168] A combination of both a pit and a stack built above it is also known.[169] The funnel-shaped and bowl-shaped tar extraction pits are known archaeologically from the area around Uppsala in central Sweden, where many tar extraction pits of varying sizes have been excavated. Several of these features have been dated to the Viking Age and High Middle Ages.[170]

The bottoms of both pits and stacks were lined with gravel, sand, clay and birch bark or in more recent times with plastic and roofing felt.[171] A pipe or a channel issued from the bottom of the funnel.[172] Often, a pipe[173] and a channel[174] were used at the same time, and the tar was tapped through this double outlet.[175] In the lined pit or stack, the uniformly dimensioned pieces of root, log and branch[176] were stacked pointing towards the bottom of the funnel (fig. 19).[177]

Fig. 19. Left: Cross-section of a pit dug for tar-burning. After Surminski 1997: 117. Right: A cross-section of a stack for tar-making built on a slope. After Egenberg 1997: 143.

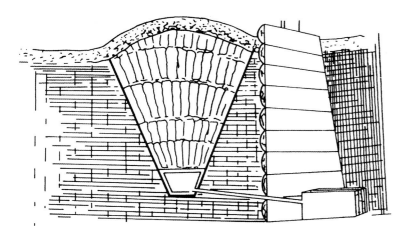

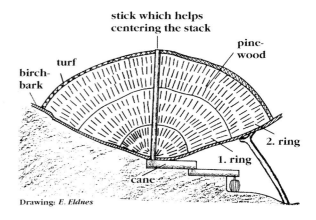

Fig. 20. The making of wood tar in a small stack by the charcoal-burning guild Eskilstrup Kulsvierlaug in 2013.
Top left: The stack, consisting of a funnel-shaped pit, which was then covered with a stack of pieces of wood – traditionally pine roots – of uniform size. Over the wood, turf has been laid, with the whole construction supported by stone paving.
Top right: The stack seen from the other side, where a gutter made of half a birch log, traditionally called the 'throat' runs out from the funnel-shaped pit into a bucket (this can be seen in more detail at bottom left). An incomplete burning first draws out pyroligneous acid, then the light wood tar, and finally the dark wood tar from the wood, which is tapped into the bucket through the cleft birch log.
Photos: The author, Viking Ship Museum in Roskilde.

The stack or pit was then covered with turf, soil, damp sawdust, twigs or a combination of several of these materials, and lit.[178] Removing covering floors or adding them to the stack or pit made the burning process controllable.[179] In the course of a few days – depending on the size of the stack or pit, as well as wind and weather – the pieces of wood were burnt and the tar was gathered at the bottom of the stack or pit, and tapped out through pipes or channels at the bottom (figs. 20 & 21).

The above-mentioned archaeological traces of the extraction of tar show that the extraction devices of the Late Viking Age varied in size and shape. Archaeological experiments and ethnological studies further demonstrate that both the quality and quantity of the tar extracted varied considerably.[180] For example, the smallest extraction units converted about 1 m³ of wood to about 10 litres of pure tar,[181] while the largest stacks can convert around 60 m³ of wood into around 2000 litres of pure tar.[182]

The individual tar product is evaluated by present-day traditional tar-burners by tasting, smelling, feeling and looking at the tar during production.[183] We can imagine a similar method of quality control being used by the 11th-century tar-burners. Besides the tar, the process produces a small amount of charcoal. A stack containing 60 m³ of pine wood has a by-product of about 2 m³ of charcoal.[184]

177. Jespersen 1986: 123–124; Egenberg 1997: 142.
178. Egenberg 1997: 142; Nielsen, S. 2002: 4–5; Glastrup 2010: 152.
179. Nielsen, S. 2002: 5–8.
180. Ihlen 1932.
181. Personal communication from Hans P.J. Nielsen. As a member of the guild involved in the Skuldelev 3 reconstruction *Sif Ege,* Hans Nielsen has participated in tar-burning experiments in collaboration with the Aggebo Charcoal Burning Guild.
182. Nielsen, S. 2002: 8.
183. Ihlen 1932: 20; Nielsen, S. 2002: 8–9.
184. Nielsen, S. 2002: 8.

General processes	Procurement	Preparation	Primary production	Modification, testing and modification	Use and mainte-nance
Processes in connection with the making of wood tar	Suitable resources are felled or produced by debarking and felling.	The raw materials are chopped and dressed to various dimensions. The stack or pit is built. The wood is put in the stack or pit.	The stack or pit is lit and a controlled burning produces tar.	The quality of the tar is assessed and mixtures are made.	The tar is used to protect and decorate.
Processes in connection with the making of grease/fats	Linseed or fat from a ruminant is collected.	Linseed is cold- or warm-pressed and the fat is heated.	The impure linseed oil and tallow are made.	The linseed oil is purified.	Linseed oil and tallow are ready for use as binder, lubrication etc.
Processes in connection with the making of pigments	Raw materials are procured locally or imported.	Some minerals and plants are crushed or grounded.	Minerals or plants are burnt or heated and an extract is produced. Ready-made pigments (primary products) are presumably also imported.	Colour extracts are used in different mixtures.	Can be used mixed with a binder as paint or to dye other primary products such as yarn.

Fig. 21. The processes in connection with the surface treatment of hull and fittings. Table: The author, Viking Ship Museum in Roskilde.

185. Lyngstrøm 2011a; Winther Olesen 2011: 83.
186. Lyngstrøm 2008: 70–99.
187. Personal communication from Henriette S. Lyngstrøm. Henriette S. Lyngstrøm is an archaeologist and associate professor at the Saxo Institute, Department of Archaeology, Copenhagen University.
188. Contains less than 0.1% phosphorus or carbon, see Lyngstrøm 2008: 9–14.
189. Contains 0.3% or more carbon, see Lyngstrøm 2008:9–14.
190. Contains 0.3% or more phosphorus, see Lyngstrøm 2008: 9–14.
191. Hardt 2003: 116; Lyngstrøm 2011b: 118–119.
192. Lyngstrøm 2011b: 118–119.
193. Jöns 1997: 117–119.
194. Møller 2012.

Iron parts

The processes from bog ore to finished iron product begin with the procurement of the necessary raw materials. All the resources – bog ore, clay tempered with sand or straw for the building of an extraction furnace, and wood for the production of charcoal – which are used in connection with iron extraction and forging, could be obtained and produced over more or less all of 11th-century Denmark.[185] However, metallurgical analyses make it clear that the quality of the bog ore varied from region to region.[186]

During the selection of the bog ore, the experienced prehistoric iron extractor could probably tell – by seeing, feeling and tasting it – the quality of the ore,[187] and thus also whether it was suitable for producing the three types of iron quality used in archaeological terminology; pure iron,[188] carbon iron[189] or phosphorus iron.[190]

Charcoal

Charcoal had a central role in connection with iron extraction and forging. Charcoal was produced in a pit or a stack.

If charcoal is produced in a stack, it is necessary for the pieces of wood used to have a uniform size, because the stack has to be packed tightly so that the air supply can be controlled. This control ensures a slow burn, which is a requirement for charcoal production.[192] If the charcoal is burnt in a pit, the requirements for the uniformity of the raw material are fewer, and the wood need not be stacked so carefully.[192]

After stacking, the stack or pit is lit. Turf or soil is used as a covering to ensure better control of the burning process (fig. 22). After a few days, the stack or pit can be opened and the charcoal can be taken out and used. Archaeological traces of charcoal stacks have been demonstrated at several iron extraction sites,[193] and many charcoal pits have been recorded in the present-day forests of Denmark.[194] The pro-

Fig. 22. An earth-covered charcoal stack, just lit, in connection with Eskilstrup Kulsvierlaug's annual charcoal burning in 2013, at Rønnede south of Køge. During the burning the stack is under constant supervision and is regularly beaten tighter with clubs (see picture, right) as the wood in the stack gradually collapses during burning. In this way the burning process can be controlled. Photos: The author, Viking Ship Museum in Roskilde.

duction of charcoal, considering its many uses, appears to have been very extensive in the Viking Age, both in Denmark and in the other regions of northern Europe where suitable raw materials could be procured.

Archaeologically, it would appear that deciduous trees, mainly oak, were the preferred raw material for charcoal burning in the Iron Age. It is possible that deciduous trees were also preferred in the Viking Age. Around 100 kg of air-dried deciduous wood would typically convert to between 20 and 25 kg of charcoal.[195]

Smelting

No Danish finds of iron extraction furnaces dated to the 11th century are known empirically, but metallurgical analyses of the iron objects of the time show that iron was extracted.[196] The lack of iron extraction furnaces must, therefore, be due to preservation and excavation conditions. Without direct evidence it is difficult to reconstruct the iron smelting furnace units of the time, but judging from finds of tapping slag, some of the furnaces were indeed slag-

tapping furnaces, and were built in a variety of forms and sizes.[197]

Once built, the iron smelting furnace was first pre-heated, and prior to this or at the same time, the ore was roasted. The roasting evaporates the water in the bog ore, and the mineral content is rendered uniform. The roasting process also ensures that the ore can be easily crushed into smaller pieces. After roasting and crushing, the ore can be used in the actual iron smelting process.[198]

To achieve the desired temperature[199] at which the slag flows and is separated from the iron, it would have been necessary to use charcoal. Alternately layering charcoal and roasted ore into the shaft in the proportions 1:1 or 1.5 volume of charcoal to 1 volume of bog ore, and blowing air into the furnace could create the necessary temperature. The blowing may have been done with bellows, or on a windy day the wind could be used.[200]

The time factor for the burning process would depend on the furnace type, the raw materials, wind and weather and the knowledge

195. Lyngstrøm 2002: 19; Lyngstrøm 2011b: 118–119.
196. Voss 1986: 29; Voss 1993a: 206 & 209; Voss 1995: 28; Voss 2002: 143–144; Buchwald 2008: 113; Lyngstrøm 2008: 91–92; Lyngstrøm 2013b: 122–124.
197. Buchwald 1991; Vellev 2004; Lyngstrøm 2008: 30–33; Rundberget 2015: 170–171.
198. Buchwald 1991: 2; Lyngstrøm 2002: 24; Lyngstrøm 2008: 37.
199. Around 1200 degrees Celsius.
200. Lyngstrøm 2013a: 135.

and skill of those participating. Between 10 and 30 hours is a likely suggestion for how long an extraction process may have lasted in the late part of the Viking Age.[201]

As mentioned above, 11th-century iron smelters had probably already evaluated the suitability of the ore for the production of various iron qualities in connection with the digging of the ore. Alternatively, the selection of the various qualities could be done in connection with the cleaning and refining of the 'iron sponge'.[202] In several cases, the smiths of the Viking Age and the High Middle Ages would seem to have deliberately chosen different qualities of iron in connection with the making of tools and other iron objects,[203] which underscores the great knowledge of iron production and forging at the time, as well as the ability to apply this knowledge in practice.

Cleaning

Archaeological iron research uses a guideline extraction formula where 100 kg of roasted bog ore becomes a 10 kg iron sponge, which after cleaning and refining becomes 2 kg of usable iron. The consumption of charcoal is about 50% higher than the amount of roasted bog ore. The weight of the unroasted bog ore varied depending on the type of ore used, but it is realistic to assume that the weight of the un-roasted bog ore was at least twice as much as that of the roasted ore.[204] It must however be emphasised that the iron smelters and forgers of the Late Viking Age could undoubtedly extract a larger amount of usable iron from the raw bog ore than the researchers today.[205]

In several cases, metallurgical analyses of iron would suggest that the procurement of raw materials and the extraction, forging and use of the finished product took place locally, and it is characteristic of the prehistoric[206] iron produced in Denmark that on the whole, it never appears in regular, standardised bar forms of the kind known from Norway, Sweden, England, France, Germany and Poland.[207] The iron produced from Danish bog ore, is, on the other hand, distributed over three general, but

not uniform morphologically determined groups: blocks, bars and sheets.[208] Comparing the interpretations of the sources it is likely that the Danish iron production in the Viking Age was relatively limited, and that both the iron production and the use of the finished products were mainly local phenomena.[209] We cannot preclude the possibility that iron production and forging was a specialised secondary occupation for some communities of the Viking Age[210], but generally speaking, neither refined iron nor iron tools were produced with a view to trading at the regional or supraregional level.

On the contrary, metallurgical analyses show that the Danish Viking Age communities imported iron in bar form that had been produced outside the Danish realm.[211] In southeastern Norway[212] in the areas Oppland, Telemark and in Sør-Hedmark, and in Sweden[213] in the areas Västergötland, Småland, Dalarne, Hälsingland, Västmanland and Värmland, large and small specialised ore-roasting, iron-smelting and iron-refining production sites have been identified. Several of these production sites were probably controlled by local magnates and kings, and they were particularly active from the last part of the Viking Age through the High Middle Ages.[214] Many of the products may very well have been intended as trading goods.[215]

Iron was thus both imported and produced locally. However, it is important to emphasise that the farmers' collectivities were probably responsible for much of the iron extraction and forging, both for their own households and as a secondary occupation in the many-stranded peasant economy.

Forging

Archaeological forging experiments suggest that rivets and spikes were made by selecting iron, probably in bar form, and then forging this until the required diameter on the shank of the rivet or spike was acheived. Afterwards, the shank was cut off with a hammer and chisel, then the piece was placed in a nail header, and the head of the rivet or spike was forged (fig.

201. Lyngstrøm 2008: 37.
202. Jouttijärvi 1996: 87.
203. Lyngstrøm 2008: 67–99.
204. Barbré & Thomsen 1983: 154; Lyngstrøm 2008: 116; Lyngstrøm 2015: 70–71.
205. Personal communication from Henriette S. Lyngstrøm. Henriette S. Lyngstrøm is an archaeologist and associate professor at the Saxo Institute, Department of Archaeology at Copenhagen University.
206. Iron Age, Viking Age and High Middle Ages.
207. Lyngstrøm 2008: 47–56.
208. Lyngstrøm 2008: 55–56.
209. Lyngstrøm 2011b: 116; Rundberget 2015: 180–183.
210. Martens 1995; Stoklund 1998; Bach Nielsen 2005.
211. Jensen 2004: 432; Roesdahl 1987: 132–135; Buchwald 2005: 246, 295–316; Lyngstrøm 2008: 47–56 & 91–92.
212. Rundberget 2015: 173–177.
213. Rundberget 2015: 171–173.
214. Rundberget 2015: 183.
215. Rundberget 2012.

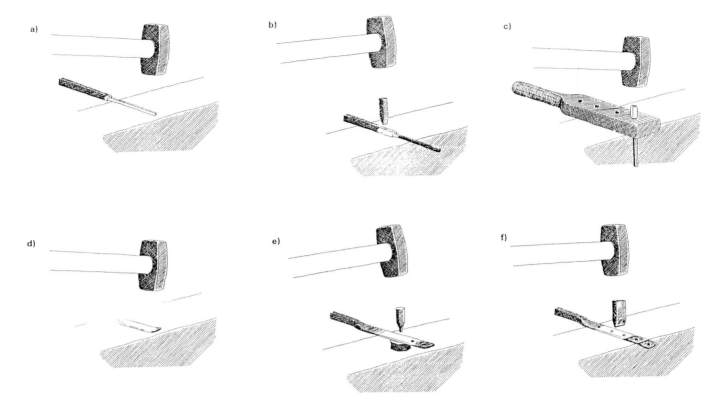

Fig. 23. Top; The process of making a rivet or a spike (a–c). Bottom: The process of making a rove (d–f). Drawing from Bill 1994: 56, Fig. 1.

23). It is still being discussed whether the rivet or spike was afterwards surface-treated with tar to give it a protective coat against rust.[216]

The roves were probably made by first selecting a suitable piece of iron in sheet form and then forging this into a flat bar with the desired dimensions. A punch was then used to perforate the bar. Finally, a hammer and chisel were probably used to knock the rove free of the flat bar (fig. 23).[217]

From the 6th century until the end of the 11th century, the shanks of rivets and spikes were almost exclusively produced in round form in southern Scandinavia. In the same period, rivets and spikes were mainly made with square shanks in the southeastern Baltic area. From the 12th century on, rivets and spikes with both round and square shanks were used for shipbuilding in southern Scandinavia.[218] To this general picture of the morphological characteristics of the rivets

and spikes the following should be added: the spikes used in the ship finds Hedeby 1 and Roskilde 3 and possibly also a few spikes and rivets in Hedeby 2 and 3, have a square cross-section. 24 of the rivets excavated at the Fribrødre Å site have a square shank, while only one rivet has a round shank (fig. 24).[219] These deviations from the general tendency can be interpreted as: 1) the use of imported objects; 2) the participation in the construction of boatbuilders with origins in the Slavic shipbuilding technology; or 3) an interaction between Nordic and Slavic techniques and methods.

In connection with all three interpretations it should be remarked that Hedeby 1, 2 and 3 and probably Roskilde 3 were built in areas (fig. 6) where both Scandinavian and southern Baltic craftsmen and merchants were active, which is why the areas can be interpreted as technological and cultural contact zones.

216. Bill 1994; Vadstrup 1997a: 41–47; Frederiksen 2009.
217. Bill 1994; Vadstrup 1997a: 41–47; Frederiksen 2009.
218. Bill 1994.
219. Klassen 2010: 199.

As for the morphological features of the roves – quadratic, rhomboid or rectangular – it is characteristic that variously formed roves were used (fig. 25). However, the traces of the roves used on Roskilde 3 are described as exclusively rectangular, and Skuldelev 5's roves are all described as slightly rhomboid (fig. 25). The empirical material offers a very scant basis for drawing conclusions, but perhaps the various morphologies of the roves were due to their production by many different smiths or workshops. In the two cases where morphologically uniform roves were used, it is possible that the roves were made by the same smith or the same workshop.

A noteworthy feature is the traces of 'barbs' or 'grooves' on the underside of some of the rivet and spike heads. These have been documented in several places on the planks from the Roskilde ships (fig. 26). The barbs and grooves may have been used during forging to get the head positioned properly on the shank.[220]

Traces of barbs are documented on Roskilde 3, where at least three different nail headers – one with four barbs, one with five barbs and one with seven barbs – were used to make the rivets for the ship.[221] In addition, traces of barbs are present on the following four ship finds: Roskilde 2,[222] where a single case is documented with eight barbs on a plank (fig. 26);[223] Roskilde 5,[224] where many traces of rivets with 4–8 barbs are documented;[225] Roskilde 6,[226] where the traces of one rivet with cross-grooves has been registered on a repair plank (fig. 26);[227] and Roskilde 9,[228] where a repair plank shows traces of a rivet with four square barbs beneath the head of the rivet.[229]

It is possible that far more rivets and spikes were made with barbs and grooves in the Viking Age and the High Middle Ages. The lack of documentation may be due to preservation conditions. Furthermore, it must also be acknowledged that the traces of barbs and grooves are extremely difficult to recognise.

The barbs and grooves appear in different numbers and in different patterns, which shows that different nail headers were used. These differences in the nail headers used can be interpreted as indicating different craft or workshop traditions. Particular smiths or workshops may perhaps have wished to show that the rivets or spikes were made as a result of their work. Alternatively, can the barbs or grooves be interpreted as indicating a particular quality of rivets and spikes?

In connection with the latter interpretation, metallurgical analyses of rivets from the Viking Age boat graves in Vestfold in Norway should be noted. These analyses suggest that particular iron qualities were used in different places in the vessels. To rivet the planks of the strakes together, rivets made of pure iron were mainly used, while the nails that were used to hold together keel and stem parts had a higher content of phosphorus.[230] Unfortunately it is not clear whether the rivets and spikes of different iron qualities were also made with morphological features that enabled immediate visual distinctions, for example with barbs or grooves.

Besides the Norwegian-found rivets, the rivets from the Viking Age site Vestby Mark near Selsø on Zealand should be mentioned. Metallurgical analyses of these rivets also show a high content of phosphorus.[231] Is it possible that phosphorus iron was preferred for the rivets that were used for shipbuilding? Theoretically, phosphorus iron was more resistant to rust, but at the same time it is clear that the brittle character of phosphorus iron may have made its use for rivets difficult.[232] An experimental archaeological testing of the hypothesis is in progress at the Viking Ship Museum in Roskilde in connection with the reconstruction project The Gislinge Boat II.[233]

Iron anchors are only sparsely represented among the object material from the Viking Age. Examples are known from Ribe,[234] from the Oseberg Ship Burial[235] and from the Ladby Ship Burial.[236] To these five anchors can be added: one from Vestnes south of Trondheim,[237] one from the Södertälje Canal in Sweden,[238] one from the harbour of London,[239] a fragment of an arm fluke from Schleswig,[240] and one unpublished find at Kolkous in Iceland.[241]

220. Frederiksen 2009: 10.
221. Bill 2006b: 10.
222. Dated to after 1185.
223. x134B, see Bill 2006a: 37.
224. Dated to after 1131–1136.
225. Bill 2007a: 11.
226. Dated to after 1015–1025.
227. x263, see Bill 2007b: 40.
228. Dated to after 1171.
229. Bill 2007c: 13.
230. Christie et al. 1979; Christensen 1995: 124.
231. Buchwald 2005: 304–306.
232. Lyngstrøm 2008: 12.
233. Sørensen et al. forthcoming.
234. Bencard 1979; Aistrup 1979; Jensen 1991: 22; Rieck 2004: 173–175.
235. Shetelig 1917: 319–320; Rieck 2004: 177.
236. Sørensen 2001: 51–55.
237. Carpenter 1995.
238. Haasum 1989: 26–27.
239. The Blackfriars Anchor, see Marsden 1994: 160–161.
240. Crumlin-Pedersen 1997b: 145.
241. Damgård-Sørensen et al. 2007: 15.

Shaft (cross-section) / Ship finds	Round	Square	Square/round	Shaft cross-section not recorded
Fotevik 1[1]	X			
Fotevik 2[2]				X
Fotevik 3[3]				X
Fotevik 4[4]				X
Fotevik 5[5]				X
Fribrødre Å[6]	X (1 rivet)	X (24 rivets)	X (4 rivets)	
Hedeby 1[7]		X (spikes)	X (rivets)	
Hedeby 2[8]			X (rivets)	
Hedeby 3[9]			X (Spikes)	
Roskilde 3[10]	X (rivets)	X (spikes)		
Skuldelev 1[11]	X			
Skuldelev 3[12]	X			
Skuldelev 5[13]	X			

Fig. 24. Shaft design of the rivets and spikes. Table: The author, Viking Ship Museum in Roskilde.

NOTES
1. Crumlin-Pedersen 1984: 35-36.
2. Crumlin-Pedersen 1984: 40-43.
3. Crumlin-Pedersen 1984: 43-45.
4. Crumlin-Pedersen 1984: 45-46.
5. Crumlin-Pedersen 1984: 46-49.
6. Klassen 2010: 197-204.
7. Crumlin-Pedersen 1997b: 224-236.
8. Crumlin-Pedersen 1997b: 237-238.
9. Crumlin-Pedersen 1997b: 250-251.
10. Bill 2006b.
11. Crumlin-Pedersen & Olsen 2002: 57 & 101-119.
12. Crumlin-Pedersen & Olsen 2002: 57 & 199-217.
13. Crumlin-Pedersen & Olsen 2002: 57 & 250-264.

Rove shapes / Ship finds	Rhomboid	Rectangular	Quadratic/ rhomboid/ rectangular	Rove shapes not recorded
Fotevik 1[1]			X	
Fotevik 2[2]				X
Fotevik 3[3]				X
Fotevik 4[4]				X
Fotevik 5[5]				X
Fribrødre Å[6]			X	
Hedeby 1[7]			X	
Hedeby 2[8]			X	
Hedeby 3[9]				X
Roskilde 3[10]	X			
Skuldelev 1[11]			X	
Skuldelev 3[12]			X	
Skuldelev 5[13]	X			

Fig. 25. Design of the roves. Table: The author, Viking Ship Museum in Roskilde.

NOTES
1. Crumlin-Pedersen 1984: 35-36.
2. Crumlin-Pedersen 1984: 40-43.
3. Crumlin-Pedersen 1984: 43-45.
4. Crumlin-Pedersen 1984: 45-46.
5. Crumlin-Pedersen 1984: 46-49.
6. Klassen 2010: 197-204.
7. Crumlin-Pedersen 1997b: 224-236.
8. Crumlin-Pedersen 1997b: 237-238.
9. Crumlin-Pedersen 1997b: 250-251.
10. Bill 2006b.
11. Crumlin-Pedersen & Olsen 2002: 57 & 101-119.
12. Crumlin-Pedersen & Olsen 2002: 57 & 199-217.
13. Crumlin-Pedersen & Olsen 2002: 57 & 250-264.

Fig. 26. Examples of imprints after barbs and grooves beneath the rivet heads. Left, the imprint of a rivet with eight barbs beneath the head, on plank 1469 x134B, from the Roskilde 2 ship find. Right: The imprint of a rivet head with cross-grooves on the underside, on plank 1482 x263, from the Roskilde 6 ship find.

Photo: Ivan Conrad Hansen, Viking Ship Museum in Roskilde.

242. Buchwald 1996.
243. Blakelock *et al.* 2009;
Rundberget 2015: 178–179.
244. Rahbek 1980.
245. Made from bog
ore or other kinds of ore.
246. Here made from
bog ore.
247. Aistrup 1979: 159;
Rahbek 1980; Wahl 1999: 20.
248. Jesch 2001: 169.
249. Jensen 1991: 22.

As for the production site and production conditions for the anchors, it should be mentioned that the provenance of the slag inclusions in the anchor from Ladby has been determined as southern Norway.[242] However, the method of determining provenance is still being developed,[243] which makes it problematic to verify the methodological factors, and in the end may compromise the validity of the result. Analyses of the Ribe anchor show that it was not made of bog ore iron, so it must have been made of iron produced outside the primary geographical area of study of this book.[244]

Despite the very limited source material it seems likely that iron anchors were not made from ore procured within the present primary geographical area of study in the 11th century. Anchors were either produced using imported iron[245] or imported as finished anchors. At the above-mentioned specialised production sites in Norway and Sweden, large quantities of iron[246] were produced. Perhaps it was at such production sites that the iron for the anchors, among other things, was produced and later

exported to both Danish and other northern European actors.

The greatest challenges when an anchor was to be forged were on the one hand the procurement of the large quantities of iron, on the other the handling of the large object in the forge and on the anvil. The procedure probably entailed first welding bars or sheets of iron together into two large pieces and then welding these two pieces together into the shank and arms of the anchor respectively.[247]

Few iron anchors are known from the Viking Age, even at the northern European level. The explanation may be both preservation conditions and the rarity of anchors in the Viking Age. The large quantities of iron that were necessary to make the anchors would have represented great value in the Viking Age. One can read in the skaldic poems that an iron anchor symbolised high social status,[248] and in the French annals from the 8th and 9th centuries that anchors could be hired before a sea voyage. Iron anchors were expensive to produce and could be owned only by the few.[249]

The relatively small, light Viking Age anchors – although the stock, anchor ring, and in some cases also buoy rings and the anchor cable should be included in the overall weight – raise issues about anchoring in the Viking Age. Did the vessels only rarely anchor? Or did boats and ships have several smaller anchors on board, such that an anchoring could be effected – in a 'V' configuration – with several small anchors? In connection with the latter possibility, it is interesting that several wood-stone anchors have been found in the Danish waters, at least two of which have been dated to the Viking Age or Middle Ages.[250]

A wood-stone anchor consists of crossed arms of wood on which one or more stones have been placed, functioning as weights, all held together by withies or other suitable material. It is usually unclear whether anchors of this type were used as ships' anchors or as net or trap anchors, but they may well have functioned as a less resource-intensive type of anchor.

Besides rivets, roves, spikes, anchors and the links of the anchor cable, iron was also used to produce hooks and swivels, rigging and stay rings, fittings, rails and various hooks.[251]

The procurement of usable iron for the production of the vessel parts was twofold in the 11th century. The raw materials were either procured by digging up bog ore which was later converted into iron by iron smelting and cleaning processes, or imported as usable iron made from bog ore or from some other type of ore (fig. 27).

The subsequent processes by which the iron was worked into the desired form for the finished product were also twofold. It is probable that the above-described barbs and grooves beneath the heads of rivets were made with a view to demonstrating the products of a particular workshop or a particular quality of rivets and spikes, which indicates that there may have been a specialised production of some iron objects. The production of iron anchors also supports this tendency, but at the same time it is likely that other iron objects were made by non-specialist craftsmen as part of the many-faceted economy of 11th-century society.

Finally, some iron objects were imported as finished products ready to be used when building, maintaining, rigging or equipping the boats and ships.

Sails

Several of the vessel finds dated to the 11th century carried sail: the hull forms and mast attachment systems point clearly to thus. However, the technical and morphological properties of the sails and the manner in which they formed part of the rigging on the vessels are far more problematic to determine.[252] To this we can add another difficult matter to elucidate – the material and quality of the sailcloth.

Sails made of wool

There are very few archaeological sail fragments from the Nordic countries.[253] From the early part of the Viking Age, one can mention the Oseberg and Gokstad ship burials, in which fragments of densely woven wool with sewn-on, finger-thick pieces of rope[254] have been interpreted as fragments of sailcloth.[255] The Oseberg and Gokstad sailcloth fragments are woven both in plain weave and in a 2/2 twill weave. The threads in both warp and weft are Z-spun, and the cloth is densely woven with 13–14 threads per cm in the warp and 8–9 threads per cm in the weft.[256] The sailcloth fragments at Trondenes Church[257] are also close-woven, and in principle, the fragments resemble preserved sailcloth from the 1700s and 1800s from Amla and Nordmøre – both in structure and thread type.[258]

Medieval sailcloth fragments of wool are known, as mentioned, from Trondenes Church in Norway,[259] and many textile fragments that were perhaps once part of sailcloths have been found in Iceland at the sites Bergþórshvoll, Stóraborg and Viðey. However, more accurate dating of the Icelandic textile fragments is problematic,[260] and since it is even doubtful whether they were parts of sailcloths, the Icelandic textile finds will not be analysed further

250. Genner Bay at Haderslev and Aggersund on the Limfjord.
251. Thorvildsen 1957: 38–39; Bischoff & Jensen 2001: 224–225.
252. Nýlen 1986; Andersen & Andersen [1989] 2007; Heide, E. 2006; Heide, V. 2006; Planke 2006; Kastholm 2009; Crumlin-Pedersen 2012; Bischoff 2016; Kastholm 2016.
253. Möller-Wiering 2002: 114–115.
254. Reef points?
255. Andersen *et al.* 1989: 13–16; Ingstad 1992b: 222–223; Andersson 2000: 166.
256. Ingstad 1992a: 1996–198.
257. Dated to 1280–1420.
258. Andersen 2009: 11.
259. Godal 1994: 271–278; Andersen 2009: 10–11.
260. Dating framework: from Viking Age to recent times.

General processes	Procurement	Preparation	Primary production	Modification, testing and modification		Use and maintenance
Processes in connection with the production of rivets, roves and spikes	Bog ore is dug up and transported to the production site. Charcoal is produced. Alternatively, refined iron is imported, after which forging begins.	Bog ore is roasted in fires and the iron-smelting furnace is built.	The direct extraction begins. Refining of iron sponge and sorting of the various iron qualities produced.	Selection of refined iron and forging to a bar size that can be handled in a nail header and sheets that can be forged into roves on the anvil.	Production of rivets, roves and spikes in a process with many modifications and tests.	Rivets and roves as well as spikes are used to hold the vessel parts together.
Processes in connection with the production of anchors and anchor cables	Possibility 1: Bog ore is dug up and transported to the production site and charcoal is produced. Possibility 2: Refined iron is imported and charcoal is produced, after which forging begins. Possibility 3: Ready-made anchors are imported.	Only possibility 1: Bog ore is roasted in fires and the iron-smelting furnace is built.	Only possibility 1: Direct extraction begins. Refining of iron sponge and sorting of the various iron qualities produced.	Only possibilities 1 and 2: Selection of refined iron and forging to a bar size suitable in length and diameter for rings, links, hooks and swivels. Selection of refined iron and forging to a bar size suitable for welding anchor shanks and arms.	Only possibilities 1 and 2: Welding of bars in two pieces: one forming the shank, one forming the arms. These two pieces are later welded together into an anchor. Forging of anchor and buoy rings and the links, hooks and swivels of the anchor cable in a process with many modifications and tests.	The anchor is used and may undergo minor modifications in connection with its use in a vessel.
Processes in connection with the production of stay and shroud rings	Bog ore is dug up and transported to the production site. Charcoal is produced.	Bog ore is roasted in fires and the iron-smelting furnace is built.	Direct extraction begins. Refining of iron sponge and sorting of the various iron qualities produced.	Selection of refined iron and forging to a bar size suitable for forging stay and shroud rings on an anvil.	Production of stay and shroud rings in a process with modifications and tests.	Stay and shroud rings are used together with the cables and ropes of the standing rigging.

Fig. 27. The processes in connection with the production of iron objects. Table: The author, Viking Ship Museum in Roskilde.

261. Möller-Wiering 2002: 149–157.
262. The ship was built around 1142 and the last repairs were done around 1167, see Bill 1997: 185.
263. Andersen et al. 1989: 28.
264. Möller-Wiering 2002: 78–80.
265. Andersen 1995: 266–267.
266. Möller-Wiering 2002: 115 & 177.
267. Möller-Wiering 2002: 115 & 177.

in this context.[261] A wool textile fragment re-used as caulking material in connection with a repair in the Lynæs Ship[262] has also been interpreted as a fragment from a wool sailcloth.[263] Since then, doubt has been cast on this interpretation and the textile fragment has instead been interpreted as part of a garment.[264] In this context it should be mentioned that both the archaeological and the ethnological source material suggests that the same weaves and thread

types were used for sailcloth and other textiles.[265] It is therefore possible that several textile fragments were part of the sails of the past, but it is extremely difficult to determine such things if details such as reef point, eyes or boltropes are not preserved.[266] It should be noted, however, that the scanty sailcloth material at least shows two common features: high thread density and a coating of the sailcloth.[267]

When the use of wool for sailmaking is to be analysed, it is necessary to know the various components of the wool. One generally distinguishes between two different types of sheep race: the primitive and the modern. The prehistoric wool finds in Scandinavia all come from sheep of the so-called primitive race. The wool from primitive sheep races consists of an outer layer, called the outer fleece, and an inner layer called the under wool.[268] Both wool types were used for sailmaking in northern Europe during the 18th, 19th and 20th centuries, and something similar may have been the case in connection with 11th century production of wool sails.

The weight of a sail varies between 400 and 1000 g per m².[269] For a small sail, a light cloth[270] would have been necessary, because a strong and heavier cloth is too stiff if it is used for a sail of small dimensions. On the other hand, a strong and heavier cloth[271] is necessary for a large sail, since a sail of large dimensions made from light cloth will quickly be destroyed.[272] Else Østergård points out that a sheep annually produces 1.5–2 kg of raw wool.[273] A small part of this raw wool is not suitable for spinning, and must therefore be left out of the calculation. In addition, not all the spinnable wool is suited as raw material for sailmaking. Archaeological experiments indicate that a sheep[274] of a size and wool type comparable to those of the 11th-century Scandinavian sheep annually produces about 500 g of wool suitable for sailcloth production.[275] The remaining spinnable wool can be used for many other purposes.

In an area like Löddeköpinge in Scania, where the archaeological traces suggest that there was extensive textile production in the 11th century, the landscape was probably dominated by multitudes of grazing sheep.[276] Shepherds, pens or pasturing on islands were probably used to tend the many sheep.[277]

In the 19th and 20th centuries, the wool in certain parts of Denmark was washed after shearing or plucking; in other places the sheep was washed before shearing of plucking; and finally there were regions where neither wool nor sheep was washed before or after shearing or plucking.[278] The practice in the 11th century cannot be determined, but it is probable that local customs, then as now, led to different local or regional practices.

After the wool has been shorn or plucked from the sheep, it is sorted. Ethnological studies and oral and written accounts from the 19th and 20th centuries show that wool was treated differently depending on local customs. It was combed or carded, beaten with thin, smooth debarked twigs, dried near a heat source, or spun directly with no further prior treatment.[279] Archaeologically, we know of finds of wool combs,[280] but by all indications wool was not carded in Scandinavia before the end of the Middle Ages.[281] The thrashing of wool produced fibres that after spinning and weaving became a uniform material, and this may have been a desirable property in the cloth for a sail. After one or more of these processes, the wool was ready to be spun.

Quality

The concept of quality has long been a topic of discussion in textile research. Professional textile production is described as being expressed materially in products that are homogeneous and of good quality.[282] But what is good quality? The problem is that quality should be viewed in relation to the purpose for which the textile is produced.[283] In connection with the quality a sailcloth should have, a high thread density is important.[284] To achieve the required density, it is necessary to use tools to beat or press the weft threads together. For this, a sword beater and a weaving comb are both suitable, and both are known archaeologically.[285] Moreover, the finishing treatment made the sailcloth highly windproof and ensured that it could endure longer as a functioning sail.[286]

From the sites Henne Kirkeby Vest,[287] Löddeköpinge II,[288] Sebbersund[289] and Selsø-Vestby,[290] the number of spindle whorls and loom weights, as well as other textile-production tools excavated, is so high, that the production was probably concentrated on textiles. It is possible that several of these textiles were used to

268. Warburg 1974: 18; Wild 1988: 13–20.
269. Andersen 1995: 259; Nørgård 2009b: app. 1.
270. For example 13–14 warp threads and 8–9 weft threads per cm with a weight of 600–800 g per m².
271. For example 8 warp threads and 5 weft threads per cm with a weight of 800–1000 g per m².
272. Nørgård 2016.
273. Østergård 2003: 40.
274. Norwegian *spelsau* and *wild-sheep*.
275. Nørgård 2009a: 9.
276. Andersson 2000: 176.
277. Hoff 1997: 217–248.
278. Højrup 1966: 178.
279. Hald 1950: 130–132.
280. Ryder 1983: 539; Østergård 2003: 42.
281. Østergård 2003: 42–43.
282. Bender Jørgensen 1992: 76; Geijer 1972: 98–99.
283. Bender Jørgensen 1992: 75–77.
284. Andersson 2000: 160.
285. Andersson 2000: 174; Nørgård 2009b: 22–27.
286. Andersen *et al.* 1989: 31–36.
287. Frandsen 2013: 165–168.
288. Andersson 2000: 182–184; Svanberg & Söderberg 2000: 319.
289. Birkedahl Christensen & Johansen 1992: 219; Nielsen, J. N. 2002: 11 & 25.
290. Ulriksen 1998: 75–77.

291. Ulriksen 1998: 75–77;
Andersson 2000: 183.
292. Andersson 2000: 183.
293. Nørgård 2009a;
Nørgård 2009b: 15.
294. Nørgård 2009b: 51;
Personal communication
from Anna Nørgård. Anna
Nørgård is a hand-loom
weaver and has been involved
in several experimental
archaeological textile projects.
295. Højrup 1966: 195–199.
296. Ravn 2012a: 145–146.
297. Østergård 2003: 58–60;
Andersen 2009: 11–13;
Nørgård 2009b: 15–19.
298. Nyberg 1984: 145–150;
Elsner 1992: 54.
299. Personal communication
from Anna Nørgård.
Anna Nørgård is a hand-
loom weaver and has
been involved in several
experimental archaeological
textile projects.

Fig. 28. The warp-weighted loom with selected parts indicated. Photo: Werner Karrasch, Viking Ship Museum in Roskilde.

make sailcloth, but it cannot be proven. In Löddeköpinge and Selsø-Vestby, other archaeological finds that can be interpreted as marlin spikes[291] and bone pins with dimensions that make them usable in the sailmaker's work,[292] indicate, however, that sail-related activities took place at the sites. This makes it seem likely that the textiles woven at the sites were to some extent used for sailcloth.

Spinning

The spinning process is the most time-consuming phase in sailcloth production. Archaeological experiments conducted by Anna Nørgård suggest that for a 25 m² sail of wool, made in 2/1 twill with 13 warp threads and eight weft threads per cm, it takes about 2000 working hours to spin the yarn and sewing thread with a spindle.[293] As a comparison, Nørgård's experiments show that it takes about 1600 working hours to weave the cloth on a warp-weighted loom.[294] The highly time-consuming spinning process may however have been done on every available occasion and often along with other chores, just

as it was done among peasants in the 18th and 19th centuries.[295] It is moreover possible that children participated in the work of spinning yarn as their contribution to the textile making of the time.[296] In these ways, the seemingly great burden of work became part of the other chores of the day and thus more manageable.

The warp-weighted loom

In 11th-century Scandinavia, the warp-weighted loom was the most commonly used loom type (fig. 28) – that is, a loom with one beam and loose-hanging, weighted warp threads.[297] It has been claimed that a tackle/block excavated in the Hedeby harbour area show that the horizontal treadle loom was also used at the end of the 10th century for weaving in southern Scandinavia.[298] However, because of the find context, the tackle/block can also be interpreted as part of a winch used in connection with the work in the harbour.[299] Nonetheless, we cannot preclude the possibility that the horizontal treadle loom had begun to be used at this juncture.

In order to describe the setting-up of the warp system and the further processes in connection with weaving on a warp-weighted loom, the starting point must be the details that can be observed in the textiles found, as well as the artefacts that can be interpreted as related to textile production. Alongside this, it is necessary to reconstruct both tools and processes that indicate how the Viking Age weavers used the warp-weighted loom.

Before the warp system can be put on the loom, it is needed to process the yarn. First the yarn is made wet and warm – either with water or with steam – and later the wet yarn is stretched, for example on a niddy-noddy.[300] Such a niddy-noddy is known from the Oseberg Ship Burial.[301] If time is not a problem, the yarn can also lie wound up for about a year, after which a similar effect will have arisen. The purpose of this preparation is to prevent the yarn winding around itself in connection with the weaving.[302]

The warp system can be made in various ways, each of which is suited to a particular weave. Moreover, the length of the warp determines how long a length of cloth can be. After the warp has been laid on the loom, the loom weights are attached to the warp threads, and heddles are used to attach some of the warp threads to the heddle rods so they can be lifted forward in connection with the weaving process.[303]

During the actual weaving, it is particularly important – and difficult – for the weaver to keep the selvedges straight and to keep a uniform distance between the warp threads. When the weft threads are laid in with the shuttle and become part of the weave, it is important to maintain an appropriate balance between tight and loose positioning of weft threads and to ensure that the weight for the warp threads is balanced for the desired quality and appearance of the finished textile.[304]

Of the frequently used and archaeologically attested tools that are used in connection with weaving on a warp-weighted loom, the sword beater and the weaving comb should be mentioned.[305] The sword beater is used to beat the weft threads together, while the weaving comb is used partly to lay the weft threads closely together and partly to hold the warp threads in place by passing them horizontally and diagonally across the threads.[306]

Loom weights and spindle whorls are the most frequently-seen archaeological traces of textile production, presumably because the weights are made of materials such as stone and glass[307] as well as fired and unfired clay, which are generally well preserved.[308]

Once the lengths of cloth are finished and taken off the loom, it is an often used practice to soak the cloth lengths in water. This process removes stiffness and tension in the cloth (fig. 29). However, neither sailcloth fragments nor the results of archaeological experiments suggest that textiles woven for use as sailcloth were fulled. Fulling is problematic because the process makes the cloth shaggy, which reduces its strength and means that the cloth absorbs too much fat during the subsequent treatments of the sailcloth.[309]

Traces of colour in the ship burials from Gokstad and Ladby,[310] as well as the representations of coloured sails in the Bayeux Tapestry,[311] make it likely that sails were to some extent coloured, and perhaps even painted with didactic images[312] in special cases.[313] The colouring was done either by dyeing the threads before weaving or the lengths of cloth before sewing. Alternatively, the sailcloth could be painted after it had been sewn together.[314]

Sewing sails

It is considered reasonable to assume that the densities of the cloth lengths varied in the 11th century, and since density is of great importance to the functionality of a sail, the selection of the positioning of the various lengths of cloth in the sail would have been important.[315] A high degree of sailing experience is necessary to be able to determine the most appropriate positioning of the various cloth lengths, which indicates that this part of the working process involved one or more particularly expert sailors.

300. Nørgård 2009b: 40–43.
301. Grieg 1928: 135–172.
302. Lightfoot & Aarø 1998; Nørgård 2009b: 41.
303. Nørgård 2009b: 29–40.
304. Nørgård 2009b: 43–48.
305. Østergård 2003: 56; Nørgård 2009b: 22–27.
306. Nørgård 2009b: 22–27.
307. Only spindle whorls.
308. Nørgård 2009b: 54–55.
309. Nørgård 2009b: 55; Andersen & Bischoff 2016.
310. Christensen 1979; Bischoff & Jensen 2001: 239–241.
311. Rud 2008: 63, 66 & 88–98.
312. Depicting for example the military achievements of kings and magnates.
313. Pentz 2014.
314. Bill et al. 2007: 27.
315. Andersen & Bjøru 2000.

The next process was to sew the lengths of cloth together and cut the sailcloth to size (fig. 29). After this, reef points were sewn into the sailcloth and the holes used for tying the sail to the yard were strengthened with edging. After this, the four sides of the sailcloth were edged and the boltrope was stitched to the sail.[316]

The relationship between sailcloth and boltrope is of great importance to the functionality of the sail. The boltrope relieves the sometimes intense traction on the sail from the bowline, sheets and tack, and defines the scope for the 'depth' of the sail under the effects of wind. In connection with this, the materials and dimensions of the boltrope and sailcloth must fit with one another, and a very fine balance is required.[317]

There are no Viking Age finds of boltropes, but the Gulating Law and ethnological studies suggest that boltropes in the 11th century were made of a variety of materials: Horsetail and cowtail hair, as well as hemp rope and rope made of skin or roots and branches.[318]

Coating

When a sail was finished and installed on the ship with the standing and running rigging, it was presumably tested in use (fig. 29). Through testing and adjustments, the sail found its form. After this process, the sail was ready to be coated. Coating stabilises, seals, conserves and decorates the sailcloth. From ethnological studies, we know of many variations on the choice of method and materials for coating sails. In Norway, both linen and wool sails were coated with a mixture of grease, tar and sometimes ochre. In other cases, linen sails were coated with a mixture of birch bark, seawater, slaked lime and wood tar.[319] The mixtures with which 11th-century sails were coated cannot be identified. However, we can reasonably assume that sails were treated, because untreated sailcloth will not function optimally and will perish after a few years.[320]

A wool sail that is well maintained – that is, which is given regular coatings and repairs –

can remain functional for around 15–30 years, while a linen sail – again carefully maintained – can be used for about eight to ten years. The boltropes of both sail types were probably replaced after five to ten years.[321]

Sails made of linen

No flax-based textiles dated to the Viking Age or High Middle Ages can be related to use as sailcloth. However, written sources suggest that linen was used for sailcloth production in the High Middle Ages and perhaps also in the later part of the Viking Age.[322] Furthermore, finds of retting wells[323] and clothing made of linen[324] show that the raw material was part of the textile production of the 11th century. It thus seems reasonable that some of the flax-based textiles were used to make sailcloth.

Farming

The first process in connection with the use of flax for textile production is the cultivation and harvesting of the flax plant (fig. 29). Flax can only be grown with poor results on very damp or very dry soil. If the flax is grown on sandy soil, the linen textiles produced tends to be coarser and more hard-wearing than if it is grown on hard clayey soil, where the produced textiles often become soft and less hard-wearing. Flax thrives – that is, produces the best yield for use in textile production – in a cool, moist climate with plenty of sunlight and wind.[325] Ethnological sources and archaeological experiments with the cultivation of flax show that it is problematic to grow flax in the same place year after year. Rotation periods of six to eight years where the field area can be planted with other crops in the intervening period are most productive. It may also be necessary to fertilise the soil.[326]

Flax seed is sown very densely, and its cultivation involves a great deal of weeding. If the flax is harvested as a young, still-green plant, one has a basis for the production of very fine fibres and unripe seeds, while a late harvest produces coarser fibres and ripe seeds. Flax is harvested by pulling up the whole plant with the

316. Nørgård 2009b: 55–57.
317. Andersen 2009: 14.
318. Svabo [1781–1782] 1959: 77–87; Kristjánsson 1982: 202–206; Lightfoot & Aarø 1998; Miller 1889: 284–285; Gulatingslovi, XIII, chapter 14, section 308 [Robberstad 1952: 278].
319. Personal communication from Erik Andersen. Erik Andersen is a ship reconstructor at the Viking Ship Museum in Roskilde; Eldjarn & Godal 1988: 223–227.
320. Cooke & Christiansen 1999; Hvid & Ravn 2016.
321. Personal communication from Erik Andersen. Erik Andersen is a ship reconstructor at the Viking Ship Museum in Roskilde; Personal communication from Anna Nørgård. Anna Nørgård is a hand-loom weaver and has been involved in several experimental archaeological textile projects.
322. Falk [1912] 1995: 76–78; Thier 2002: 92–95; Andersen 2009: 5.
323. Møller Hansen & Høier 2000: 78–80.
324. Fentz 1998.
325. Ejstrud et al. 2011: 9.
326. Ejstrud et al. 2011: 9.

root, because the fibres used for textile production extend deep into the soil.[327]

Preparation

Once the flax plants have been harvested, they are dried in the sun and wind, either in bundles in the open field or on frames in a process called airing. After this drying, the seeds are removed either with the bare hands or by using a ripple – a short-handled rake with tines of wood or iron.[328] Fragments of such an implement are known archaeologically from Coppergate in York, dated to the 12th or 13th century,[329] but it is not clear whether the ripple was used in Viking-Age Scandinavia. From a rational perspective, however, it does seem likely.

The next process releases the fibre bundles from the flax stalks. To take out the fibres one must remove the adhesive – consisting of pectin A and lignin – that holds the fibres together. This process is called retting, and can be done either with water or with dew (fig. 29). If the retting is done with cold water the water has to be slightly running and the water temperature at least 12 degrees Celcius, otherwise the process stops. Archaeological experiments have shown that water-retting takes 5–10 days if the water temperature is 17–20 degrees Celcius. The lower the temperature, the longer the retting processes takes, and if the temperature is lower than 12 degrees Celcius, the processes stops.[330] A small proportion of 'old' retting bacteria is also important in new retting processes. The content of 'old' retting bacteria may, however, also be too high, which makes the retting processes impossible.[331]

If the flax is dew-retted, the stalks are spread in a thin layer and turned over either each week or every other week, depending on wind and weather. Experiments have shown that dew-retting can be done more or less throughout the year, but that the ideal season is late summer to early autumn. At this time of year, the air humidity is high and the temperature generally well suited to the dew-retting processes.[332]

After retting, the stalks must be made 'bone-dry', and this is done in the sun, close to the heat of a kiln or over a pit containing heated stones.[333]

After drying, the outer skin and woody fibre of the stalks are beaten from the released bast fibres. Clubs and other suitable implements can be used in this process.[334] The wooden clubs from the Oseberg Ship burial are often described as clubs used for scutching flax, but in connection with archaeological experiments at the Ribe Viking Centre reconstructions of these wooden clubs have proved poorly suited to the purpose.[335] Perhaps a so-called flax breaker was used in connection with the scutching of the flax stalks. During the excavation of the Iron Age settlement site at Feddersen Wierde an object was found that has been interpreted as a flax breaker.[336]

Afterwards, the flax threads are combed out and are then ready to be spun into thread.[337] The spinning and weaving process is, generally speaking, the same, whether flax or wool is used. The above description of the spinning and weaving processes in connection with the production of sails of wool therefore covers the further process of production leading to a finished linen sail. (fig. 29).

Rigging

Most rope finds from Hedeby and Schleswig have been identified as made of oak and elm bast.[338] However, there are a number of problematic factors in the identifications that will be presented here.

Ole Magnus has conducted a comparative analysis of the lime bast rope material from Højbro Plads and the rope finds from Hedeby and Schleswig. These analyses indicate that the many specimens from Hedeby and Schleswig were not made from oak or elm bast, but from lime bast.[339] It should be mentioned here that archaeological experiments with ropemaking have shown that oak bast is extremely difficult to use to make rope.[340] When we add to this that the differences between oak bast, elm bast and lime bast are very difficult to determine

327. Møller Hansen & Højer 2000: 79.
328. Møller Hansen & Højer 2000: 79; Ejstrud *et al.* 2011: 9.
329. Rogers 1997: 1724.
330. Mannering 1996: 77–80.
331. Møller Hansen & Højer 2000: 80–81.
332. Ejstrud & Thomsen 2012: 18–21.
333. Møller Hansen & Højer 2000: 81.
334. Ejstrud *et al.* 2011: 10.
335. Ejstrud *et al.* 2011: 27; Ejstrud & Thomsen 2012: 23.
336. Haarnagel 1979: table 28.4.
337. Mannering 1996: 77–80; Andersson 2000: 161.
338. Körber-Grohne 1977: 73.
339. Magnus 1999: 4 & 31.
340. Magnus 1999: 29–31.
341. Crumlin-Pedersen 1997b: 188; Kalmring 2010: 373–374.
342. Magnus 1998a: 3.
343. Crumlin-Pedersen 1997b: 188–191 & table 8.6; Magnus 1999: 4.

General processes	Procurement	Preparation	Primary production	Modification, testing and modification		Use and maintenance
Processes in connection with the production of wool sails	Sheep breeding (perhaps also goat-breeding). Plucking or shearing.	The wool is sorted, probably by combing. The wool may have been washed.	Spun into sewing thread and yarn. The yarn is woven into lengths of cloth.	Some sails were coloured. Either the lengths of cloth were dyed or the yarn was dyed before weaving. The finish sailcloth could also be painted.	The lengths of cloth are sewn together and cut to shape. The sail is edged and reinforced. Boltropes, seizing etc. are sewn on. The holes for the reef-earing gaskets and for attaching the sail to the yard are reinforced.	Testing and greasing and barking of sailcloth. Maintained with regular greasing and barking and repairs.
Processes in connection with the production of linen sails	Cultivation and harvesting of flax.	Retting of plant stalks, which are afterwards broken, scutched and hackled so the fibres can be released and sorted.	Spun into sewing thread and yarn. The yarn is woven into lengths of cloth.	Some sails were coloured. Either the lengths of cloth were dyed or the yarn was dyed before weaving. The finish sailcloth could also be painted.	The lengths of cloth are sewn together and cut to shape. The sail is edged and reinforced. Boltropes, seizing etc. are sewn on. The holes for the reef-earing gaskets and for attaching the sail to the yard are reinforced.	Testing and greasing and barking of sailcloth. Maintained with regular greasing and barking and repairs.

Fig. 29. The processes in connection with the production of sails. Table: The author, Viking Ship Museum in Roskilde.

344. Magnus 1998b: 271–275.
345. Crumlin-Pedersen & Olsen 2002: 62.
346. The database for archaeological rope material made by Ole Magnus, at the Viking Ship Museum in Roskilde.
347. Crumlin-Pedersen 1997b: 188–191 & table 8.6; Magnus 1999: 4.
348. Crumlin-Pedersen 1997b: 188–191 & table 8.6; Magnus 1999: 4.

even with a microscope, we must consider it highly likely that the majority of rope finds from Hedeby and Schleswig have been mistakenly identified as made of oak bast.[341] To sum up, this means that lime bast was the primary raw material for ropemaking in the Viking Age and the High Middle Ages. It should be noted, however, that the predominance of rope finds made of lime bast may be due to preservation conditions. Archaeological experiments have shown that in the right conditions, bast is excellently preserved in soil and under water, while rope made of hemp fibres and rope made of hair, hide and skin is broken down much more quickly.[342]

Besides lime bast, willow bast and grass have been used to make rope.[343] In addition, a rope made of hazel has been documented from Viborg Søndersø[344] and one rope fragment made of withies is known from the Skuldelev find.[345] At Horsmark, a rope has been found that was made of spun wool,[346] and seven fragments of rope from Schleswig were made of animal hair.[347] In 21 cases from Schleswig,[348] in two cases from Kalvebod Strand, and in one case from Roskilde 6, withy fragments have also been found.[349]

In the following, the focus will be on lime bast rope.

Ropes of lime bast

In the Viking Age and the early High Middle Ages, ropes were exclusively made by hand only; no turning tools were used.[350] Lime trees were presumably grown as coppice forest in the Viking Age, and the long, young shoots in the coppices would have been suitable as raw material for the extensive production of rope.[351]

After the trees had been felled, bark and bast were peeled from the logs and retted under water (figs. 30 & 32). The heartwood may have been used as firewood. After the retting and drying process the bast could be separated from the bark and finally used to make rope (figs. 30 & 32).[352] First, two or three strands were made, either by spinning threads that were later plied into strands, or by spinning the strands directly.[353] The bast layers were offset so that long threads or strands could be made,[354] and afterwards the strands were laid into a rope (figs. 30 & 32). In some cases, threads and strands were spun and plied respectively, each in its own direction, in other cases the spinning and plying directions were the same.[355] However, the rope was always laid in the opposite direction of the plying of the strands. If the strands were S-plied, the rope was laid Z-plied, and vice versa.[356]

No traces of tar or grease have been documented on the rope material analysed.[357] It is possible that fat was used to a limited extent, but a surface treatment of lime bast rope with tar as protection again moisture seems unlikely, because lime bast rope is stronger when wet than when dry.[358]

It has been discussed whether rope made of hemp was used on board boats and ships in the Viking Age. The earliest fragments of hemp rope found in a maritime context are from the Vejby Cog, dated to ca 1375.[359] However, since processing and production of hemp is documented in Norway and Sweden from the Germanic Iron Age on,[360] and since the local pollen diagrams from Fribrødre Å have a conspicuous presence of hemp in the active period of the building site, it is possible that hemp was grown with a view to ropemaking.[361] The absence of finds of hemp rope from the Viking Age may therefore be due to preservation conditions.

Ropes of skin, hide and hair

Rope was also made of animal skin, hide and hair. In his account of his voyages from the end of the 9th century, the magnate Ohthere[362] says that he received tribute in the form of rope of whale or walrus skin[363] as well as seal,[364] which is described as ship's rope.[365] In the later written sources from the High Middle Ages, rope of walrus skin is mentioned[366] as well as other hide ropes[367] made from seal, deerskin, elk or ox hide. In addition, hairs from horses'[368] and cows' tails as well as hair from pigs and outer fleece from sheep were used.[369]

Animal hair was spun into threads that were later made into strands and finally laid into rope. Hide and skin ropes were made by cutting hides into strips and treating them with hard rubbing and greasing with heated fat, and later twisting them directly either into ropes or strands (fig. 32). The strands were then made into rope.[370]

The written sources also states where in the rigging the various ropes were used. It is mentioned that rope of walrus hide and other hide ropes were used for halyards, shrouds and stays, as well as for anchor cables, while ropes of horsehair were used for boltrope, bowlines, sheets and braces.[371] Experimental archaeological use of horsehair rope has shown that the ropes do not become stiff – even in very cold weather – and are highly flexible, which makes them suitable as ropes in the running rigging, but unsuited – because of the flexibility – in the standing rigging.[372]

349. The database for archaeological rope material made by Ole Magnus, at the Viking Ship Museum in Roskilde.
350. Magnus 2006: 33–34.
351. Magnus 2006: 31; Møller 2012.
352. Magnus 1999: 9–19; Myking *et al.* 2005: 68–69.
353. Magnus 1998a: 10.
354. Magnus 1998a: 10.
355. The database for archaeological rope material made by Ole Magnus, at the Viking Ship Museum in Roskilde.
356. The database for archaeological rope material made by Ole Magnus, at the Viking Ship Museum in Roskilde; Persson 2013: 145–147.
357. The database for archaeological rope material made by Ole Magnus, at the Viking Ship Museum in Roskilde.
358. Magnus 2008: 29.
359. Crumlin-Pedersen 2010: 118.
360. Barrett *et al.* 2007: 304; Jessen & Stylegar 2012: 139–140.
361. Christensen & Fischer Mortensen 2010: 46–47 & 55.
362. See Bately 2007: 46.
363. *Hwæles.*
364. *Sioles.*
365. *Sciprapas.*
366. *Rosmalreip, svarðreip.*
367. *Hudreip.*
368. *Simereip.*
369. Andersen 1997a: 181.
370. Magnus 1998a: 14.
371. Andersen 1997a: 181.
372. Magnus 1998a: 8.

*Fig. 30. The various
working processes in
connection with the
production of lime-bast
rope. After the raw
materials have been felled,
bark and bast are peeled
from the logs. Bark and
bast are then laid out for
retting under water, and
after the retting process,
the bast is separated from
the bark. Afterwards the
bast is dried and later used
to make rope. Photos:
Werner Karrasch, Viking
Ship Museum in Roskilde.*

General processes	Procurement	Preparation	Primary production	Modification, testing and modification	Use and maintenance
Processes in connection with the production of bast rope	Trees are felled, bark and bast are cut from the trunk.	Bark and bast are retted and afterwards the bast is separated from the bark and dried.	The bast is used to make strands (spun and plied), which are later laid together into rope.	The rope can be surface-treated with grease, but probably not with tar.	Becomes part of a vessel's rigging or other cordage, and is regularly maintained, perhaps with grease.
Processes in connection with the production of rope of hair, hide and skin	Hair, hide and skin from animals is procured.	The hairs are spun into threads, while hide and skin is rubbed and greased with fat and twisted either directly into rope or strands.	The spun threads are plied into strands which are afterwards laid into rope.	The finished rope surface is not treated, or is treated with only a little grease.	Becomes part of the rigging of a vessel, or is used for another purpose on board. Regularly maintained.
Process in connection with the production of withies	A young tree with a small trunk diameter is selected.	In the spring the trunk of the young tree is twisted off and the roots are severed a small distance from the trunk.	The withy can either be used directly or stored for later use.	The withy may be surface-treated before use. If a withy has been stored for later use, it must first be laid in water for a few days to regain its flexibility.	The withy is used as a means of fastening rigging to hull and rudder to rudder frame.

Fig. 32. The processes in connection with the production of ropes and withies. Table: The author, Viking Ship Museum in Roskilde.

373. The database for archaeological rope material made by Ole Magnus, at the Viking Ship Museum in Roskilde; Crumlin-Pedersen 1997b: 188–191 & table 8.6; Magnus 1999: 4; Crumlin-Pedersen & Olsen 2002: 62.
374. Shetelig 1917: 309.
375. With a diameter of about 5 cm.
376. Nielsen 2011: 78; Englert *et al.* 2013: 54–55.
377. Hjelm Petersen 2012: 23.
378. Often Z-plied.
379. Crumlin-Pedersen & Olsen 2002: 60–61.
380. Möller-Wiering 1997: 304; Crumlin-Pedersen & Olsen 2002: 60–61.
381. Möller-Wiering 1997.

Making withies

Withies made of hazel, birch, oak and juniper have been documented.[373] In addition, a pine root had been used to attach the rudder to the rudder frame in the Oseberg Ship.[374] Withies were used as a medium for attaching rigging to hull as well as attaching the rudder to the rudder frame.

A withy was made by selecting a suitable young tree,[375] which, in the course of the spring, when the sap was rising, was twisted from the top down to ca 20–30 cm from the root (fig. 31). Afterwards, the roots were cut off a little way out from the trunk, and the withy was used directly afterwards. A withy could also be kept for later use, but then it had to be laid in water for some days before use to regain its flexibility (fig. 32).[376]

Caulking

Judging from the empirically known caulking material, the plank-built vessels of the 11th century were mainly caulked with wool from several sheep races. The wool was S-spun into coarse yarn or strands. In the following analysis, these will simply be referred to as strands, following the terminology developed by Anette Hjelm Petersen and Carsten Hvid.[377] The strands were later laid together,[378] coated with tar and then used as caulking material.

Caulking materials

The diameters of the individual strands vary considerably from 1.5 to 10 mm,[379] but the most frequently used thread thickness was between 2 and 5 mm.[380] Besides sheep wool, cow

Fig. 33. Description of the caulking material from the analysed ship finds. Table: The author, Viking Ship Museum in Roskilde.

NOTES
1. Crumlin-Pedersen 1984: 36.
2. Klassen 2010: 423.
3. Crumlin-Pedersen 1997b: 227.
4. Crumlin-Pedersen 1997b: 97.
5. Crumlin-Pedersen 1997b: 101-102.
6. Hjelm Petersen 2012.
7. Crumlin-Pedersen & Olsen 2002: 60-61.
8. Crumlin-Pedersen & Olsen 2002: 60-61.
9. Crumlin-Pedersen & Olsen 2002: 60-61.
10. Humbla 1934: 1-21; Åkerlund 1948.

Ship finds	Caulking materials
Fotevik 1[1]	Twisted sheep's wool probably first dipped in tar.
Fribrødre Å[2]	Plank PL 40: Caulking material of sheep's wool and moss.
Hedeby 1[3]	Consists of sheep's wool treated with pine tar. Pollen analyses have shown that the sheep grazed in meadow areas close to a forest with many beeches. Primarily coarse S-spun wool strands.
Hedeby 2[4]	Not possible to identify.
Hedeby 3[5]	Not possible to identify.
Roskilde 3[6]	Wool. 26 specimens from the caulking were analysed. Seven different types of caulking identified: (1) felt sheet; (2) two strands plied together; (3) three strands plied together; (4) four strands plied together; (5) five strands plied together; (6) six strands plied together; and (7) seven strands plied together. They are plied together with between one and two coils per 10 cm. 20 of the samples had S-spun strands, which had later been Z-plied, while four samples consisted of S-spun strands that had later been S-plied. The last two samples were felt sheet.
Skuldelev 1[7]	In connection with either repair phase 1 or 2 caulking material consisting of both cow hair and wool is mentioned. It consists not of spun strands, but of felt sheets.
Skuldelev 3[8]	A caulking groove can be demonstrated on all the planks and in it there are many occurrences of tarred woollen strands laid together as caulking (S-spun, Z-plied, 3-4 strands, 2.5-4 mm thick). The caulking was laid in the groove before the riveting of the planks. In the scarfs usually only a small quantity of caulking was used, probably because the scarfs were so accurately fitted that sealing material was only necessary to a limited extent.
Skuldelev 5[9]	In the construction phase wool was used for strands which are S-spun, and later four strands were Z-plied. The diameters of the strands are between 4 and 10 mm. For repairs wool was used: S-spun strands, later laid together Z-plied, as well as felt.
Äskekärr 1[10]	Tarred animal hair. Not much caulking material in the lands, but more in the scarfs.

General processes	Procurement	Preparation	Primary production	Modification, testing and modification		Use and maintenance
Processes in connection with the direct production of caulking material	Animal hair (mainly sheep's wool) is plucked or shorn from the animals.	Sorted, some probably combed, some used directly without combing.	Spun into strands which are plied together into cords of caulking material.	Greased or dipped in tar.	Laid in lands and scarfs.	Used as sealing material. In the event of repairs, new caulking can be inserted or hammered in.
Processes in connection with the use of residual products or unworked materials as caulking	Residual products from other production or plucked or shorn animal hair (mainly wool).			Greased or dipped in tar.	Laid in lands and scarfs.	Used as sealing material. In the event of repairs, new caulking can be inserted or hammered in.

hair was used in a few cases,[381] and both coarse and fine, as well as spun, rolled or felted fibres were used (fig. 33).[382]

In general, caulking material for the individual ship appears to have been non-homogeneous, with Skuldelev 3 as an exception. It is even likely that Skuldelev 3 was caulked with identically made material in both the construction and the repair phase.[383]

Since it is difficult to imagine that the preferred, coarse-spun, relatively thick wool yarn could be used for making textiles, it is highly likely that the strands were spun for direct use as caulking material.[384] In other cases, the non-homogeneous caulking material indicates that re-used and residual products were used as caulking material. Whereas plied strands were almost exclusively used in the lands, plied strands and felt[385] were both used in the scarfs.

Besides animal hair, moss was used as caulking material at the Fribrødre Å site (fig. 34). Moss is usually seen as caulking material in connection with the Slavic shipbuilding technology,[386] while animal hair is usually used in the Nordic shipbuilding technology.[387] The combined use of moss and animal hair as caulking material, which is documented from the plank PL 40 (fig. 33), has therefore been interpreted as a mixture of the two shipbuilding technologies.[388]

To sum up, the caulking material for the plank-built vessels was both made directly for use as caulking material, and residual as well as plucked or shorn untreated wool and other animal hair were also used. The caulking was greased or dipped in tar and later laid into scarfs and lands before the vessel parts were assembled. (fig. 34).

Fig. 34. The processes in connection with the production of caulking material. Table: The author, Viking Ship Museum in Roskilde.

382. Möller-Wiering 1997; Crumlin-Pedersen & Olsen 2002: 60–61.
383. Crumlin-Pedersen & Olsen 2002: 60–61.
384. Möller-Wiering 1997: 304.
385. Felt was only used to a limited extent.
386. See chapter II, section: Shipbuilding technology and regionally delimited shipbuilding practices, for a more detailed description.
387. See chapter II, section: Shipbuilding technology and regionally delimited shipbuilding practices, for a more detailed description.
388. Klassen 2010: 204–205.

III. Resources

For all production, and thus also for shipbuilding, both natural and human resources are needed. In this chapter, the natural resources will be analysed first, partly in an analysis of the tree species and qualities with which the Viking-Age shipbuilders built ships, and partly in an analysis based on experimental archaeology exploration of the amounts of natural resources necessary to build the various ship types of the Viking Age. Later, there will be an analysis of the working hours involved in building the different ship types and sizes in the Viking Age. The analyses of the amounts of necessary natural resources and human resources are based on empirical data resulting from building full-scale ship reconstructions at the Viking Ship Museum in Roskilde.

Tree species used in late Viking-Age shipbuilding, and their qualities

The first part of the investigation of resources use in connection with Viking-Age shipbuilding focuses on the choice of tree species and qualities. The suitability of tree species for shipbuilding is analysed and there is a discussion of the intentions that the boatbuilders of the time may have had in connection with their use of wood resources.

Alder[1]
Alder was used to make components for Hedeby 1, Hedeby 3 and Skuldelev 5 (fig. 35). In Hedeby 1, two side frames and a *biti* or thwart stanchion were made of alder. In Hedeby 3, a long keelson knee, two *biti* knees, three *bitis*, a futtock and a floor timber were made of alder. Finally, a stringer from Skuldelev 5 was also made from the same material.

Today, alder is not considered a suitable wood for shipbuilding, because timbers of alder have an extremely limited life when subjected to a combination of humidity and drying. Such factors are basic conditions for the wood components in an open clinker-built ship.[2] Other properties of alder would, however, have been advantageous in connection with use for shipbuilding. In connection with drying-out the raw material does not change shape, and wood from alder is easy to work.[3]

Experimental archaeological experience of the use of alder for shipbuilding is good, also in terms of its longevity.[4] These positive results must, however, be viewed in relation to the fact that all ship parts are treated with wood tar before they are installed in a ship, and that a ship is regularly treated with wood tar.

Ash[5]
In some cases, tree species were presumably chosen for special ship parts on the basis of the physical properties of the wood. The ash plank with oar ports in Skuldelev 5 is an example of this. The physical properties of ash, which include high resistance to mechanical wear, which for example arises between oar and oar port during rowing, make this wood particularly suitable as raw material for the strakes where the oar ports sit (fig. 35).[6] Ash was also chosen for floor timbers, side frames, stanchions, *bitis*, beams and knees in Hedeby 1, and for knees in Hedeby 3 (fig. 35).

It is notable that ash was used in such relatively large quantities to make frame timbers in Hedeby 1. In general, Hedeby 1 is built of raw materials of the best quality – that is, without knots and twisted growth.[7] The choice of ash can therefore be seen as expressing a deliberate choice of particular trees, which, because of

1. *Alnus glutinósa.*
2. Wagner 1986: 133; Moltesen 1988: 84.
3. Wagner 1986: 133; Moltesen 1988: 84.
4. Nielsen 2012.
5. *Fraxinus* sp.
6. Wagner 1986: 132; Moltesen 1988: 103–108.
7. Crumlin-Pedersen 1997b: 183.

their optimal form, were especially well suited to the purpose at hand, and not as indicating any shortage of more suitable wood types.

Beech[8]

The resistance of beech wood to variations in humidity is low and its drying shrinkage is high.[9] In addition, it should be mentioned that fresh beech wood can be difficult to work with an axe.[10]

With these factors in mind, it is noteworthy that beech was used to make vessel parts. It is documented that beech was used to make fenders and rowlocks at the Fribrødre Å site, and in Skuldelev 3 the outside cleats are made of beech (fig. 35). Moreover, Hedeby 2 was built with some planks made of beech (fig. 35).

One explanation of the use of this not eminently suitable wood for shipbuilding may be that the boatbuilders had to use the materials that were directly available. The planks of beech in Hedeby 2 may serve as an empirical indication of this. Otherwise, it should be noted that beech was only used in connection with the building of ships of modest size and usually for ship components that probably had to be replaced several times in the course of the ship's active use. It should also be noted that beech is highly resistant to attacks of shipworm and crustaceans, and is generally highly durable if the wood is kept well soaked.[11]

Hazel[12]

A single stanchion from Hedeby 1 has been identified as made of hazel (fig. 35). The use of hazel as raw material for anything but treenails is rarely seen, but precisely the shape of the stanchions may have made pollarded hazels well suited as raw material.

Maple[13]

In Hedeby 1 and 3, maple was used to make knees. In addition, a frame fragment from Hedeby 3, probably from a floor timber, was made of maple (fig. 35). It may be that maple was used to make ship components for two of the ship finds from Hedeby because maples, with suitable dimensions for shipbuilding, grew locally in the area around Hedeby. It was probably Norway maple[14] that was used for shipbuilding, since Norway maple can grow to tree size, while common maple[15] is bush-sized and only rarely grows to tree size.[16]

Oak[17]

Oak was the raw material of choice for shipbuilding in 11th-century Denmark (fig. 35), with the production of treenails being the only case where oak was not the most frequently used wood type (fig. 35). However, there were great differences in the types of oaks that were preferred as raw material for the different vessel parts. For the planks, the longitudinal reinforcements, the keel and the keelson, erect, high-boled oaks would have been preferred, while the crooked timber resources from low-boled, curved trees would normally be used for frame parts.

Written and ethnological sources dealing with shipbuilding in the 19th and 20th centuries[18] describe dense-growing durmast oak[19] as the most suitable resource for planks, while common oak[20] growing in open-canopy woodland such as hedgerows, was regarded as the most suitable resource for frame parts. The durmast oaks are described as having a tendency to grow tall and straight, which makes it especially suitable as a resource for planks, keels, keelsons and stringers. The common oak, on the other hand, often developed large, strong side branches, which in shipbuilding can be preferable as a resource for floor timbers, knees and stems.[21]

The practical observations made by the 19th- and 20th-century boatbuilders are partly supported by the scientific research indicating that durmast oak has a tendency to grow more erect and high-boled in dense stands than common oak. In addition, durmast oak has fewer knots than common oak. Furthermore, both durmast oak and common oak in open canopies have a low bole and crooked growth.[22] It should

8. *Fagus* sp.
9. Wagner 1986: 134; Moltesen 1988: 67–68.
10. Vadstrup 1997a: 40.
11. Wagner 1986: 134; Moltesen 1988: 67–68.
12. *Corylus* sp.
13. *Acer* sp.
14. *Acer platanoides*.
15. *Acer campestre*.
16. Wagner 1986: 135; Moltesen 1988: 81–82.
17. *Quercus* sp.
18. Frost 1985.
19. *Quercus petraea*.
20. *Quercus robur*.
21. Frost 1985: 2.
22. Wagner 1986: 132; Moltesen 1988: 95; Crumlin-Pedersen 1997b: 179–184; Møller 2012.

be emphasised, however, that there are exceptions to these general tendencies: erect, high-boled common oaks and durmast oaks are also found in open-canopy woodland habitats, and low-boled and crooked common oaks and durmast oaks can be found in closed-canopy woodland habitats.

Whether the boatbuilders of the 11th century distinguished between common oak and durmast oak like the historical boatbuilders described above cannot be determined. It has not been possible to say whether archaeological finds of oak were common oak or durmast oak. The difference cannot be determined on the basis of wood anatomy or pollen analysis.[23] Even with DNA analyses, the contamination of later times with modern DNA and the fact that common oak and durmast oak have a tendency to hybridise makes identification problematic.[24]

An English investigation of differences in chloroplast DNA among present-day old stands of British common and durmast oak shows that it is possible to see differences in haplotypes among the stands of common oak and durmast oak within a region. However, the investigation also shows that a haplotype, which in one region is seen among the stands of common oak, can be found in another region among stands of durmast oak.[25] Whether it will be possible to distinguish common oak from durmast oak on the basis of DNA analysis of fossil oak in Denmark is thus unclear.

Old, free-standing and crooked oaks can achieve a diameter at breast height of about 3 m,[26] but these oaks would not have been suitable for shipbuilding. The oaks that were suitable as a resource for shipbuilding are unlikely to have had a diameter at breast height that was greater than 1.5–2 m – and such a diameter was probably extremely rare.[27]

In the 11th century, oaks with a breast-height diameter of more than 1 m were by all indications not numerous.[28] Among the erect, high-boled oaks, the largest trunks probably reached heights of around 15 m and a total height of around 30 m.[29]

Compared with oak trees today, those of the Viking Age were generally of slower growth.[30] A slowly grown oak has less strength and durability, less density and volume weight, as well as a lower ultimate stress under pressure.[31] On the face of it, it seems that the Viking-Age boatbuilders had access to 'poorer' raw materials than present-day boatbuilders and ships' carpenters. However, the slow-growing oaks have a higher degree of flexibility, which is an advantage when vessels are built with the Viking-Age wet deciduous wood technology where long radially cleft planks are used.[32] What is today regarded as a poor quality of oak for shipbuilding may thus have been considered a good quality for shipbuilding in the Viking Age.

Pine[33]

Some of Hedeby 2's planks are made of pine, as are four planks and a single floor timber in Skuldelev 5 (fig. 35). It is possible that the raw materials for the smaller pine planks in Skuldelev 5's 4th strake in the port side, which respectively measure 0.20 m in width and 2.0 m in length and 0.28–0.30 m in width and 2.6 m in length,[34] could have been felled in the woodlands of 11th-century Denmark.[35] The same is the case with the smaller pine planks[36] from Hedeby 2.[37] As for the floor timber in Skuldelev 5, it is also likely that it could have been made of raw materials from 11th-century Danish woodlands. In contrast, it seems less likely that the very long planks in Skuldelev 5's 5th and 6th strake on the port side – which respectively measure 14 and 10.5 m and are both between 0.30 and 0.32 m in width[38] – could have been made of pines that grew in the woods within the area investigated here in the 11th century.

Woods used for treenails

The preferred wood for making treenails in 11th-century southern Scandinavia was willow (fig. 35). It is difficult to determine which type of willow was used, but sallow[39] has been suggested as a likely type.[40] Willow would have

23. Personal communication from Claus Malmros. E-mail correspondence, November 2012. Claus Malmros is a museum curator and senior consultant at the Natural Science Department of the National Museum of Denmark.
24. Personal communication from Niels Bonde. E-mail correspondence, November 2012. Niels Bonde is a dendrochronologist and senior researcher at the Natural Science Department of the National Museum of Denmark.
25. Cottrell *et al.* 2002.
26. Moltesen 1988: 95.
27. Wagner 1986: 132.
28. Christensen 1995: 125; Vadstrup 1997a: 38; Englert *et al.* 2013: 51.
29. Wagner 1986: 132; Moltesen 1988: 95.
30. Møller 2012.
31. Moltesen 1988: 95–102; Poulsen 2005: 67.
32. Nielsen 2012.
33. Crumlin-Pedersen & Olsen 2002: 252–253.
35. See chapter IV for a more detailed description of the woodlands of 11th-century Denmark.
36. Width ca 0.23 m.
37. Crumlin-Pedersen 1997b: 238–239.
38. Crumlin-Pedersen & Olsen 2002: 252–255.
39. *Salix caprea.*
40. Christensen 1996a: 21; Jensen 2002: 1.

	Keel components	Keelson & Mast-fish	Stem components	Planks	Floor timbers	Intermediate frames	Stanchions	Bitis	Thwarts	Beams	Knees	Futtucks	Stringers	Treenails	Wedges in treenails	Other ship components
Fotevik 1[1]	Oak	–	–	Oak	Oak	–	Oak	–	–	–	Oak	–	Oak	Willow & pomaceous fruit	–	–
Fotevik 2[2]	–	–	–	Oak	–	–	–	–	–	–	Oak	–	Oak	–	–	–
Fotevik 3[3]	–	–	–	Oak	Oak	–	–	–	–	–	Oak	–	–	–	–	–
Fotevik 4[4]	–	–	–	Oak	–	–	–	–	–	–	–	–	–	–	–	–
Fotevik 5[5]	–	–	–	Oak	Oak	–	–	–	–	–	Oak	Oak	Oak	–	–	–
Fribrødre Å[6]	Oak	-	Oak	Oak	-	-	-	-	-	-	-	-	-	*1	*2	*3
Hedeby 1[7]	Oak	–	Oak	Oak	Oak (3), ash (4)	Ash (4), red alder (2)	Ash (1), hazel (1), red alder (1)	Ash	–	Ash	Maple, oak, ash	–	–	Willow	Oak	–
Hedeby 2[8]	–	Oak	–	Oak (15), beech (4), pine 6)	Oak	–	–	–	–	–	–	–	–	Juniper	–	–
Hedeby 3[9]	–	Oak	–	Oak	Red alder, maple	--	–	Red Alder	–	–	Oak (6), red alder (3), maple (1), ash (1)	Red alder	–	Willow	Oak	Rudder frame: Oak
Roskilde 3[10]	Oak		Oak	Oak	Oak	Oak	–	–	–	–	–	–	–	Conifer	Oak	–
Skuldelev 1 (repair phase 2)[11]	Oak	–	–	Oak	--	–	–	--	–	–	–	--	--	Willow	Pine	–
Skuldelev 3[12]	Oak	Oak	Oak	Oak	Oak	–	Oak	Oak	Oak	–	Oak	Oak	Oak	Willow & hazel	Oak & Willow	*4
Skuldelev 5[13]	Oak	Oak	Oak	*5	Oak, pine (1)	–	Oak	Oak	–	–	Oak	Oak	Oak, Red ald-er	Willow	Oak	*6
Äskekärr 1[14]	Oak	Oak	Oak	Oak	Oak	–	–	Oak	Oak	–	Oak	Oak	–	Juniper	Pine	*7

Fig. 35. The tree species used for shipbuilding in 11th-century Denmark. The specific number of ship components is only given in the cases where several different woods were used, since the intention is to illustrate the primary and secondary tree species used.

Key to the figure: The number of documented ship components is given in brackets: -: means either that the ship element was not found or that the tree species used has not been identified: *1: willow (42 units), oak (6 units), hazel (61 units), elder (1 unit), hawthorn (1 unit), buckthorn (6 units), ash (4 units), maple and lime; *2: oak (103 units), willow (13 units), beech (3 units) and red alder (1 unit); *3: Fender: beech; Tholepins: beech (2 units), hazel (1 unit), maple (1 unit); Breasthooks: oak; *4: Outside cleats: beech or oak; Inside cleats: beech; Bulkheads: oak; Bitt: oak; *5: Mainly oak but also pine (4 units) and ash (1 unit); *6: Oar port bung: oak; *7: Wale: oak; Fender beam: oak. Table: The author, Viking Ship Museum in Roskilde.

NOTES

1. Crumlin-Pedersen 1984: 27-60; Bill 1997: 167-168; Jensen 1999: B36-B37; Crumlin-Pedersen & Olsen 2002: 241; Rosborn 2004: 198.
2. Crumlin-Pedersen 1984: 27-60; Bill 1997: 167-168.
3. Crumlin-Pedersen 1984: 27-60; Bill 1997: 167-168.
4. Crumlin-Pedersen 1984: 27-60; Bill 1997: 167-168.
5. Crumlin-Pedersen 1984: 27-60; Bill 1997: 167-168.
6. Bonde 1984; Skamby Madsen 1984; Skamby Madsen & Klassen 2010.
7. Crumlin-Pedersen 1997b: 81-95, 179-186 & 224-236 & 2010: 83-85; Jensen 1999: B22-B23.
8. Crumlin-Pedersen 1997b: 96-99, 179-186 & 236-241.
9. Bill 1997: 175-176; Crumlin-Pedersen 1997b: 99-104, 179-186 & 242-251; Jensen 1999: B24-B25; Englert 2000: 167.
10. Daly 1999:2-5; Bill et al. 2000: 229-231; Englert 2000:169; Bill 2006b: 3-35.
11. Olsen & Crumlin-Pedersen 1969: 131; Bartholin 1998; Jensen 1999: B28-B29; Englert 2000: 170; Crumlin-Pedersen & Olsen 2002: 65-66 & 97-140; Crumlin-Pedersen 2010: 109-110.
12. Bonde 1998; Jensen 1999: B30-B31; Englert 2000: 174; Crumlin-Pedersen & Olsen 2002: 67 & 195-243; Crumlin-Pedersen 2010: 110.
13. Olsen & Crumlin-Pedersen 1969: 131; Jensen 1999: B26-B27; Crumlin-Pedersen & Olsen 2002: 67-68 & 245-278; Crumlin-Pedersen 2010: 86-87.
14. Humbla 1934: 1-21; Åkerlund 1948; Bråthen 1998: 13-15; Borg et al. 2000; Englert 2000: 165; Jakobsson 2003.

41. The treenail type dominantly used for shipbuilding, cf. Westphal 2006: 89.
42. Salix sp.
43. Quercus sp.
44. Corylus sp.
45. Rhamnus cathartica.
46. Fraxinus sp.
47. Sambucus sp.
48. Crataegus sp.
49. Acer sp.
50. Tilia sp.
51. Juniperus sp.
52. Wagner 1986: 134; Vadstrup 1997a: 41.
53. Quercus sp.
54. Salix sp.
55. Fagus sp.
56. Alnus glutinósa.
57. Pinus sp.
58. For example more or less all the vessel parts in Hedeby 1. See Crumlin-Pedersen 1997b: 183–184 & 224–236.
59. For example several of the Skuldelev 5 planks. See Crumlin-Pedersen & Olsen 2002: 269–273.
60. Crumlin-Pedersen & Olsen 2002: 205; Nielsen 2012.
61. Crumlin-Pedersen & Olsen 2002: 252; Nielsen 2012.

been easy to procure in the Danish forests of the time, and it is even likely that willow was cultivated by the coppicing method, which would have produced willow in dimensions suitable for treenail production.

Treenails were also made of several other woods. The analysed type 1 treenails[41] from the Fribrødre Å site are made of willow[42] in 42 cases, of oak[43] in six cases, of hazel[44] in 61 cases, of buckthorn[45] six times, of ash[46] four times, and finally a few treenails are made of elder,[47] hawthorn,[48] maple[49] and lime[50] (fig. 35).

In other cases, juniper[51] and unspecified conifer and pomaceous trees were used as raw material for treenail production (fig. 35). A treenail must be soft and flexible so it does not split the vessel parts its fixes in place, yet also strong and hard so it can resist the motion of the vessel without breaking itself.[52]

Woods used for wedges
Oak[53] was the most common choice of raw material for the treenail wedges. Besides this, willow[54] was used in Skuldelev 3 and at the Fribrødre Å site. At Fribrødre Å wedges in tree-nails were also made of beech[55] and red alder.[56] The treenail wedges in Skuldelev 1's repair phase 2, and in Äskekärr 1, were made of pine (fig. 35).[57] In general, it seems that a harder wood was chosen for wedges than for the treenails (fig. 35), probably because such wedges could more easily split the treenails and thus 'lock' them.

Qualities of raw materials
The boatbuilders of the 11th century used timber of both high[58] and lower quality.[59] In this context, quality must be understood to mean having strength and appearance that were especially suitable as raw material for a specific vessel part. Good quality timber for planks is defined as having few knots and straight growth, such that long, wide, strong and light planks can be made from the raw materials (fig. 36).[60] By contrast, poor quality raw materials for planks have the consequence that the planks can more easily crack, and the many flaws and the twisted growth make it difficult to work the raw material, and nearly impossible to make long and wide planks (fig. 36).[61]

Tree species used in late Viking-Age shipbuilding, and their qualities

Fig. 36. Top: A plank (1482-x006) with a wavy pattern suggesting that the tree from which the plank was made was of irregular and twisted growth. Note the knots, also. Bottom: A plank (1482-x242) in which the medullary rays can hardly be seen, suggesting that the tree from which the plank was made was of more regular, straight growth. Both planks are of oak, and are from the Roskilde 6 ship find. Photos: Ivan Conrad Hansen, Viking Ship Museum in Roskilde.

As regards good raw material quality for crooked timbers, it is important that the fibre direction follows the desired form of the vessel component, which gives the component strength and a fine appearance.[62] Finally, it is important, as outlined above, that the vessel components are made of a wood suitable for shipbuilding.

In figure 37, an assessment of the raw material qualities used has been drawn up. It must be stressed that it has only been possible to propose a generalised assessment, and that in sev-

eral cases the state of preservation of the vessel parts makes it extremely difficult to evaluate the quality of the raw material. In the cases where this is considered impossible, or if the vessel parts have not been preserved, this is indicated in the figure by a dash.

Hedeby 1 and Skuldelev 3 in particular appear to have been built with raw materials of good quality (fig. 37). This is interesting, because the two ships are different in terms of both type and size: Hedeby 1 is a large person-

62. Crumlin-Pedersen 1997b: 180–181.

Ship finds	Keel components	Keelson & mast-fish	Stem components	Planks	Frame components
Fotevik 1[1]	Good	-	-	Average & poor	Average & poor
Fotevik 2[2]	-	-	-	-	-
Fotevik 3[3]	-	-	-	Average & poor	Average & poor
Fotevik 4[4]	-	-	-	-	-
Fotevik 5[5]	-	-	-	-	-
Fribrødre Å[6]	-	-	-	Average & poor	Average & poor
Hedeby 1[7]	Good	Good	Good	Good	Good & average
Hedeby 2[8]	-	Average	-	Poor	Poor
Hedeby 3[9]	-	Average	-	Good (only two planks excavated)	Average
Roskilde 3[10]	Average	-	Average	Average	Average
Skuldelev 1 (repair phase 2)[11]	Average	-	-	Average	-
Skuldelev 3[12]	Average	Good	Good	Good	Good
Skuldelev 5[13]	Average	Average	Average	Poor & average	Average
Äskekärr 1[14]	Good	Average	-	Good & average	Good & average

Fig. 37. Generalised descriptions (good, average and poor) of the qualities of the raw materials from which the ship components were made. The good qualities are emphasised with darker blue shading. Table: The author, Viking Ship Museum in Roskilde.

NOTES
1. Crumlin-Pedersen 1984: 27-60.
2. Crumlin-Pedersen 1984: 27-60.
3. Crumlin-Pedersen 1984: 27-60.
4. Crumlin-Pedersen 1984: 27-60.
5. Crumlin-Pedersen 1984: 27-60.
6. Klassen 2010: 65-213 & 367-431.
7. Crumlin-Pedersen 1997b: 85-89 & 183.
8. Crumlin-Pedersen 1997b: 96-97 & 183.
9. Crumlin-Pedersen 1997b: 101-102 & 183.
10. Bill 2006b: 3-35.
11. Crumlin-Pedersen & Olsen 2002: 101, 105-107.
12. Crumlin-Pedersen & Olsen 2002: 199-220.
13. Crumlin-Pedersen & Olsen 2002: 250-276.
14. Humbla 1934: 1-21.

nel carrier, and Skuldelev 3 is a medium-sized cargo ship. It was thus not exclusively the largest ships that were built with high-quality materials. Otherwise, most of the vessel finds analysed appears to have been built with raw materials with a mixture of good and medium qualities (fig. 37). Some slight gradations are, however, evident: Hedeby 3, Roskilde 3 and Äskekärr 1 were built with good raw materials (fig. 37), but without approaching Hedeby 1's and Skuldelev 3's level of quality, while the raw materials for the Fotevik ships, the Fribrødre Å ships, Skuldelev 1's repairs in phase 2 and Skuldelev 5 are all of medium or poor quality (fig. 37). Finally, Hedeby 2's raw materials appear to be of the poorest quality (fig. 37).

Resources required for shipbuilding

The second part of the analysis of the use of materials in Viking-Age shipbuilding focuses on the required resources. The systematically documented experimental archaeological reconstruction projects which began in Scandinavia in the 1980s[63] make it possible to propose approximate quantities of raw materials and manpower invested in the building of the various vessel types. The reconstructed vessels are hypothetical representatives of vessel types and sizes, which means that the proposed quantities

of raw materials and working hours are only to be regarded as indicating probable resource consumption. There is also great variation in the detail with which the resource consumption is documented, and the premises for the published assessment. Nevertheless, the reconstruction projects must be viewed as the most precise method that can be used to suggest the quantities of resources consumed – primarily because the process of building the reconstructions makes otherwise hidden issues clear.

Specifically, in the case of sailcloth production it must be noted that it has only been possible to suggest a likely resource requirement for the production of wool sails. This is noted because linen sails were probably produced and used alongside wool sails in the 11th century.[64]

Natural resources

Several factors could have influenced the procurement of natural resources for shipbuilding. On the one hand, the availability and knowledge of, and access to, potentially suitable resources created the framework for what constituted the suitable resources. On the other hand, the range of sociocultural norms and individual skills among those involved would have influenced the selection of appropriate resources. The selection and procurement led to the use of a raw material in a specific context (fig. 38).[65]

63. The documentation, reporting and publication of the preliminary work and the actual building of the Viking Ship Museum in Roskilde's Skuldelev 3 reconstruction, *Roar Ege,* is an early example of a systematic, reflective scientific practice in connection with the reconstruction of the vessels of the past. See Andersen *et al.* 1997.
64. An analysis of the quantity of flax fibre and the amount of manpower invested in the production of linen sails has not been possible within the framework of this book. For more on the making of linen sails and resource consumption, see for example Bender Jørgensen 2012; Ravn *et al.* (eds.) 2016.
65. Andrus & Menard 1980.

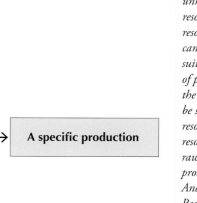

Fig. 38. The relationships within the total volume of resources consisting of unknown and known resources as well as the suitable resources. The known resource can be worked into resources suitable for a specific type of production. Alternatively the suitable resources can be selected from the known resources. The suitable resources can be worked into raw materials for a specific production type. Based on Andrus & Menard 1980. Redrawn and adapted by the author, Viking Ship Museum in Roskilde.

66. Damgård-Sørensen &
Sørensen (eds.) unpublished.
67. See chapter II, section:
Iron parts, for a more
detailed account of the issue.
68. The density of deciduous
wood in air-dried condition is
ca 730 kg per m³. Specifically
durmast oak: 730 kg per m³;
common oak: 760 kg per m³;
ash: 720 kg per m³; beech:
720 kg per m³, see Petersen
1957: 50.
69. See chapter II, section:
Iron parts, for a more
detailed account of the issue.
70. See chapter II, section:
Sails.
71. See chapter II, section:
Sails.
72. Damgård-Sørensen &
Sørensen (eds.) unpublished.

Small cargo ship

In terms of size Skuldelev 6 can be used as a representative of the ship type characterised today as a small cargo ship. However, since the ship has been determined as having been built at Sognefjorden in Norway, the suitable wood resources would have been considerably different from those considered in this book's field of investigation. The wooden raw material consumption in connection with the building of small cargo ships in 11th-century Denmark therefore cannot be estimated on the basis of reconstructions of Skuldelev 6.

The Viking Ship Museum's reconstruction of Skuldelev 6, *Kraka Fyr*, can, however, be used to suggest the consumption of bog ore for rivets, roves and spikes as well as the amount of wool used for sails. In addition, the resources necessary for the ropes and cordage can be indicated.

In all, 970 rivets and spikes as well 865 roves were produced in connection with the building of *Kraka Fyr*. The total weight of rivets, roves and spikes is 32,417 g, or ca 32 kg.[66] If this quantity of iron is converted to bog ore, following the method drawn up in chapter II, the necessary quantity of bog ore was 50 × 32 = 1,600 kg of roasted bog ore and 2 × 1,600 = 3,200 kg of unroasted bog ore. However, by all indications the quantity of bog ore needed has been overestimated, because the iron smelters of the 11th century could have extracted a larger quantity of usable iron from bog ore than the researchers today.[67] The consumption has therefore been estimated here as being lower – that is, as ca 1,400 kg of roasted bog ore and 2,800 kg of unroasted bog ore (fig. 39).

If we calculate the consumption of charcoal for iron smelting on the basis of the model drawn up in chapter II, the result is that 1,400 + 700 = 2,100 kg of charcoal was used. Converted to air-dried deciduous wood[68] the consumption becomes 2,100 × 4 = 8,400 kg or 8,400/600 = 14 m³ of air-dried deciduous wood (fig. 39).

As indicated, iron anchors were probably not used aboard the smaller vessel types.[69] Instead, wood-and-stone anchors were used, which makes a calculation of the amount of bog ore used unnecessary in this context.

It is assumed that a small cargo ship carried a sail of a size more or less matching that of *Kraka Fyr*'s sail of 25 m². As described above,[70] there is a connection between sailcloth quality and size in terms of the size of the vessel that the sail had to propel. A sail of 25 m² was probably made of cloth weighing 600–800 g per m². The consumption then becomes between 600 × 25 = 15,000 g and 800 × 25 = 20,000 g of processed wool (fig. 39). As described above[71] a 'Viking-Age sheep' yielded ca 500 g of wool suitable for sailcloth production, which means that a stock of ca 30–40 sheep was necessary to produce the needed raw material in a year.

In connection with the production of the rigging for *Kraka Fyr*, 72 m of rope was produced for the standing rigging, while 115 m of rope and cordage was produced for the running rigging. In addition, 87 m of rope was made for other ropes such as boltrope and reef points (fig. 39). For *Kraka Fyr*, both lime bast, hemp and horsetails were used to produce rope.[72]

Fig. 39. Consumption of raw materials in connection with the building of the Skuldelev 6 reconstruction Kraka Fyr. Table: The author, Viking Ship Museum in Roskilde.

	Quantities of wood utilised	Quantities of bog ore utilised	Quantities of fibres utilised
Small cargo ship	**Charcoal**: ca 8,400 kg or 14 m³ hardwood (air-dried)	**Rivets and spikes:** ca 1,400 kg (roasted); ca 2,800 kg (unroasted)	**Sailcloth**: 15-20 kg of wool (sheep needed: 30-40) **Standing rigging**: 72 m **Running rigging**: 115 m **Other ropes**: 87 m

Medium-sized cargo ship

Two reconstructions of Skuldelev 3 – *Roar Ege* and *Sif Ege* – can be used to indicate the raw material consumption for the production of medium-sized cargo ships. The construction of *Roar Ege* can be used to estimate the consumption of the raw materials – wood and bog ore – for the hull of the ship type, while *Sif Ege* can be used to suggest the raw material consumption in connection with the making of the standing and running rigging of the ship type. Figure 41 shows a theoretical calculation[73] of the raw materials necessary to build a ship with the same dimensions and the same raw materials as Skuldelev 3. It should be noted that the calculations only express an estimated consumption, which means that other log diameters and lengths may have been used to build a medium-sized cargo ship. For example, the radially cleft planks could have been made of oak trees with a smaller log diameter, but in that case, more oaks had to be felled. The theoretical calculation is thus an expression of one among several possible specific raw material requirements.

A count of the rivets, roves and spikes in the hull of *Roar Ege* made by Tom Nicolajsen from the Viking Ship Museum in Roskilde and the author, has resulted in 1204 rivets and roves as well as 323 spikes. In connection with the count, efforts were made to arrive at a result that describes the ship when it was launched, so the rivets and roves used in connection with repairs were not included. Since extra rivets, roves and spikes were probably made in connection with the construction, an extra 50 rivets and roves and 50 spikes have been added to the documented ones. Spikes and rivets were mainly made with a length of 80 mm, but longer ones were made in a few cases if this was considered necessary.[74]

In the following, an average weight of 27 g is used as the basis of calculation for a rivet and a spike with a length of 80 mm, and 7.9 g for a rove. An overall estimate of the iron consumption then becomes $1,254 + 373 \times 27 = 11,325$

$+ 1,254 \times 7.9 = 110.391$ kg. If this amount of iron is converted to bog ore, in accordance with the method outlined above, the necessary amount of bog ore becomes respectively $50 \times 110.391 = 5,519.55$ kg of roasted bog ore and $2 \times 5,519.55 = 11,039.1$ kg of unroasted bog ore. The bog ore requirement has, however, probably been set too high, since the iron smelters of the Viking Age could extract a larger amount of iron than the researchers today.[75] The consumption is therefore estimated to have been less – ca 5,000 kg of roasted bog ore and 10,000 kg of unroasted bog ore (fig. 40).

The consumption of charcoal in connection with iron extraction can now be estimated on the basis of the calculation model shown in chapter II, and $5,000 + 2,500 = 7,500$ kg of charcoal is the estimated consumption. Since wood from deciduous trees was probably the preferred raw material for making charcoal in the field of investigation in this book, the charcoal amount can be converted to deciduous wood as $4 \times 7,500 = 30,000$ kg. If we use the density of the deciduous wood in air-dried condition,[76] the consumption becomes ca 41 m³ of air-dried deciduous wood (fig. 40).

It can be reasonably assumed that some medium-sized cargo ships had an anchor of iron, while others only used wood-and-stone anchors. However, since the raw materials for making iron anchors were probably not procured within the present primary geographical area of study in the 11th century,[77] but were either imported as iron used for the production of anchors or as finished anchors, a calculation of the raw material consumption for these will not be relevant in this context.

For making of the lime bast rigging for *Sif Ege* – both the standing and the running rigging – 58 lime trees were used, which yielded ca 600 m of bark or, converted to kilograms, ca 126 kg of usable bast.[78]

As for an indication of the raw material consumption of wool for the medium-sized cargo ships' sails, the sail size of *Roar Ege* of 45 m² is used. Such a sail is estimated to have had

73. Based on Andersen 1997a: 179; Vadstrup 1997a: 38; Vadstrup 1997b: 85 & 135.
74. Vadstrup 1997a: 44.
75. See chapter II, section: sails, for a more detailed account of the issue.
76. The density of deciduous wood in air-dried condition is ca 730 kg per m³. Specifically durmast oak: 730 kg per m³; common oak: 760 kg per m³; ash: 720 kg per m³; beech: 720 kg per m³, see Petersen 1957: 50.
77. See chapter II, section: Iron parts, for a more detailed account.
78. Magnus 2008: 17.

a weight per m² of sailcloth between 600 and 800 g.[79] The estimated consumption then becomes between 600 × 45 = 27,000 g and 800 × 45

= 36,000 g of processed wool, corresponding to what a stock of ca 54–72 sheep can yield annually of wool suitable for sailcloth (fig. 40).[80]

Fig. 40. Consumption of raw materials in connection with the building of the Skuldelev 3 reconstructions Roar Ege and Sif Ege. Table: The author, Viking Ship Museum in Roskilde.

	Quantities of wood utilised	Quantities of bog ore utilised	Quantities of fibres utilised
Medium-sized cargo ship	**Keel**: 1 log of oak, ca 9.5 m long and 0.35-0.40 m in diameter **Stems**: 2 logs of oak, ca 4 m long, 0.35-0.40 m in diameter **Planks**: 4 logs of oak, ca 6-10 m long and ca 1 m in diameter **Stringers**: 2 logs of oak, ca 10-12 m long and ca 0.5-0.6 m in diameter **Frame components**: ca 20 pieces of large crooked timbers of oak, and 60 pieces of small and medium-sized crooked timbers of oak **Other hull components**: Produced using the wood remaining from the conversion of the hull components mentioned above **Oars**: 3-6 logs of pine or red alder, ca 4.5 m long and 0.15-0.35 m in diameter **Mast**: 1 log of pine, ca 9.2 m long and 0.2 m in diameter **Yard**: 1 log of pine, ca 7.1 m long and 0.15 m in diameter **Charcoal**: ca 30,000 kg or 41 m³ hardwood (air-dried)	**Rivets and spikes**: ca 5,000 kg (roasted); ca 10,000 kg (unroasted)	**Sailcloth**: 27-36 kg of wool (sheep needed: 54-72) **Standing and running rigging**: ca 58 lime trees (600 m or 126 kg of lime bast)

Large cargo ship

To indicate the raw material consumption in connection with the construction of the largest cargo ships of the 11th century, the following sources have been used: Ole Crumlin-Pedersen's theoretical estimates of raw material consumption in connection with the building of Hedeby 3[81] and the experimental archaeological estimates of raw material consumption in connection with the building of the Skuldelev 1 reconstructions *Saga Siglar*[82] and *Ottar*.[83]

On the basis of the ship parts from Hedeby 3 and the results of archaeological experiments[84] Ole Crumlin-Pedersen estimated the raw material consumption for the building of a ship the size of Hedeby 3. The consumption is mainly expressed in metres, not in the number of logs,[85] and the missing dimensional figures have therefore been sought by comparing the data to the results gleaned from the building of the Skuldelev 1 reconstruction *Ottar*.[86]

In order to make a keel for a ship the size of Hedeby 3, one or two logs with a total length of ca 18 m and a diameter of ca 0.5 m would have been necessary. To make the stems, two oak logs with a length of 4 m and a diameter of 0.5 m would probably have been needed. The keelson could be made of an oak log ca 9.5 m long with a diameter of 0.5 m. To make the planks, ca 315 m of oak planks had to be procured from logs with a diameter between 0.8 and 1.0 m. The ca 95 m of stringers could be produced using logs with a diameter of ca 0.6 m. It is likely that 3–4 stringers were made of one log. For frame parts, around 144 crooked timbers in various sizes would have been necessary. For treenails, 10–15 willow trees with a diameter of 0.2–0.25 m had to be felled,[87] while the other parts in the hull and the wooden elements in the rigging could be made of cleft wood left over from the making of the already-mentioned vessel parts (fig. 41).

It has been estimated that the mast for a ship the size of Skuldelev 1 would have been made of a pine or spruce log of ca 14 m with a minimum diameter of 0.30 m. The yard would have been made of a pine or spruce, and in this case,

the minimum raw material dimensions have been determined as ca 10.1 m in length and ca 0.20 m in diameter.[88] Since Hedeby 3[89] is larger than Skuldelev 1[90] its mast and yard were presumably larger. The estimated lengths and diameters of the logs are thus (for the mast) ca 14.5 m in length and a minimum if ca 0.35 in diameter, and (for the yard) ca 10.5 m in length and a minimum of ca 0.25 m in diameter (fig. 41).

4,000 rivets and spikes and 3,160 roves were made for the Skuldelev 1 reconstruction *Ottar*. The total weight of rivets, roves and spikes is 115.141 kg.[91] Since Hedeby 3 is a larger vessel than Skuldelev 1, a further 20 kg has been added to the iron consumption. The total estimated consumption thus becomes ca 135 kg.

If the amount of iron is converted to the necessary amount of bog ore, the result is that $50 \times 135 = 6{,}750$ kg of roasted bog ore and $2 \times 6{,}750 = 13{,}500$ kg of unroasted bog ore were used. By all indications, the amount of bog ore required has, however, been set too high, since the iron smelters of the Viking Age could extract a larger quantity of iron from the bog ore than the researchers today.[92] The consumption is therefore estimated to have been less, that is ca 6,000 kg of roasted bog ore and 12,000 kg of unroasted bog ore (fig. 41).

The consumption of charcoal in connection with the iron extraction can now be calculated, again on the basis of the calculation model. The estimated consumption thus amounts to 6,000 + 4,500 = 10,500 kg of charcoal. Converted to deciduous wood this becomes $4 \times 10{,}500 = 42{,}000$ kg or ca 58 m^3 of air-dried deciduous wood (fig. 41).[93]

It can be reasonably assumed that on board the large cargo ships, there were one or more anchors of iron. However, since the raw materials for making iron anchors were probably not procured within the primary geographical area studied here,[94] but were either imported as iron or as finished anchors, a calculation of the raw material consumption for these will not be relevant in this context.

81. Crumlin-Pedersen 1997b: 179–185.
82. Andersen 1997a: 179.
83. Damgård-Sørensen & Sørensen (eds.) unpublished.
84. Experience from the building of the reconstructions *Saga Siglar* and *Roar Ege*.
85. Crumlin-Pedersen 1997b: 180.
86. Damgård-Sørensen & Sørensen (eds.) unpublished.
87. Crumlin-Pedersen 1997b: 180.
88. Andersen 1997a: 179.
89. Length 22 m and width 6.3 m.
90. Length 16 m and width 4.8 m.
91. Damgård-Sørensen & Sørensen (eds.) unpublished.
92. See chapter II, section: Iron parts, for a more detailed account of the issue.
93. The density of deciduous wood in air-dried condition is ca 730 kg per m^3. Specifically durmast oak: 730 kg per m^3; common oak: 760 kg per m^3; ash: 720 kg per m^3; beech: 720 kg per m^3, see Petersen 1957: 50.
94. See chapter II, section: Iron parts, for a more detailed account of the issue.

95. Crumlin-Pedersen
1997b: 191.
96. See chapter II, section:
Sails, for a more detailed
account of the relationship
between a ship's dimensions
and the quality of the sailcloth.
97. See chapter II, section:
Sails, for a more detailed
account.

Fig. 41. Theoretical and
experimental archaeologi-
cal calculation of the
consumption of raw
materials in connection
with the building of
Hedeby 3. Table: The
author, Viking Ship
Museum in Roskilde.

The sail of Hedeby 3 has been estimated as having had an area of ca 150 m². [95] Such a sail would have required a strong sailcloth, and the weight per m² has thus been estimated as between 800 and 1,000 g. [96] A probable raw material consumption in connection with the making of a sail for a large cargo ship then becomes between 800 × 150 = 120,000 g and 1,000 × 150 = 150,000 g of processed wool (fig. 41), which corresponds to what a stock of 240–300 sheep could yield annually in the Viking Age. [97]

	Quantities of wood utilised	Quantities of bog ore utilised	Quantities of fibres utilised
Large cargo ship	**Keel**: 1-2 logs of oak, in all ca 18 m long and 0.50 m in diameter **Stems**: 2 logs of oak, ca 4 m long, 0.50 m in diameter **Keelson**: 1 log of oak, ca 9.5 m long and 0.50 m in diameter **Planks**: ca 315 m of planks, using logs of oak with a diameter of 0.8-1.0 m **Stringers**: ca 95 m of planks, using logs of oak with a diameter of 0.6 m. **Frame components**: ca 144 pieces of crooked timbers of oak or red alder **Other hull components**: Produced using the wood remaining from the conversion of the hull components mentioned above **Treenails**: 10-15 logs of willow, ca 0.20-0.25 m in diameter **Mast**: 1 log probably of pine or spruce, ca 14.5 m long and 0.35 m in diameter **Yard**: 1 log probably of pine or spruce, ca 10.5 m long and 0.25 m in diameter **Charcoal**: ca 42,000 kg or 58 m³ hardwood (air-dried)	**Rivets and spikes**: ca 6,000 kg (roasted); ca 12,000 kg (unroasted)	**Sailcloth**: 120-150 kg of wool (sheep needed: 240-300)

Medium-sized personnel carrier

The Viking Ship Museum's Skuldelev 5 reconstruction *Helge Ask* has been chosen as a case study in connection with an estimate of the raw material consumption needed to build the medium-sized personnel carriers. As the raw material for the keel, an oak log ca 12 m in length and 0.35–0.40 m in diameter had to be procured. The stems could be made of two oak logs, both a minimum of 2 m long and around 0.90 m in diameter.[98]

Characteristic of Skuldelev 5, are the many re-used planks and the fact that oak, pine and ash were all used to make the ship's planks.[99] In connection with the building of the reconstruction *Helge Ask*, these original raw material choices were all followed. Three radially cleft planks were made of two 7–9 m long oak logs with a diameter of ca 0.90 m, six planks were made by tangentially cleaving one pine log 4 m long and 0.40 m in diameter; one pine log 11 m long and 0.40 m in diameter; and one pine log 14 m long and 0.40 m in diameter; and finally four planks were tangentially cleft from two ash logs of 4 and 8 m respectively, both with a diameter of 0.40 m (fig. 42).[100]

Mast and yard were made of pines with lengths between 8 and 10 m and with a diameter of 0.15–0.20 m.[101] For frame parts, ca 130 pieces of crooked timbers were felled and the other vessel parts in the hull as well as the wooden elements in the rigging were made of cleft wood left over from the making of the above-mentioned vessel parts (fig. 42).[102]

Finally, the keelson was made from a 4 m long oak log with a diameter of 0.40 m, while stringers and shield-racks were made of two oak logs respectively 8 and 12 m in length and both with a diameter of 0.50 m (fig. 42).[103]

Tom Nicolajsen from the Viking Ship Museum in Roskilde and the author made a count of all rivets, roves and spikes in *Helge Ask*. The result of this count was 1,389 rivets and roves and 381 spikes. To these must be added a further 50 rivets, roves and spikes, representing the extra rivets, roves and spikes that were probably produced for the construction.

An average weight of 27 g for a rivet or spike, and 7.9 g for a rove, was used in the following calculations. The total weight of rivets, roves and spikes is 61,858 g. This weight is an indication of the amount of iron, and on this basis the bog ore consumption can be estimated as $50 \times 61.858 = 3{,}092.9$ kg of roasted bog ore and $2 \times 3{,}092.9 = 6{,}158.8$ kg of unroasted bog ore. However, the amount of bog ore required has probably been set too high since the iron smelters of the 11th century could extract a larger amount of iron than the researchers today.[104] The consumption has therefore been adjusted downwards to ca 2,900 kg of roasted bog ore and 5,800 kg of unroasted bog ore (fig. 42).

The charcoal consumption can now be estimated as $2{,}900 + 1{,}450 = 4{,}350$ kg of charcoal. If the charcoal consumption is converted to deciduous wood the result becomes that $4 \times 4{,}350 = 17{,}400$ kg or 24 m^3 of air-dried deciduous wood[105] would have been necessary for the charcoal production (fig. 42).

Aboard the medium-sized personnel carriers, anchors of both iron, and wood-and-stone, were probably used. However, since the raw materials for making iron anchors, judging from the metallurgical analyses, were not procured within the present primary geographical area of study in the 11th century,[106] but were either imported as iron or as finished anchors, an estimate of the raw material consumption will not be relevant in this context.

The following proposed raw material consumption of wool for the sails of the medium-sized personnel carriers is based on a sail size of 48 m^2 with a weight per m^2 of sailcloth between 600 and 800 g.[107] An estimated consumption then becomes between $600 \times 48 = 28{,}800$ g and $800 \times 48 = 38{,}400$ g of processed wool (fig. 42). A consumption of this volume corresponds to the amount of wool suitable for sailcloth that can be yielded by ca 58–77 sheep annually.[108]

98. Damgård-Sørensen & Sørensen (eds.) unpublished.
99. Crumlin-Pedersen & Olsen 2002: 251–255.
100. Damgård-Sørensen & Sørensen (eds.) unpublished.
101. Damgård-Sørensen & Sørensen (eds.) unpublished.
102. Damgård-Sørensen & Sørensen (eds.) unpublished.
103. Damgård-Sørensen & Sørensen (eds.) unpublished.
104. See chapter II, section: Iron parts, for a more detailed account of the issue.
105. The density of deciduous wood in air-dried condition is ca 730 kg per m^3. Specifically durmast oak: 730 kg per m^3; common oak: 760 kg per m^3; ash: 720 kg per m^3; beech: 720 kg per m^3, see Petersen 1957: 50.
106. See chapter II, section: Iron parts, for a more detailed account of the issue.
107. See chapter II, section: Sails, for a more detailed account of the relationship between a ship's dimensions and the quality of the sailcloth.
108. See chapter II, section: Sails, for a more detailed account.

Fig. 42. Consumption of raw materials in connection with the building of the Skuldelev 5 reconstruction Helge Ask. Table: The author, Viking Ship Museum in Roskilde.

	Quantities of wood utilised	*Quantities of bog ore utilised*	*Quantities of fibres utilised*
Medium-sized personnel carrier	**Keel**: 1 log of oak, ca 12 m long and 0.35-0.40 m in diameter	**Rivets and spikes**: ca 2,900 kg (roasted); ca 5,800 kg (unroasted)	**Sailcloth**: 28.8-38.4 kg of wool (sheep needed: 58-77)
	Stems: 2 logs of oak, ca 2 m long, 0.9 m in diameter		
	Keelson: 1 log of oak, ca 4 m long and 0.40 m in diameter		
	Radially-oriented planks: 2 logs of oak, ca 7-9 m longs and 0.90 m in diameter		
	Tangentially-oriented planks: 3 logs of ash, ca 4, 11 and 14 m long and 0.40-0.50 m in diameter, and 2 logs of pine, ca 4 and 8 m long and 0.40-0.50 m in diameter		
	Stringers and shield -racks: 2 logs of oak, ca 8 and 12 m long and ca 0.5 m in diameter		
	Frame components: ca 130 pieces of crooked timbers of oak or red alder		
	Other hull components: Produced using the wood remaining from the conversion of the hull components mentioned above		
	Oars: 3-6 logs of pine or red alder, ca 4.5 m long and 0.15-0.35 m in diameter		
	Mast and yard: 2 logs of pine, ca 8-10 m long and 0.15-0.20 m in diameter		
	Charcoal: ca 17,400 kg or 24 m^3 hardwood (air-dried)		

Large personnel carrier

Only one of the large personnel carriers, dating from the 11th century, has been experimentally reconstructed – the Skuldelev 2 reconstruction *The Sea Stallion from Glendalough*. The documentation of this project was highly detailed in terms of the consumption of raw materials and working hours, and the consumption has been published in several contexts.[109] The following estimate of the use of raw material takes its point of departure in the published work.

Six oak logs between 8 and 10 m long and 0.5–0.7 m in diameter were used to make the keel, keelson and mast-fish. For the planks, 14 oak logs between 8 and 10 m long and ca 1 m in diameter were used, and four ash logs ca 10 m long and ca 0.35 m in diameter were cleft and dressed. The stringers were made of three oak logs, ca 12 m long and ca 0.6 m in diameter, while the ca 285 frame parts were made of crooked timbers of oak. The treenails were made from ten willows with a diameter of 0.2–0.25 m (fig. 43).[110]

The rudder was made from one log ca 4 m long and 0.4–0.5 m in diameter, and the oars were made of 35 pine logs ca 5 m long and

109. Damgård-Sørensen *et al.* 2004: 44–45; Nielsen 2011: 71; Englert *et al.* 2013: 51.
110. Damgård-Sørensen *et al.* 2004: 44–45; Nielsen 2011: 71; Englert *et al.* 2013: 51.
111. Damgård-Sørensen *et al.* 2004: 44–45; Nielsen 2011: 71; Englert *et al.* 2013: 51.

	Quantities of wood utilised	Quantities of iron ore utilised	Quantities of fibres utilised
Large personnel carrier	**Keel, stems, keelson and mast fish:** 6 logs of oak, 8-10 m long and 0.5-0.7 m in diameter **Planks:** 14 logs of oak, ca 8-10 m long and 1 m in diameter, and 4 logs of ash, ca 10 m long and 0.35 m in diameter **Stringers:** 3 logs of oak, ca 12 m long and 0.6 m in diameter **Frame components:** ca 285 pieces of crooked timbers of oak **Other hull components:** Produced using the wood remaining from the conversion of the hull components mentioned above **Oars:** 35 logs of pine, ca 5 m long and 0.30-0.35 m in diameter **Rudder:** 1 log of oak, ca 4 m long and 0.4-0.5 m in diameter **Mast:** 1 log of pine, ca 15 m long and 0.3 m in diameter **Yard:** 1 log of pine, ca 13 m long and 0.3 m in diameter **Treenails:** 10 logs of willow, ca 0.20-0.25 m in diameter **Charcoal:** ca 69,000 kg or 95 m^3 hardwood (air-dried) **Tar (ca 500 l):** ca 18 m^3 of pine (branches, logs and roots)	**Rivets and spikes:** ca 11,500 kg (roasted); ca 23,000 kg (unroasted)	**Sailcloth:** 89.6-112 kg of wool (sheep needed: 180-224) **Standing and running rigging and other ropes:** 4,500 branches or small logs of lime trees and 600 horse tails

Fig. 43. Consumption of raw materials in connection with the building of the Skuldelev 2 reconstruction Sea Stallion from Glendalough. Table: The author, Viking Ship Museum in Roskilde.

0.3–0.35 m in diameter. The mast was made of one pine log ca 15 m long and ca 0.3 m in diameter, while the yard was made from one pine log that was ca 13 m long and ca 0.3 m in diameter (fig. 43).[111]

The total weight of all the rivets and spikes made for the building of *The Sea Stallion from Glendalough* is 204.226 kg. The roves for *The Sea Stallion from Glendalough* weigh a total of 49.146 kg. The total weight of all rivets, spikes and roves is thus ca 253 kg.[112] Converted from iron to bog ore in accordance with the method shown in chapter II, the necessary amount of bog ore becomes respectively $50 \times 253 = 12,650$ kg of roasted bog ore and $2 \times 12,650 = 25,300$ kg of unroasted bog ore. By all indications the amount of bog ore required has, however, been set too high since the iron smelters of the Viking Age could extract a larger amount of iron than the researchers today.[113] The consumption has therefore been set lower, to ca 11,500 kg of roasted bog ore and ca 23,000 kg of unroasted bog ore (fig. 43).

An estimated consumption of charcoal in connection with the iron extraction can now be calculated:[114] $11,500 + 5,750 = 17,250$ kg. Converted to air-dried deciduous wood this becomes $4 \times 17,250 = 69,000$ kg or ca 95 m³ of air-dried deciduous wood (fig. 43).[115]

It can reasonably be assumed that at least one anchor of iron was on board the large personnel carriers. However, since the raw materials for making iron anchors were probably not procured within the present primary geographical area of study in the 11th century,[116] a calculation of the raw material consumption is not relevant in this context.

For the probable raw material consumption of wool for the sails of the large personnel carriers the point of departure is a sail of 112 m² with a weight between 800 and 1,000 g per m² of sailcloth.[117] Thus an estimated consumption between $800 \times 112 = 89,600$ g and $1,000 \times 112 = 112,000$ g of processed wool would have been necessary (fig. 43). About 180–224 sheep can yield such an amount of wool suitable for sailcloth annually.[118]

Human resources

An analysis of the manpower invested in building the various ship types can be conducted by examining the probable number of working hours that were spent on the process. It is necessary not only to analyse the total number of working hours involved, but also to turn the focus on how many of the invested working hours required special knowledge and skills. By all indications, certain tasks demanded a high degree of specialisation, while other aspects of the construction process could be dealt with by a labour force with no special qualifications.

The experimental archaeological reconstructions of ship finds are undoubtedly the most important source for the analysis of the quantity and character of the manpower that was invested in building and equipping the ships of the 11th century. However, several source-critical considerations must be noted.

The boatbuilders of the 11th century probably participated marginally or peripherally in shipbuilding from childhood and thus gradually became engaged in the work,[119] whereas, the experimental archaeological boatbuilders today learn the methods and techniques of the craft during their training as adults. Later, in their experimental archaeological practice, the boatbuilders must try to disregard modern knowledge and concrete techniques and methods while at the same time applying their fundamental craft knowledge and skills. This dialectic is important, because the archaeological finds make it clear that the boatbuilders of the 11th century were able craftsmen, but also that their conceptual understanding and their use of techniques and methods was different from today.

Furthermore, when the number of working hours invested in building the various vessel types is analysed through reconstruction projects, it should be noted that the experience and craftsmanship of the participants are different, both in the individual project and from project to project. This diversity can be illustrated by drawing up the different reconstruction projects' statements of time consumption in connection with the felling of trees with axes.

112. Damgård-Sørensen & Sørensen (eds.) unpublished.
113. See chapter II, section: Iron parts, for a more detailed account of the issue.
114. See chapter II, section: Iron parts, for a more detailed account.
115. The density of deciduous wood in air-dried condition is ca 730 kg per m³. Specifically durmast oak: 730 kg per m³; common oak: 760 kg per m³; ash: 720 kg per m³; beech: 720 kg per m³, see Petersen 1957: 50.
116. See chapter II, section: Iron parts, for a more detailed account of the issue.
117. See chapter II, section: Sails, for a more detailed account of the relationship between a ship's dimensions and the quality of the sailcloth.
118. See chapter II, section: Sails, for a more detailed account.
119. Ravn 2012a; Ravn 2012b.

When building a reconstruction of a Viking-Age hall, 'Salshuset', in the *Viking Village in Albertslund* a time consumption of two hours is recorded for felling one oak with a breast-height diameter of 60 cm. The felling of the tree involved four men.[120] Those involved, as far as this author knows, were neither boatbuilders, forestry workers, carpenters nor in any other way had extensive knowledge of work with trees. For a "flock of half-trained axe-swingers" it took two hours and 22 minutes to fell an oak 70 cm in diameter in connection with the building of the Skuldelev 3 reconstruction *Roar Ege*.[121] And finally, it took four of the Viking Ship Museum's boatbuilders one hour to fell a tree with a breast-height diameter of 75 cm. For the boatbuilders at the Viking Ship Museum it also took four men three and a half hours to fell a tree with a diameter at breast height of 100 cm.[122]

Several of the reconstruction projects have been conducted in a museum context and have involved a high degree of dissemination. The stated time consumption in connection with the building of a reconstruction has therefore generally been set too high. It is estimated that between 30% and 40% of the working hours spent on the actual building site were spent on communication.[123]

It should also be noted that all the reconstruction projects have, to a greater or lesser extent, used modern tools and other aids alien to the 11th century, which means that the time consumption may have been set too low.

This means that the time-consumption indications of the reconstruction projects set up both too few and too many hours compared with those spent in the 11th century. The potential sources of error are many and extremely difficult to make allowances for. In general, the stated time consumption is considered higher than the time that the boatbuilders of the 11th century would have spent. It is therefore most appropriate to list the number of hours used as a range[124] where the highest value is determined by the total recorded consumption, while the lowest value is stated as 10% less than the total recorded consumption.

The following remarks should be made on the calculation of working hours spent on the making of sailcloth. Only the spinning and weaving processes have been calculated, which means that the processes up to the procurement of fibres for spinning the thread are not included in the following case studies.

If the results are used to analyse how long a construction process took, and how many people were involved, other factors become problematic. The modern distinction between work, leisure time and rest cannot be applied to the society of the 11th century. The length of a working day was probably governed by how long it was possible and productive to work on that day. Other chores may have stopped the building process, and in particular, wind and weather and the number of hours of light would have limited the length of the working day. In addition, the physical and mental strain of the work, as well as the techniques and methods used in the specific working sequence, would have influenced the length of the working day, and thus how long a construction took.

Finally, it is problematic to view the number of working hours as an expression of a direct value for the society of the time. Such an assumption is modern, and is to a great extent determined by the mode of life and production.[125]

Small cargo ship

In order to analyse the investment of time in connection with the building of the small cargo ships, the building process for the Skuldelev 6 reconstruction *Kraka Fyr* has been chosen.

It has been estimated that the building of the hull of *Kraka Fyr*[126] took ca 7,500 hours.[127] Correlated with the above-mentioned time span this gives a time consumption of between 6,750 and 7,500 hours (fig. 44).

The time consumption in connection with the making of charcoal and tar cannot be reliably estimated. On the other hand, the time consumption in connection with the making of a sailcloth for a small cargo ship[128] can be

120. Poulsen 2005: 82.
121. Vadstrup 1997a: 39.
122. Damgård-Sørensen *et al.* 2004: 27.
123. Personal communication from Søren Nielsen. Søren Nielsen is a boatbuilder and head of maritime crafts, reconstruction and public activities at the Viking Ship Museum in Roskilde. (Damgård-Sørensen & Sørensen (eds.) unpublished.).
124. With a margin of uncertainty.
125. Højrup 2003: 138–143.
126. This includes the forging of rivets, roves and spikes.
127. Personal communication from Søren Nielsen. Søren Nielsen is a boatbuilder and head of maritime crafts, reconstruction and public activities at the Viking Ship Museum in Roskilde. (Damgård-Sørensen & Sørensen (eds.) unpublished.).
128. A sail of 25 m² in 2/1 twill with 13–14 warp threads and 8–9 weft threads per cm.

Fig. 44. Estimated consumption of hours in connection with the building of a cargo ship the size of the Skuldelev 6 reconstruction Kraka Fyr. Table: The author, Viking Ship Museum in Roskilde.

Process	Hours (ca)	References
Building the hull and forging the rivets, roves and spikes (procurement of raw materials included)	7,500	Nielsen 2010: pers. comm.[1]
Production of sail	Spinning: 2,000 Weaving: 1,600	Calculations are based on Nørgård 2009b

NOTE 1. Personal communication from Søren Nielsen. Søren Nielsen is a boatbuilder and head of maritime crafts, reconstruction and public activities at the Viking Ship Museum in Roskilde. (Damgard-Sørensen & Sørensen (eds.) unpublished.).

estimated as ca 2,000 spinning hours and ca 1,600 weaving hours (fig. 44).[129]

As indicated above, large parts of the work of building plank-built ships could probably be done by a non-specialised workforce, but at least one person involved would need to have a more detailed knowledge of shipbuilding.

It is furthermore important to emphasise that the production of primary products may to some extent have taken place in connection with the other practices of the society,[130] and that the total construction period would therefore be less than stated here (fig. 44). It is thus estimated that five full-time[131] boatbuilders could have built a small cargo ship in ca 6 months.

Medium-sized cargo ship

The building of the Skuldelev 3 reconstructions *Roar Ege* and *Sif Ege* has been used to suggest the time consumption in connection with the building of the medium-sized cargo ships. It appears from an unpublished minute of a meeting of the steering group for the construction work that it took 16,000 hours to build the hull, which includes the making of rivets, roves and spikes as well as spars.[132] More specifically it is mentioned that 8,000 hours were spent by the construction group,[133] 6,000 hours on working hours[134] and 2,000 hours on construction supervision.[135]

The building of *Roar Ege* was a pioneering project[136] which for the first time systemati-

cally and scientifically sought knowledge of the shipbuilding technology of the Viking Age through archaeological experiments. The reflective practice undoubtedly meant that the building of *Roar Ege* took longer than the time spent in the Viking Age to build a similar ship type. A more realistic, if still estimated time consumption in connection with the building of the hull has therefore been set at ca 12,000 hours,[137] or with the margin of uncertainty stated above, between 10,800 and 12,000 hours (fig. 45).

The total time consumption in connection with the making of lime bast rigging[138] for the Skuldelev 3 reconstruction *Sif Ege* has been set at ca 1,190 working hours (fig. 45). The whole process from the felling of trees in the forest until the cordage was ready for use has been included.[139] The time consumption in connection with the making of a sailcloth for a medium-sized cargo ship[140] can be estimated, on the basis of the experience of making a sail of 25 m^2,[141] as ca $45/25 \times 2,000 = 3,600$ spinning hours, and ca $45/25 \times 1,600 = 2,880$ weaving hours (fig. 45).

The time consumption in connection with producing iron, charcoal and tar, and sewing a sail cannot be reliably estimated.

For the building of the medium-sized cargo ships, the quantity of invested resources, both raw materials and manpower, reaches a level that requires a high degree of advance planning with sub-goals, and monitoring that these sub-

129. See chapter II, section: Sails, for a more detailed account of the relationship between a ship's dimensions and the quality of the sailcloth.
130. See chapter II for a more detailed account of the issue.
131. Ca 200 hours a month each.
132. Vadstrup 1984.
133. That is, for the actual construction.
134. Assumed to be the manufacture of basic products, including the forging of the iron objects.
135. Vadstrup 1984.
136. Took place in 1982–1984.
137. Personal communication from Søren Nielsen. Søren Nielsen is a boatbuilder and head of maritime crafts, reconstruction and public activities at the Viking Ship Museum in Roskilde.
138. Both standing and running rigging.
139. Magnus 2008: 18.
140. A sail of 45 m^2, woven in 2/1 twill with 13–14 warp threads and 8 weft threads per cm.
141. Nørgård 2009b.

Process	Hours (ca)	References
Building the hull, forging the rivets, roves and spikes, and manufacturing some equipment (procurement of raw materials included)	12,000	Vadstrup 1984; Crumlin-Pedersen 1985; Nielsen 2013: pers. comm.[1]
Production of ropes and sail	Ropes: Standing and running rigging: 1,200 Sail: Spinning: 3,600 Weaving: 2,880	Calculations are based on Magnus 2008; Nørgård 2009a; Nørgård 2009b

Fig. 45. Estimated consumption of hours in connection with the building of a cargo ship the size of the Skuldelev 3 reconstructions Roar Ege and Sif Ege. Table: The author, Viking Ship Museum in Roskilde.

NOTE 1. Personal communication from Søren Nielsen. Søren Nielsen is a boatbuilder and head of maritime crafts, reconstruction and public activities at the Viking Ship Museum in Roskilde. (Damgard-Sørensen & Sørensen (eds.) unpublished.).

goals are achieved. Moreover, the size of the ship makes the construction supervisor's work more complex.

Since several of the necessary raw materials and primary products could have been procured and produced over an extended period, the actual continuous shipbuilding process has been assessed as ca 8,000 hours, which means that ten boatbuilders working 200 hours a month could build the hull of the ship in around 4 months.

Large cargo ship

No large cargo ships (over 20 m in length) from the 11th century have yet been reconstructed in full size, so the investment of time in connection with the building of the largest cargo ships in the southern Scandinavia of the 11th century has been estimated in a different way. The working hours spent on the building of the Viking Ship Museum's Skuldelev 1 reconstruction *Ottar*[142] is the point of departure from which the additional consumption of working hours has been estimated.

An approximate total time consumption on the building of *Ottar* has been set at ca 16,000 hours.[143] To this we add a further 2,000 hours considered necessary to build a large cargo ship. With the margin of uncertainty, the time span becomes between 16,200 and 18,000 hours (fig. 46).

To this we must add the spinning and weaving work in connection with the making of the sail of a large cargo ship. The size of the sail of Hedeby 3[144] has been estimated as 150 m², and it was probably made of strongly woven cloth. Archaeological experiments with the making of a 90 m² sailcloth in a strong quality[145] make it likely that it takes ca 4,710 hours to spin yarn and sewing thread with a hand spindle for such a sailcloth. In addition it takes ca 3,140 weaving hours to make and tie up the warp on the loom for both sailcloth and reinforcements of the sailcloth.[146] On this basis, a probable time consumption on the making of a 150 m² sailcloth in a similar quality has been estimated as ca 150/90 × 4,710 = 7,850 spinning hours and ca 150/90 × 3,140 = 5,233 weaving hours (fig. 46).

In addition, iron would have to be produced or imported, and the iron objects would have to be forged. Large quantities of charcoal, wood tar and rope also had to be made, but it has not been possible to make a reliable estimate of the time consumption in connection with this production.

The total building period would therefore probably have been shorter than the estimated 16,200–18,000 working hours for the total construction of the hull of a large cargo ship. It is estimated that ten boatbuilders, each working 200 hours a month, could build the hull of the ship in six to seven months.

142. A medium-sized cargo ship, with a length of ca 16 m.
143. Nielsen 2003.
144. The Hedeby 3 ship is representative in size of the large cargo ships.
145. Woven in 2/1 twill with 8 warp threads and 5 weft threads per cm.
146. Nørgård 2009a: 8.

Process	Hours (ca)	References
Building the hull, forging the rivets, roves and spikes, and manufacturing some equipment (procurement of raw materials included)	18,000	Nielsen 2003
Production of sail	Spinning: 7,850 Weaving: 5,233	Calculations are based on Nørgård 2009a

147. In Olav Tryggvason's Saga, it is stated that the building of the large personnel carrier *Ormen Lange* was built over the course of one winter, see Snorri Sturluson's *Heimskringla*, Olav Tryggvason's saga [Hødnebø & Magerøy (eds.) 1979a: 186]. Perhaps, also other large ships were built over the course of winter?

148. See chapter II, for a more detailed account.

149. Vadstrup 1991.

150. Vadstrup 1993b; Vadstrup 1993c; Vadstrup 1993d; Vadstrup 1995.

151. Vadstrup 1993a: 143.

152. Nørgård 2009b

153. Woven in 2/1 twill with 13–14 warp threads and 8 weft threads per cm.

It is possible – as indicated by written sources[147] – that large cargo ships were built during the course of a winter, but this would have required a comprehensive plan including sub-goals and monitoring of the achievement of these sub-goals. The ability – prior to the actual construction process – to define the shape of the hull would also have been necessary. Several raw materials and primary products could be procured and produced as part of the other work in the various groups in society.[148]

Specialised boatbuilders were necessary to supervise the building; on the one hand to select the suitable resources, on the other to design the most difficult technical details of the ship, and to sew the sail and get all the rigging to work optimally in relation to the hull. Besides the specialised boatbuilders a large number of craftsmen with more general skills would have been involved. By all indications, the construction of the largest cargo ships of the 11th century must be regarded as a major task for the community, with great investment of resources, both raw materials and manpower.

Medium-sized personnel carrier

Skuldelev 5 is considered representative of the medium-sized personnel carrier. The process in connection with the building of *Helge Ask* is the most detailed documentation of a Skuldelev 5 reconstruction to date, but unfortunately the time consumption involved cannot be determined from either the unpublished construction journal[149] or the similarly unpublished *Helge Ask* reports.[150] The construction supervisor on the *Helge Ask* project, Søren Vadstrup,

mentions 'the actual shipbuilding' as having lasted ca 12,000 working hours.[151] In this context the 'actual shipbuilding' should presumably be understood as the selection and procurement of raw materials as well as cutting and rough dressing, the supervision of the work, the finer dressing of the ship components, the testing and adjustment of the components, and the laying and placing of the ship components – this also including the riveting work – until the finished hull was ready at the building site. In addition, the making of the ship's equipment was also included. Stated as a time span, including the margin of uncertainty discussed above, this provides a time consumption for the actual shipbuilding of 10,800–12,000 hours (fig. 47).

It has not been possible to present a reliable estimate of the time consumption in connection with the production of iron or the making of charcoal, tar and ropes on the basis of the available documentation material. The time consumption in connection with the production of the sailcloth, which is 48 m² and woven in a light quality, can be indicated by using Anna Nørgård's experience[152] of making a 25 m² light sailcloth.[153] The result is that ca $48/20 \times 2,000 = 3,840$ spinning hours and ca $48/25 \times 1,600 = 3,072$ weaving hours were spent making a sailcloth for a medium-sized personnel carrier (fig. 47).

The monitoring of the design of the ship, the selection of the suitable resources and the final establishment of the dimensions of the ship parts were, along with the sailmaking work and the rigging of the ship, probably dealt with, by

Process	Hours (ca)	References
Building the hull and manufacturing some equipment (procurement of raw materials included)	12,000	Vadstrup 1993a: 143
Production of sail	Spinning: 3,840 Weaving: 3,072	Calculations are based on Nørgård 2009b

Fig. 47. Estimated consumption of hours in connection with the building of a personnel carrier the size of the Skuldelev 5 reconstruction Helge Ask. Table: The author, Viking Ship Museum in Roskilde.

specialised craftsmen. The remaining majority of the workforce probably consisted of both specialised and non-specialised craftsmen and assistants. In addition, it is important to point out that the raw materials and primary products could be procured and produced as part of other work, and that the total period within which the medium-sized personnel carriers were built would therefore have been shorter than the 10,800–12,000 working hours. Therefore, it is considered likely that ten boatbuilders, working ca 200 hours a month, could build a medium-sized personnel carrier in about five months.

Large personnel carrier

In order to analyse the probable time consumption in connection with the building of the largest personnel carriers, the process of building the Skuldelev 2 reconstruction *The Sea Stallion from Glendalough* has been chosen. The building process is documented in detail and several articles about the time consumption concerning the procurement of raw materials, the rough-dressing of the vessel parts and the actual building process, have been published.[154]

The time consumption associated with the making of the ship's equipment, rigging and sail, the forging processes and the making of wood has also been published[155], and the hours involved in these phases within the context of the overall shipbuilding process is shown in figure 48.

Prior to the actual building of the largest personnel carriers, there were numerous related production processes that must be carried out.

Charcoal for iron smelting and forging could be produced long before it had to be used. The same applies to rivets, roves and spikes, wood tar and rope as well as textile for sailcloth. On the other hand, the sewing and trimming of the sailcloth was probably only begun at the time when the basic dimensions of the ship were known.

The apparently huge time consumption (fig. 48) must be seen in this light. It must be understood in a context where the work was probably distributed over the year, or several years, and over the many individuals and groups involved. In addition, several production processes would have taken place concurrently, while the actual work of testing and adjusting the ship components and designing the shape of the ship was being done.

Archaeological experiments make it seem likely that a maximum of ten boatbuilders could work at the same time.[156] The work of fine-cutting, testing and adjusting the various ship parts and finally of installing the parts in the ship took about 1,400 hours per boatbuilder in connection with the building of *The Sea Stallion from Glendalough*.[157] This time consumption makes it seem likely that the largest of the personnel carriers could be built in around seven months if the ten boatbuilders each worked a good 200 hours a month.[158] However, it was only possible to build the ship within this timescale if many production processes and other preparations had preceded the actual building process, and if the boatbuilders and workers involved did not have to do other work at the same time.[159]

154. Damgård-Sørensen *et al.* 2004; Bill *et al.* 2007; Nielsen 2011; Nielsen 2013a; Englert *et al.* 201
155. Damgård-Sørensen *et al.* 2004: 43–44; Nielsen 2011: 72; Nielsen 2013a: 141–144; Englert *et al.* 2013: 52–53;
156. For the sake of the organisation of the work, see Nielsen 2013a: 142–144.
157. Nielsen 2013a: 142–144.
158. Nielsen 2013a: 144.
159. Nielsen 2013a: 144.

Fig. 48. Estimated
consumption of hours in
connection with the
building of a personnel
carrier the size of the
Skuldelev 2 reconstruc-
tion Sea Stallion from
Glendalough. Table: The
author, Viking Ship
Museum in Roskilde.

Process	Hours (ca)	References
Building the hull (procurement of raw materials included)	32,700	Damgård-Sørensen et al. 2004; Bill et al. 2007; Nielsen 2011; Nielsen 2013a; Nielsen 2013b; Englert et al. 2013
Manufacturing mast, yard, oars and shields	1,800	Damgård-Sørensen et al. 2004; Bill et al. 2007; Nielsen 2011; Nielsen 2013a; Nielsen 2013b; Englert et al. 2013
Forging (iron parts)	1,300	Damgård-Sørensen et al. 2004; Bill et al. 2007; Nielsen 2011; Nielsen 2013a; Nielsen 2013b; Englert et al. 2013
Production of tar	1,600	Damgård-Sørensen et al. 2004; Bill et al 2007; Nielsen 2011; Nielsen 2013a; Nielsen 2013b; Englert et al. 2013
Production of ropes	9,000	Damgård-Sørensen et al. 2004; Bill et al. 2007; Nielsen 2011; Nielsen 2013a; Nielsen 2013b; Englert et al. 2013
Production of sail	Spinning: 5,861 Weaving: 3,908 Sewing: 500	Beregninger baseret på Nørgård 2009a; Nielsen 2013a

160. Snorri Sturluson's *Heimskringla,* Olav Tryggvason's saga [Hødnebø & Magerøy (eds.) 1979a: 186].

161. Compared with the amount of daylight in the winter months in Denmark today.

162. Danish Meteorological Institute's website: http://www.dmi.dk/dmi/hvor_meget_kan_solen_skinne. The content of the website was used on 29 July 2013.

163. See chapter II for a more detailed account.

164. See chapter II, section: Shipbuilding technology and regionally delimited shipbuilding practices, for a more detailed account.

It is evident that the organisational structure around the building of the largest personnel carriers must have been comprehensive. Long-term planning with sub-goals and monitoring of the achievement of the sub-goals were necessary. In Olav Tryggvason's Saga, which deals with the building of the large personnel carrier *Ormen Lange*, it is stated that the ship was built over the course of one winter in southern Norway.[160]

If winter was often the time for shipbuilding, the number of hours of light becomes relevant. A monthly work effort of 200 hours would only just have been possible over the winter, at least if the work was done in daylight[161] and without the use of fire for lighting.[162]

The long, comprehensive planning and the coordination of working processes and tasks make it likely that parts of the production were in the hands of specialised craftsmen. The planning of the construction work and the actual construction management, the selection of the suitable resources, the work of making the sails and rigging of the vessel, the forging of the many iron objects and laying of ropes were probably done by such specialists. Other parts of the work such as the making of charcoal, wood tar, iron and sailcloth, as well as felling, splitting, rough-dressing and the transport of raw materials to the building site would not necessarily have involved specialised craftsmen. Many of the latter processes could be done alongside other ongoing chores in the village communities,[163] and if the magnate, by virtue of the obligations entailed in the relationship between ruler and subjects,[164] could demand products such as lengths of cloth and iron from the farmers of the community, the workload and the resource consumption would have been spread both geographically and temporally.

Building and maintaining war fleets

With a point of departure in the probable resource requirements suggested above, this section analyses resource-based aspects of the building and maintenance of a war fleet.

Attempts have previously been made to estimate the extensive logistical preparations prior to William the Conqueror's cross-channel operation in 1066, based on theoretical estimates of the resource consumption in connection with the building of the Gokstad Ship and the Skuldelev 1 ship respectively.[165] Along with even older analyses of the resource consumption and organisation of Viking Age shipbuilding,[166] these make up a group of studies for which it was not possible to include the results of the later systematically documented experimental archaeological reconstruction projects. Therefore, the results of the earlier analyses are

problematised as regards to certain factors. For example, the practical experiments have enabled a more detailed understanding of the character and volumes of the many different, carefully selected resources, and the total amount of resources used.[167] Another example of this is the considerable increase in the knowledge of the tools that Viking-Age boatbuilders employed and the manner in which they were used (fig. 49).[168]

The most difficult resource to procure was the erect, high-boled oak trees,[169] especially oak trees with a breast-height diameter of around 1 m. The procurement of these can therefore form a starting point for an analysis of the necessary resource areas. In the mixed forests of the Late Viking Age, which in many cases were strongly affected by the grazing and pasturing of domestic and wild animals,[170] it is likely that within a habitat of primarily closed-canopy

Fig. 49. Reconstructed Viking-Age tools used by the boatbuilders at the Viking Ship Museum in Roskilde. Photo: Werner Karrasch, Viking Ship Museum in Roskilde.

165. Gillmor 1985: 115–119.
166. See for example Brøgger & Shetelig 1951, and Olsen & Crumlin-Pedersen 1969.
167. Andersen et al. 1997; Damgård-Sørensen et al. 2004; Nielsen 2013a; Ravn 2014; Damgård-Sørensen & Sørensen (eds.) unpublished.
168. Finderup 2006a; Finderup 2006b; Damgård-Sørensen & Sørensen (eds.) unpublished.
169. Jessen 2015: 200.
170. See chapter IV for a more detailed account.

woodland of 500 hectares, there were only a couple of erect, high-boled oaks that were suitable for making planks.[171] As a comparison, today there is an average of 2.5 oaks with a breast-height diameter over 40 cm per hectare,[172] but very few of these would have been suitable for the shipbuilding of the Viking Age.

As shown in chapter II it was mainly – but not exclusively – oaks with straight growth and without many knots that were used. Moreover, the trees used were often of considerable dimensions. However, as mentioned above, planks with the archaeologically-found dimensions could also be made of trees with a lower breast-height diameter than the 80–100 cm often given as the necessary dimensions of a tree for the Viking-Age shipbuilding – but in that case more trees would have to be felled.

While the diameter of the trunk could thus be less than 80–100 cm, a straight, high-boled growth would have been crucial if the archaeologically-found dimensions of keel, planks and stringers were to be produced.

To sum up the various statements, it is estimated that somewhere between one and four oaks suitable for shipbuilding could have been felled within an area of 500 hectares of primarily closed-canopy forest, and this estimate will be used as a basis for the further analysis. In this estimate I have also attempted to allow for the fact that new suitable straight and high-boled oaks would be able to grow up.

The number of straight, high-boled oaks calculated to be necessary to make the various ship types' radially cleft planks, keel and keelson elements and stringers indicates that ca 23 large, straight and high-boled oaks without twisted growth and many knots would have to be felled for a large personnel carrier.[173] To build a medium-sized personnel carrier about six large, straight and high-boled oaks would have been necessary,[174] while for a large cargo ship about 16 large, straight, high-boled oaks would have been needed.[175] Finally, about seven large, straight, high-boled oaks would be necessary if a medium-sized cargo ship was to be built.[176]

Besides the straight, high-boled oaks, many other resources had to be procured: crooked timbers and raw materials for other hull parts, mast and yard; for wood tar, charcoal, the iron objects of the ship, ropes, caulking material and other equipment. All these resources could be procured either by utilising other resources within the stated resource area or by importing raw materials, primary products and finished goods (fig. 50). Finally, it has been possible to set up a calculation of the necessary grazing areas[177] for the sheep whose wool was used for the production of sailcloth (fig. 51).

The manpower necessary for the building of the various vessel types can be expressed in working hours. As the analysis in section: Resources required for shipbuilding in chapter III shows, it has been possible to draw up a detailed account of the time consumption in connection with the building of the Skuldelev 2 reconstruction *The Sea Stallion from Glendalough*. It should be noted in this respect that the source value of the probable time consumption compared with the actual time consumption in the 11th century will allways be subject to a certain degree of uncertainty. The following statements of average time consumption in connection with the building of the various ship types and sizes must therefore only be considered as indicative.

Building a large personnel carrier required a total of ca 55,000 working hours.[178] As regards the calculation of the number of working hours spent on the building of the medium-sized personnel carriers as well as the large and medium-sized cargo ships, the available data are less adequate and thus problematic to use in connection with a statement of the probable time consumption. In the light of the detailed registration of the building of *The Sea Stallion from Glendalough*, however, an approximate time consumption can be established: ca 30,000 hours for a medium-sized personnel carrier or cargo ship, and 45,000 hours for a large cargo ship.

In chapter V, the war fleet sizes of the Late Viking Age are analysed in detail. The following categorisation of the war fleets of the time

171. Personal communication from Søren Nielsen. Søren Nielsen is a boatbuilder and head of maritime crafts, reconstruction and public activities at the Viking Ship Museum in Roskilde. See also Møller 1992 for a general account of the trees of the natural forest.
172. Bastrup-Birk *et al.* 2008: 90.
173. See chapter III, section: Resources required for shipbuilding.
174. See chapter III, section: Resources required for shipbuilding.
175. See chapter III, section: Resources required for shipbuilding.
176. See chapter III, section: Resources required for shipbuilding.
177. Areas with commons, open-canopy woodlands and other places where sheep can find food.
178. See chapter III, section: Resources required for shipbuilding.

Resource area: woodlands

War fleet sizes	Numbers of ships	Ship-types Based on the probable ship-type composition from the Fribrødre Å site (Klassen 2010: 116-119)	The required amount of large, straight and high-boled oak trees with a diameter of ca 1 m A large personnel carrier: 23 A medium-sized personnel carrier: 6 A large cargo ship: 16 A medium-sized cargo ship: 7	The average required amount of large and straight grown oak trees with a diameter of ca 1 m a year A ship is estimated operational for 10 years (in average)	Estimated required resource area (primarily closed canopy woodlands) in ha
Small	8	3 large personnel carriers 3 medium-sized personnel carriers 1 large cargo ship 1 medium-sized cargo ship	$23 \times 3 = 69$ $6 \times 3 = 18$ $16 \times 1 = 16$ $7 \times 1 = 7$ In all = 110	110/10 = 11	1 appropriate oak tree pr. 500 ha = 5,500 4 appropriate oak trees pr. 500 ha = 1,375 Average: 3,400
Medium-sized	40	15 large personnel carriers 15 medium-sized personnel carriers 5 large cargo ships 5 medium-sized cargo ships	$23 \times 15 = 345$ $6 \times 15 = 90$ $16 \times 5 = 80$ $7 \times 5 = 35$ In all = 550	550/10 = 55	1 appropriate oak tree pr. 500 ha = 27,500 4 appropriate oak trees pr. 500 ha = 6,875 Average: 17,000
Large	160	60 large personnel carriers 60 medium-sized personnel carriers 20 large cargo ships 20 medium-sized cargo ships	$23 \times 60 = 1,380$ $6 \times 60 = 360$ $16 \times 20 = 320$ $7 \times 20 = 140$ In all = 2,200	2,200/10 = 220	1 appropriate oak tree pr. 500 ha = 110,000 4 appropriate oak trees pr. 500 ha = 27,500 Average: 68,750

Fig. 50. The calculations shown in the figure are based on published and unpublished data generated through the Viking Ship Museum's more than 30 years of experimental archaeological practice building reconstructions of Viking-Age ships. For a more detailed account of the analysis, see chapter III. The interpretation of the data has been discussed with the Viking Ship Museum's head of maritime crafts, reconstruction and public activities, Søren Nielsen. Table: The author, Viking Ship Museum in Roskilde.

into three different sizes is based on this analysis. A small war fleet is defined today as consisting of eight ships, while the number of ships participating in a medium-sized war fleet has been set at 40. Finally, the number of ships participating in a large war fleet has been set at 160.

In chapter V, section: The fleet from Fribrødre Å, it is demonstrated that the large war fleet that was repaired and prepared at Fribrødre Å at the end of the 11th century, probably

consisted of about three times as many personnel carriers as cargo ships, as well as approximately as many medium-sized and large ships. On the basis of such a composition of ship types and sizes a small war fleet with eight ships would have consisted of three large personnel carriers, three medium-sized personnel carriers, one large cargo ship and one medium-sized cargo ship. A medium-sized war fleet with 40 ships would have been made up of 15 large and

Fig. 51. The calculations shown in the figure are based on published and unpublished data generated through the Viking Ship Museum's more than 30 years of experimental archaeological practice building reconstructions of Viking-Age ships. For a more detailed account of the analysis, see chapter III. The interpretation of the data has been discussed with the Viking Ship Museum's head of maritime crafts, reconstruction and public activities, Søren Nielsen. Table: The author, Viking Ship Museum in Roskilde.

Resource area: grazing grounds for sheep

War fleet sizes	Numbers of ships	Ship-types Based on the probable ship-type composition from the Fribrødre Å site (Klassen 2010: 116-119)	The required amount of sheep A large personnel carrier: 180-224 (ca 200) A medium-sized personnel carrier: 58-77 (ca 68) A large cargo ship: 240-300 (ca 270) A medium-sized cargo ship: 54-72 (ca 65)	The average required amount of sheep a year A wool sail is estimated operational for 15 years (in average)	Estimated required resource area (grazing grounds) in ha A sheep eat ca 700 kg hay a year (Østergård 2003: 40). In a farming community similar to the situation in present day Denmark (without modern day farming methods and techniques) a sheep needs ca. 1 ha as grazing ground to obtain a food source that equals the 700 kg of hay (Austrheim *et al.* 2008: 15)
Small	8	3 large personnel carriers 3 medium-sized personnel carriers 1 large cargo ship 1 medium-sized cargo ship	$200 \times 3 = 600$ $68 \times 3 = 204$ $270 \times 1 = 270$ $65 \times 1 = 65$ In all = 1,139	1,139/15 = 76	76/1 = 76
Medium-sized	40	15 large personnel carriers 15 medium-sized personnel carriers 5 large cargo ships 5 medium-sized cargo ships	$200 \times 15 = 3,000$ $68 \times 15 = 1,020$ $270 \times 5 = 1,350$ $65 \times 5 = 325$ In all = 5,695	5,695/15 = 380	380/1 = 380
Large	160	60 large personnel carriers 60 medium-sized personnel carriers 20 large cargo ships 20 medium-sized cargo ships	$200 \times 60 = 12,000$ $68 \times 60 = 4,080$ $270 \times 20 = 5,400$ $65 \times 20 = 1,300$ In all = 22,780	22,780/15 = 1,519	1,519/1 = 1,519

15 medium-sized personnel carriers as well as five large and five medium-sized cargo ships, while a large war fleet with 160 ships would consist of 60 large and 60 medium-sized personnel carriers as well as 20 large and 20 medium-sized cargo ships (figs. 50, 51 & 52). However, it must be pointed out that the number of ships and ship types in the war fleets posited here is based on a type composition related to the specific situation at Fribrødre Å. The com-position and size of a war fleet depended on the intention of the sea transport, what was transported, the available resources, the distance from the destination, the duration of the transport and the waters where the transport was to take place. This means that each 11th-century war fleet was most likely unique in composition and size.

To this, it should be added that the ships, sails and other equipment of the war fleets were

Resource area: human resources

War fleet sizes	Numbers of ships	Ship-types Based on the probable ship-type composition from the Fribrødre Å site (Klassen 2010: 116-119)	Estimated required amount of hours spent building and maintaining the ships in the fleets A large personnel carrier: 55,000 A medium-sized personnel carrier: 30,000 A large cargo ship: 45,000 A medium-sized cargo ship: 30,000	Estimated annual required amount of hours spent building and maintaining the different fleet sizes A ship is estimated operational for 10 years (in average)
Small	8	3 large personnel carriers 3 medium-sized personnel carriers 1 large cargo ship 1 medium-sized cargo ship	$55,000 \times 3 = 165,000$ $30,000 \times 3 = 90,000$ $45,000 \times 1 = 45,000$ $30,000 \times 1 = 30,000$ In all $= 330,000$	$330,000/10 = 33,000$
Medium-sized	40	15 large personnel carriers 15 medium-sized personnel carriers 5 large cargo ships 5 medium-sized cargo ships	$55,000 \times 15 = 825,000$ $30,000 \times 15 = 450,000$ $45,000 \times 5 = 225,000$ $30,000 \times 5 = 150,000$ In all $= 1,650,000$	$1,650,000/10 = 165,000$
Large	160	60 large personnel carriers 60 medium-sized personnel carriers 20 large cargo ships 20 medium-sized cargo ships	$55,000 \times 60 = 3,300,000$ $30,000 \times 60 = 1,800,000$ $45,000 \times 20 = 900,000$ $30,000 \times 20 = 600,000$ In all $= 6,600,000$	$6,600,000/10 = 660,000$

Fig. 52. The calculations shown in the figure are based on published and unpublished data generated through the Viking Ship Museum's more than 30 years of experimental archaeological practice building reconstructions of Viking-Age ships. For a more detailed account of the analysis, see chapter III. The interpretation of the data has been discussed with the Viking Ship Museum's head of maritime crafts, reconstruction and public activities, Søren Nielsen. Table: The author, Viking Ship Museum in Roskilde.

used over a number of years, and that ship components, sails and other equipment were re-used. All these factors must be considered when the resources invested on an annual basis to build and maintain the various war fleets are to be estimated.

The operational life of a Viking-Age ship has been estimated as a maximum of 20–40 years[179] An average useful life[180] for the individual ship and its equipment has been set at ten years, which means that a magnate or king who wanted to maintain an operational war fleet[181] consisting of ten vessels would have had an annual average consumption of raw materials and working hours corresponding to the building of

about one vessel. A fleet consisting of 20 vessels would have had an annual estimated building requirement of about two vessels – and so on.

Since the war fleets probably consisted of different ship types and sizes, the annual requirement for raw materials and working hours would not have been the same year after year. And in some years it is likely that more than one vessel was built, while in other years no ships were built. It is thus only possible to draw up an average of necessary annual resources.

In figures 51, 52 and 53 the various factors are shown, and the overall result indicates a resource area of ca 3,400 hectares[182], primarily of closed-canopy woodlands, ca 76 hectares of

179. Crumlin-Pedersen & Olsen 2002: 333–334.
180. With an estimation of wreckage and other losses of ships as well as wear and re-use of ships' components.
181. Both newbuilding and maintenance.
182. On average.

Fig. 53. Estimated resource areas and annual time consumption for the building and maintenance of small, medium-sized and large war fleets with a ship-type composition as suggested by the Fribrødre Å site. Table: The author, Viking Ship Museum in Roskilde.

War fleet sizes	Numbers of ships	Ship-types Based on the probable ship-type composition from the Fribrødre Å site (Klassen 2010: 116-119)	Estimated resource area in ha (ca) A: Woodland B: Grazing area	Estimated annual amount of hours (ca)
Small	8	3 large personnel carriers 3 medium-sized personnel carriers 1 large cargo ship 1 medium-sized cargo ship	A: 3,400 B: 76	33,000
Medium-sized	40	15 large personnel carriers 15 medium-sized personnel carriers 5 large cargo ships 5 medium-sized cargo ships	A: 17,000 B: 380	165,000
Large	160	60 large personnel carriers 60 medium-sized personnel carriers 20 large cargo ships 20 medium-sized cargo ships	A: 68,750 B: 1,519	660,000

grazing area for sheep and ca 33,000 annually invested working hours were necessary to build and maintain a small war fleet of eight ships (fig. 53).[183]

In order to build and maintain a medium-sized war fleet of 40 ships[184] a resource area of ca 17,000 hectares[185] of primarily closed-canopy woodland, ca 380 hectares of grazing area for sheep and ca 165,000 working hours a year would have been necessary (fig. 53).

Finally, a resource area of ca 68,750 hectares[186] of primarily closed-canopy woodland, ca 1,519 hectares of grazing area for sheep and ca 660,000 annual working hours would have been necessary if a large war fleet of 160 ships[187] was to be built and maintained (fig. 53).

As a comparison, it should be mentioned that the total forest area in Denmark today has been calculated as 608,078 hectares and of this 61,836 hectares are covered with oaks.[188] Since oak was the preferred tree species for shipbuilding in southern Scandinavia the resource area necessary for a large war fleet in the late part of

the Viking Age corresponds to having to search through all the forest areas in present-day Denmark[189] to select the suitable resources. In addition, it should be noted that several large war fleets were probably operational at the same time in the 11th century, which means that far more then 160 ships had to be built and maintained.[190]

It is thus important to emphasise that not all the wood resources within the stated necessary resources areas were felled and used for shipbuilding; the stated resource areas express an approximate area of primarily closed-canopy woodlands that had to be searched through if the resources suitable for shipbuilding were to be procured. This means that woodland management or the protection of suitable resources[191] may have minimised the size of the necessary wood resource areas.

Finally, it must be stressed that it is exclusively resource area sizes and manpower for shipbuilding that have been indicated. If the other production of the communities were to

183. With a vessel-type composition as suggested by the Fribrødre Å site.
184. With a vessel-type composition as suggested by the Fribrødre Å site.
185. On average.
186. On average.
187. With a vessel-type composition as suggested by the Fribrødre Å site.
188. Johannsen *et al.* 2013: 29, table 1.4.
189. With the present distribution of tree species.
190. More on this in chapter V.
191. More on this in chapter IV.

be included, the resource areas would on the one hand have been larger in area, and on the other hand would consist of several other landscape types than woodlands and grazing areas, and the necessary manpower would have been far greater. See for example Lise Bender Jørgensen's estimates of the wool resources and working hours needed to make rugs and clothing for the crew on board a medium-sized cargo ship and a large personnel carrier respectively.[192]

The analysis suggests that the raw materials and labour necessary to build and maintain a small war fleet could be procured by a single magnate or king. The medium-sized war fleets required a particularly powerful magnate or king with a large domain, if the necessary raw materials and manpower were to be procured. Alternatively, the medium-sized war fleets could have been established by associations of magnates – sometimes also involving the king. Finally, it seems unlikely that a single magnate or the king could manage the building, maintenance and use of a large war fleet. It would only have been possible to establish by virtue of associations between magnates and the king.

192. Bender Jørgensen 2012.

IV. Woodland management

Access to suitable resources was a basic requirement if magnates or kings were to build and maintain their ships. As suggested in chapters II and III, the Scandinavian shipbuilding technology of the 11th century would have required specially selected raw materials. The special needs for the raw materials probably meant that the suitable resources were very valuable.

In the following, the woodland landscapes of the Late Viking Age within the primary geographical area of study are analysed. Against this background, there will be a discussion of how magnates and kings in the last part of the Viking Age, and High Middle Ages, protected the tree resources that were suitable for shipbuilding.

The woodlands of Late Viking-Age Denmark

The species composition of Late Viking-Age Danish woodlands cannot be determined unambiguously. It is problematic to determine the diffusion and general character of the woodlands of the time. The sources are few and by no means country-wide. Some areas are relatively well elucidated by numerous pollen analyses and historical-geographical and archaeological investigations, while for other regions within the area of investigation there are hardly any useful sources. Forestry researchers agree that more pollen analyses are necessary if more precise analyses of the prehistoric and historical development of the woodlands are to be conducted.[1]

Figure 54 sums up the analysed sources for the woodlands of the Viking Age and High Middle Ages and against this background, their

diffusion and character have been suggested. The results of the analysis will be summed up and put in perspective in the following.

In general, the landscape was wetter in the Viking Age than it is today. In such a landscape, oak, birch and alder had good growth conditions, and this meant that the competition between oak and beech was more equal than it is today, when beech often has the best conditions for growth.[2] Nevertheless the pollen analyses show that beech was in general the dominant tree species in the 11th century (fig. 54).[3]

Besides beech, oak, alder, birch, maple, yew, hazel, aspen, hornbeam, ash, lime, elm, willow, pine and various fruit trees would have been present in the Danish forests of the time.[4] However, neither sycamore nor larch were part of the tree landscape of the time (fig. 54).[5]

The wet landscape meant that the trees grew more slowly than they do today, but other factors were also significant for the growth of the trees. The genetics of the individual tree, the soil conditions, the water level, climatic conditions, weather, the dynamics of nature itself and the ecological dynamics would have been important to the growth of the individual tree.[6]

The forests of the Late Viking Age with their mixture of trees were characterised by many kinds of exploitation. Trees were cut and felled for use as construction timber and leaf forage, for fuel and in connection with the production of charcoal and tar. The woodlands were also used as grazing and pannage areas for animals.[7] This utilisation meant that in many places the woodlands consisted of scattered and irregular tree growth as well as many grassy clearings, some of which were cultivated.[8] Alongside this there was also forestry. Through coppicing, raw

1. Odgaard 1990; Berglund (ed.) 1991; Aaby 1990 & 1992; Fritzbøger 2004: 15–20; Fritzbøger 2011; Dam 2009; Odgaard & Nielsen 2009.
2. Berglund *et al.* 1991: 439–441; Møller 2012.
3. Odgaard 1990: 122–124; Aaby 1992: 215, 220 & 232; Hoff 1997: 249–250; Møller 2012.
4. Odgaard and Nielsen 2009; Møller 2012.
5. Møller 2012.
6. Møller 2012; Breuning-Madsen *et al.* 2013b: 6–8.
7. Hoff 1997: 248–249 & 359.
8. Berglund *et al.* 1991: 442–443; Dam 2009: 52.
9. Voss 1993b: 105–108; Poulsen 2005: 68–69.

Fig. 54. Analysis of woodlands of late Viking-Age Denmark. Table: The author, Viking Ship Museum in Roskilde.

Abbreviations:

LPD: Local Pollen Diagrams;
RPD: Regional Pollen Diagrams;
HGA: Historical Geographical Analysis;
AA: Archaeological Analysis;
DA: Dendrochronological Analysis.

CCW: habitat with primarily closed-canopy woodlands;
COCW: habitat with both closed and open-canopy woodlands;

OCW: habitat with only a small area of woodland, all open-canopy;
FST: habitat with a few free-standing trees.

Site; region	Source type	General woodland structure	Dominant tree species	Other frequently appearing tree species	References
Säröhalvøen; North Halland	RPD	COCW	Birch, oak & pine	Red alder, elm, lime, ash & hazel	Jönsson 2003: 12-13
Berg; Middle Halland	RPD	OCW	Birch & hazel	Oak	Sköld 2006: 21-33
North Scania	RPD, LPD & AA	CCW	Birch, pine & oak	Spruce	Karlsson 2000; Ödman 2000; Robertsson 1973
Ageröds Mose; Middle Scania	RPD	COCW	Beech, oak, hazel & red alder	Lime, birch & pine	Nilsson 1964: 17-24
South Scania	RPD, AA & DA	COCW	Beech, oak, red alder, birch, hazel & juniper	Pine	Berglund 1991: 82; Berglund (ed.) 1991: 109-271
Lund; South-west Scania	RPD, LPD, AA & DA	COCW	Oak, ash & lime		Bartholin 1976: 168
Store Gribsø; North-east Zealand	RPD	CCW	Beech	Red alder, oak & birch	Odgaard & Nielsen 2009: 47-49
Avnsø; Middle Zealand (south-west of Roskilde)	RPD	CCW	Beech	Red alder, oak & birch	Odgaard & Nielsen 2009: 47-49
South of Lammefjorden	HGA	COCW			Gøgsig Jakobsen & Dam 2009: 43
West coast of Zealand	HGA	COCW			Gøgsig Jakobsen & Dam 2009: 43
Gundsømagle Sø; East Zealand (west of Jyllinge)	RPD	COCW	Beech, red alder & birch		Odgaard & Nielsen 2009: 52-53
Horns Herred; Zealand	HGA & AA	COCW & OCW			Fritzbøger 2011: 43 & 47
Voldborg Herred; Zealand	HGA & AA	COCW & OCW			Fritzbøger 2011: 43 & 47; Ulriksen 1998: 76
Even Sø; South Zealand	RPD, AA & HGA	COCW	Beech	Birch, hazel, oak & pine	Aaby 1992: 215-217; Mikkelsen 1949: 28-33
Borre Mose; Møn	RPD, AA & HGA	COCW	Red alder & hazel	Oak, beech & birch	Mikkelsen 1949: 39-43 & tavle XVII
Holmegårds Mose; South Zealand	RPD	COCW	Beech	Birch, pine, hazel, elm, oak, red alder & ash	Andersen *et al.* 1983: 186-188; Aaby 1992: 212-214
Slagelse; South-west Zealand	RPD	COCW	Beech	Oak, ash, lime, elm, birch, red alder & hazel	Jørgensen 1989; Aaby 1992: 225-228
Northern Falster	LPD, RPD & DA	COCW	Beech	Red alder, oak. Numerous hemp pollen (for rope?)	Christensen & Fischer Mortensen 2010: 46-47 & 55-56

Grishøjgårds Krat; Vendsyssel (north Jutland)	LPD	FST			Nielsen 1993: 26-27
St. Økssø; Himmerland (north Jutland)	RPD	OCW	Oak, hazel, birch & red alder	Beech	Odgaard & Nielsen 2009: 49-50
Løvenholm; Djurs (east Jutland)	RPD	COCW	Beech	Oak & birch	Andersen et al. 1983: 189-190
Skånsø; North Jutland	RPD	FST	Oak, birch & red alder		Odgaard 1994: 84-85 & 150-151
Navnsø; Himmerland (north Jutland)	RPD	FST	Oak, birch & red alder		Odgaard & Nielsen 2009: 53-55
Kragsø; Middle Jutland	RPD	FST	Beech	Oak, birch, red alder	Odgaard 1994: 116-117 & 150-151; Odgaard & Nielsen 2009: 55-56
Bos Sø; West Jutland	RPD	FST	Birch, hazel & red alder	Pine	Odgaard 2000
Solsø; West Jutland	RPD	FST	Oak, hazel & red alder		Odgaard 1994: 54-55 & 150-151; Odgaard 2000
Børglumvej, Århus; East Jutland	LPD & RPD	COCW		Beech, oak, red alder, lime, birch, pine, hazel & elm	Aaby et al. 1994: 81-90
Dallerup Sø; East Jutland	RPD	OCW	Red alder, beech, oak & hazel		Odgaard & Nielsen 2009: 50-52
Gudme Sø; South-east Funen	RPD	OCW	Beech, red alder, birch, hazel & oak		Odgaard & Nielsen 2009: 50-52
Vorbasse; Middle Jutland	LPD	FST			Brorson Christensen 1981: 108-110
Esbjerg; West Jutland	LPD & RPD	OCW	Red alder, oak, hazel, birch & beech		Kolstrup 2009: 367
Barved Syssel; South Jutland	HGA & AA	COCW	Conifer (pine?) and other tree species not possible to determine		Oppermann 1922: 180; Poulsen 2003: 377; Feveile 2010
Abkær Mose; South Jutland	RPD	COCW	Beech	Red alder, hazel, birch & oak	Aaby 1990: 132-134
Guderup; South Jutland	RPD	OCW	Beech, red alder & birch	Lime, elm, ash & pine	Hardt 2003: 41
Angelhalvøen; Schleswig-Holstein (North Germany)	HGA & AA	OCW & COCW			Poulsen 2003: 376-381
Svans; Eckernförde & Kiel, Schleswig-Holstein (North Germany)	HGA	CCW			Poulsen 2003: 376-381
Nørre and Sønder Gøs; Schleswig-Holstein (North Germany)	HGA & AA	CCW			Lüdtke 1987: 72-74; Crumlin-Pedersen 1997b: 38; Poulsen 2003: 376-381
Hedeby and Schleswig; Schleswig-Holstein (North Germany)	LPD, RPD & AA	FST surrounding the cities; COCW further away from the cities	Beech & oak		Behre 1983: 80-84, 126-128 & 183-188; Crumlin-Pedersen 1997b: 179-184

materials were produced and used to make charcoal as well as fencing and tools.[9]

The open-canopy woodlands with grazing and browsing animals would have consisted of many different tree species. If grazing was very intensive and consistent in terms of place, there would hardly have been any undergrowth. The trees in such open grazing woodlands mainly have short, curving trunks and large tops as well as many thick and crooked branches (fig. 55).[10] At Langå, south west of Randers, such a grazing forest with old oaks can still be studied today.

Despite the intensive grazing by animals, there could still be a limited amount of naturally occurring regeneration. Sheltered in thorny scrub from the biting of the animals, small trees could grow large.[11]

Open-canopy woodlands marked by grazing and browsing were not the only type of woodland in Late Viking-Age Denmark. The planks, keels and stringers in the Viking-Age ship finds as well as timbers for the other large construction works of the time[12] testify that straight, high-boled oaks with trunk lengths of at least 14 m, and with diameters between 50 and 100 cm at breast height, were among the trees of the forests. These old, straight, high-boled trees mainly grew in landscapes with dense tree growth (fig. 55).[13]

Woodland composition and structure

Earlier studies have shown that the division of the historical landscape into forest-rich and forest-poor areas remained unchanged on the whole, from the Bronze Age right up to the end of the 18th century.[14] A single exception to this tendency should be mentioned – the eastern part of Vendsyssel was probably[15] more richly wooded before the establishment of the clearance villages at the end of the Viking Age and in the High Middle Ages.[16]

The early-occurring division into, and the long continuity of, richly and poorly wooded areas can be explained by topographical and soil-related factors. For example, one often finds the well-wooded areas in hilly terrain and in places where the soil is less fertile, while the poorly wooded areas are often to be found where the soil is fertile and the terrain more even.[17]

The analysis summed up in figure 54 makes it seem likely that in a wide belt in northern Scania, in northeastern Zealand, and in the area south west of Roskilde, and in the areas west, south and south east of Hedeby, there were large areas with closed-canopy woodlands. However, at the same time it is clear that in the same areas there were habitats with open-canopy woodlands affected by grazing and browsing.

In the northern part of Halland, the Scanian area in general, the western and southern parts of Zealand, in eastern Møn and the northern part of Falster, as well as the eastern part of Jutland and the area around Hedeby and Schleswig, the landscape would have consisted of habitats with both closed and open-canopy woodlands.

In Vendsyssel and on Funen, Lolland, Langeland, Samsø, Læsø, Ærø, Anholt and other small islands, in parts of western Jutland and on the west coast of Halland, the source material for the wooded landscapes in the Late Viking Age is so limited that it is considered impossible to indicate the overall appearance of the woodlands.[18] However, place-names and soil analyses make it seem likely that there were large woodland areas on Funen, Langeland and Samsø.[19] Moreover, the western part of Jutland – from the Limfjord down to the area west of Hedeby – were mainly dominated by open-canopy woodland habitats or few, free-standing trees. Furthermore, the occurrence of a habitat with both closed- and open-canopy woodlands east of Ribe needs mentioning. The area is called Farrisskoven, and in the Viking Age, the forest landscape probably extended through large parts of Barved Syssel from Kolding in the east to Kalvslund in the west.[20]

Fig. 55. Left: Naturally curved tree used for the production of frame components and other crooked timbers. Right: Straight, high-boled tree with a large breast-height diameter used for the production of keels, planks, stringers and other straight timbers. Photos: Werner Karrasch, Viking Ship Museum in Roskilde.

10. Bartholin 1976; Crumlin-Pedersen 1997b: 179–184.
11. Møller 2012.
12. For example magnates' halls, see Jørgensen, L. 2008, bridges, see Schou Jørgensen 1997 and fortifications, see Hellmuth Andersen 1998.
13. Bartholin 1976; Crumlin-Pedersen 1997b: 182.
14. Rasmussen et al. 1998; Dam 2009.
15. The place-name -tved indicates this. See figure 88.
16. Dam 2009: 84.
17. Rasmussen et al. 1998: 112–113.
18. That is, if the woodlands were characterised by open or closed canopy and whichever tree species predominated.
19. Dam 2009: 83–84; Breuning-Madsen et al. 2013a: 2–5.
20. Feveile 2010: 25.

Dominant tree species

When a pollen diagram is to be drawn up – locally or regionally – the pollen from the area to be investigated must be separated from the other pollen emitted – also called background pollen. Some tree species emit considerably more pollen than others, and the ability of the pollen particles to spread varies greatly. To deal with this, several models have been developed which are subject to adaptation as the empirical material grows and the theoretical calculation methods develop.[21] The following analysis allows for these factors. It should be pointed out, however, that the interpretation of pollen specimens can always be discussed, and that knowledge of the diffusion and emission of the pollen of the various trees is undergoing continuous development.[22] The accounts of the tree landscapes and their species composition must therefore only be viewed as guidelines.

Beech was the dominant species in central and southern Scania, on Zealand and Funen and in the eastern part of Jutland, as well as in southern Jutland and the area around Hedeby (fig. 54). On the wet soils near Navnsø in Himmerland and Skånsø east of Venø Bay, however, oak had a growth advantage over both beech and ash (fig. 54).[23]

In general, the pollen diagrams show that oaks grew over all of the present primary geographical area of study in the Late Viking Age and that oaks were present in considerable numbers in the tree landscape (fig. 54). Oak is water-level-tolerant and can grow on both sandy and clayey soil as well as in peat. Only a raw chalky soil gives oak problems – there beech reigns supreme. The thick bark on oaks also means that they can resist light forest fires, unlike most other tree species.[24]

The deciduous trees: lime, alder, ash, hazel and willow were all relatively frequently occurring in the mixed woodlands of the Late Viking Age and probably both grew 'wild' and were cultivated as coppiced woodland (fig. 54).

Most remarkable is the fact that pine pollen is present in relatively many, and geographically scattered, pollen diagrams (fig. 54). Although pines do not grow in such large numbers and in the same dimensions and qualities as known for example from the Sognefjord area in Norway, there are grounds to challenge the general assumption that pine – because there were few trees and these trees were of limited size – was not used at all for shipbuilding in southwestern Scandinavia in the Late Viking Age.[25] Jan Bill has earlier pointed out the problematic aspects of this assumption,[26] and the ship finds analysed in this context also have ship components that may have been made of pine that grew in the Danish forests of the Late Viking Age (fig. 35).

In Oppermann's large work *Skovfyr i Midt- og Vestjylland*[27] from 1922, place-names and written sources from the Middle Ages, Renaissance and recent times were used to show that the mixed forest of the Viking Age and later of the High Middle Ages also probably included pines. In some cases, it is likely that the pine trees had dimensions that made them suitable as resources for both construction timber and shipbuilding.[28] Oppermann's conclusion was that place-names with first elements like *Tan-, Bar-, Faar-, Grøn-, Skib-, Stok-, Tøll-, Del-, Brand-, Bram-* and *Tar-* may suggest vegetation with considerable numbers of conifers, with name formations between 800 and 1200 AD.[29]

Straight, high-boled pines could be felled in northern Scania (fig. 54). In Halland, the Baltic area and in Norway, it would also have been possible to procure suitable resources of pine, either through direct possession of the land or ownership of areas with suitable resources, or by procuring them indirectly, that is through trade.[30] In addition, it was probably possible to fell suitable resources for masts and yards in the form of spruce in Norway – especially in the large forest areas north of Oslo.[31] It is also likely – but subject to discussion – that small stands of spruce grew in the large forest areas in northern Scania bordering on Småland (fig. 54).

21. Tauber 1965; Sugita 1994; Odgaard & Nielsen 2009: 41–43.
22. Wagner 1986: 135–137.
23. Møller 2012.
24. Møller 2012.
25. Crumlin-Pedersen 1997b: 179–184; Vadstrup 1997a: 35; Crumlin-Pedersen & Olsen 2002: 138–139.
26. Bill 2006b: 13.
27. Forest pine in central and western Jutland.
28. Oppermann 1922.
29. The place-name *Barved*, which has given its name to the district (a *syssel*) where the large forest area Farrisskoven between the rivers Kongeåen, Gram Å and Ribe Å lies, may indicate that the otherwise primarily closed-canopy woodlands consisted of many conifers, see Oppermann 1922: 180 &190; Poulsen 2003: 377.
30. Møller 2012.
31. Godal 2012.

Areas with appropriate wood resources for shipbuilding

In summary, it can be concluded that resources suitable for shipbuilding were present in many forests within the present primary geographical area of study in the 11th century. However, the suitable resources were unevenly distributed in terms of their volume. In the northern part of Halland, the Scania area in general, the northeastern, western and southern parts of Zealand, on eastern Møn, the northern part of Falster, in some areas of the eastern part of Jutland, large areas in southeastern Jutland, the large forest, Farrisskoven, between the rivers Kongeåen, Gram Å and Ribe Å, and the area around Hedeby and Schleswig, it may well have been possible to fell both straight, high-boled, and crooked, low-boled oaks (fig. 56). Suitable resources for making the raw materials for all the different wooden parts in a vessel were thus present in these areas.

Large parts of western Jutland – from the Limfjord down to the area west of Hedeby – and probably also large areas along the west coast of Halland, appear to have been characterised by open-canopy woodlands or only a few free-standing trees. In these areas suitable resources for shipbuilding were probably highly limited (fig. 56), but since the analysis has to rely on a limited source basis, smaller forest areas with wood resources suitable for shipbuilding cannot be precluded. For Vendsyssel and Funen, Lolland, Langeland, Samsø, Læsø, Ærø, Anholt and other small islands, the source material is so scant that a detailed account of the wooded landscapes of the later part of the Viking Age is not possible.

Shipbuilding sites

The boats and ships of the 11th century were probably built in areas with suitable resources. We cannot preclude the possibility that raw materials were, to some extent, transported to the building site, but true long-distance wood raw material transport probably only began in the middle of the 13th century.[32]

The sources for where the shipbuilding of the time took place are limited. It is only possible to point to three places where activities undoubtedly took place that can be related to the building or repairing of boats and ships: at Fribrødre Å on Falster,[33] Eskelund near Viby south west of Aarhus,[34] and in the area around Schleswiger Stadthalbinsel at Holmer Noor on the northern side of Slien.[35]

At all three places, judging from the pollen analyses, there was a reasonable basis for the procurement of shipbuilding resources – that is, the straight, high-boled and the crooked, low-boled trees (fig. 56). It should also be pointed out that in all three places there are *snekke* place-names. At Fribrødre Å there are Nørre and Sønder Snekkebjerg as well as Snekke Tofter, at Eskelund Snekkeeng and Snekkeagre, and at Holmer Noor Schnickstedt (fig. 57). *Snekke* place-names should be noted in this context because in several cases they indicate ship-related activities, including building, repairs or fitting-out that can probably be dated to the Late Viking Age and early High Middle Ages. However, not all *snekke* place-names can be assigned to the last part of the Viking Age and the High Middle Ages. For example, several *snekke* place-names have arisen in connection with the romantic reintroduction of the term in the 18th and 19th century, and in this context the term was often used descriptively of legendary or landscape features.[36] Finally, it has been proposed that the *snekke* names in the present-day northern German areas may be derived from the German word *Schnecke*, which means 'snail'.[37]

Snekke place-names occur within the areas, which in the Viking Age and the High Middle Ages, had a Norse language. They can be found on the Orkney and Shetland Islands,[38] in southwestern and southern Norway,[39] in Finland,[40] along the east coast of Sweden and on Gotland as well as in Scania, Halland and Blekinge,[41] and finally in Denmark as well as Schleswig and Holstein.[42]

32. See chapter II, secition: Wooden parts, for a more detailed account.
33. Skamby Madsen & Klassen 2010.
34. Skamby Madsen & Vinner 2005: 94–95.
35. Crumlin-Pedersen 1997b: 179.
36. Holmberg & Skamby Madsen 1998: 204–206.
37. Laur 1992: 580.
38. Holmberg & Skamby Madsen 1998: 202–203.
39. Holmberg & Skamby Madsen 1998: 202.
40. Valtavuo-Pfeifer 1989: 405.
41. Olsson 1972: 180–208; Westerdahl 1989: 139–148.
42. Kalmring 2005; Klassen 2010: 318–319.

Fig. 56. Map showing the distribution of wood resources suitable for shipbuilding in late Viking-Age Denmark. Green markings: Areas with a probable presence of wood resources suitable for shipbuilding. Red markings: Areas probably without wood resources suitable for shipbuilding. The encircled areas are only approximate, and the areas with no map indications for the presence or absence of wood resources for shipbuilding are the result of an insufficiency of source material. Layout and additions by Narayana Press, Morten Johansen and the author, Viking Ship Museum in Roskilde.

The *snekke* place-names have been interpreted as relating to military organisation[43] and thus described as places where naval vessels were kept, repaired and fitted out.[44] The subdivisions of the Danish realm into the administrative units *skipæn* and *havner* in the provincial laws of the High Middle Ages have been compared to the *snekke* place-names, but no clear correlation has been demonstrated.[45] For example, there are areas where no *snekke* place-names occur, and areas where many *snekke* place-names occur within a very small geographical area (fig. 57). The concentration of *snekke* place-names, Lutz Klassen argues, can be explained by a permanent and massive presence of warships in these areas, which were meant to defend strategically important places in the realm.[46] The absence of *snekke* place-names in western and southwestern Jutland is explained by Klassen as indicating that the king did not administer the military organisation of these areas.[47] However, this requires the *snekke* place-names to be interpreted as places with direct relations with the monarchy. In an attempt to analyse this particular situation, Klassen has compared the positioning of the *snekke* place-names to the lists of the monarchy's lands and estates in *Valdemars Jordebog* (fig. 58).[48] Klassen arrives at the conclusion that there is a clear correlation between the positioning of the royal possessions and the *snekke* place-names – although there are a few exceptions.[49] As a result of this, Klassen interprets the *snekke* place-names as localities with maritime activities under the control of the king.[50]

Klassen's analysis and his conclusion seem well-argued, but the author considers it problematic that Klassen views all *snekke* place-names as directly related to the monarchy. There are several areas where the posited geographical match between the positioning of the monarchy's possessions and the *snekke* place-names is difficult to see. An example that can be mentioned is the central part of Halland, where no *snekke* place-names occur, but where *konunglef* and *patrimonium* both appear, and on Samsø there are numerous *snekke* place-

names, but there is no *konunglef* or *patrimonium* (fig. 58).

In my opinion, the source basis can only support that a *snekkja* was a ship that was operational in the Viking Age and Middle Ages, but neither whether it was only used for military purposes nor who owned or had the right to use the ship.[51] From this, it follows that the *snekke* place-names can only be used as a general indication of localities with ship-related activities in the 11th century.

Snekke place-names and areas with appropriate wood resources

In an article from 1998, Bente Holmberg and Jan Skamby Madsen point out that *snekke* place-names that occur together with woodland-related words may refer to areas where wood resources for shipbuilding were felled.[52] In the following, I will investigate this in more detail by comparing the geographical distribution of the *snekke* place-names with the areas where there was probably a basis for the procurement of the resources suitable for shipbuilding (fig. 59).

First and foremost, the *snekke* place-names are often absent from the places where the resources suitable for shipbuilding were also absent (fig. 59). In addition, there is a convergence between areas with many *snekke* place-names and areas where the resources suitable for shipbuilding were present. In relation to the latter it should be mentioned that *snekke* place-names and the place-names indicating forest clearings from the Late Viking Age and High Middle Ages, ending in *-rud* and *-tved,* are often found in the same general areas, presumably because habitats with a significant degree of closed-canopy woodlands occurred in these areas in the Late Viking Age and Early High Middle Ages.[53] Other medieval woodland-indicating place-names such as *-skov* and *-ved* partly support this tendency,[54] but it should be mentioned that place-names that suggest the occurrence of woodlands are also found in areas

43. The character of Scandinavian military organisation in the Viking Age and High Middle Ages is much debated, see Thestrup 1756; Rothe 1781 & 1782; Jahn 1825; Erslev [1898] 1972; Arup 1914; Christensen 1965a & 1965b; Crumlin-Pedersen 1988 & 1996b; Malmros 1988 & 2010; Skamby Madsen 1995; Lund 1996 & 2003; Gelting 1999; Hermanson 2000; Price 2002; Sawyer 2002; Varenius 2002; Williams 2002; Bill 2009; Dobat 2009; Ravn 2014; Holm forthcoming.
44. Crumlin-Pedersen 1996b: 188–193; Crumlin-Pedersen & Olsen 2002: 316–320.
45. Klassen 2010: 316–317.
46. Klassen 2010: 326–330.
47. Klassen 2010: 334.48. In the written sources called *konunglef* and *patrimonium*.
49. Klassen 2010: 314–335.
50. Klassen 2010: 335.
51. See chapter V, secition: Fleet composition, for a more detailed account of the issue.
52. Holmberg & Skamby Madsen 1998: 205.
53. Jørgensen, B. 2008: 239 & 307; Dam 2015: 129–141.
54. Dam 2015: 143–146 & 161–165.

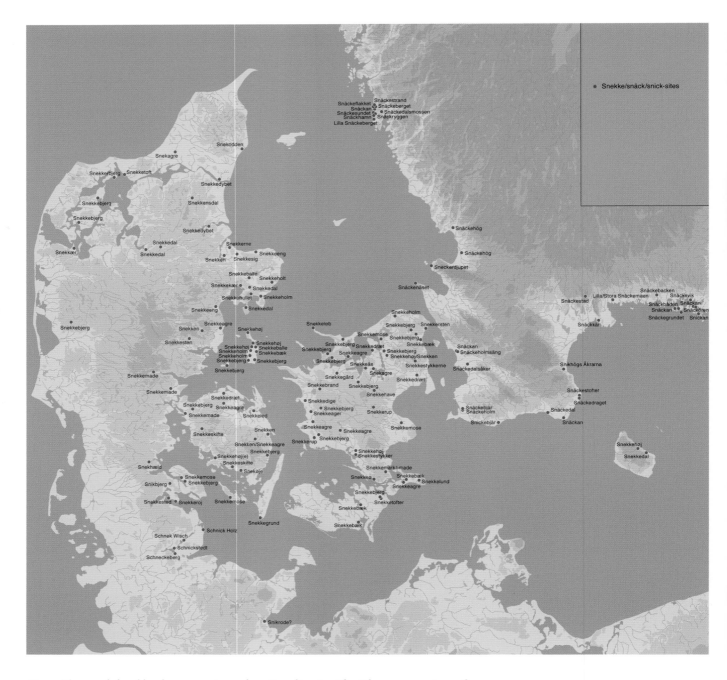

Fig. 57 The recorded snekke place-names in southern Scandinavia. After Klassen 2010: 318-319, fig. 192.

IV. Woodland management

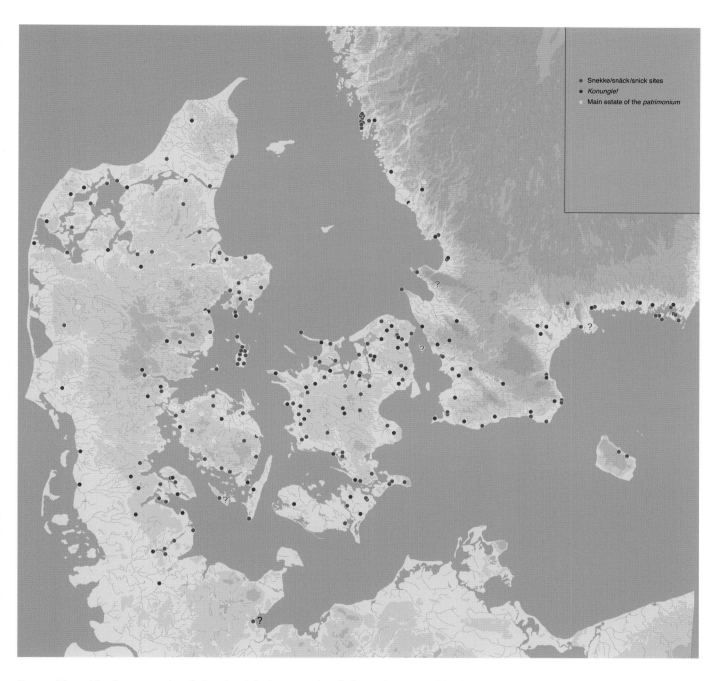

Fig. 58. The snekke place-names (marked with red dots) compared with the royal estates and lands called konunglef (marked with blue dots) and patrimonium (marked with yellow dots). After Klassen 2010: 332-333, fig. 196.

Fig. 59. The snekke place-names (marked with yellow dots) compared with areas where wood resources for shipbuilding were probably procured in late Viking-Age Denmark. Green markings: Areas with a probable presence of wood resources suitable for shipbuilding. Red markings: Areas with a probable absence of wood resources suitable for shipbuilding. The encircled areas are only approximate. Layout and additions by Narayana Press, Morten Johansen and the author, Viking Ship Museum in Roskilde.

where there are no *snekke* place-names. How-ever, these place-names, *-holt, -ris* and *-lund,* mainly indicate habitats with open-canopy woodlands, where trees suitable for shipbuild-ing were probably not easy to procure.[55]

On Funen and Samsø, and in Vendsyssel and Djursland, the absence of source material means that the character and species composi-tion of the woodlands cannot be analysed. The absence of indications of woodland in these areas (fig. 59) must therefore be seen solely as an expression of the source situation, not of an absence of woodland. This must be mentioned because *snekke* place-names are numerous on Samsø, evenly distributed on Funen, and pre-sent in Vendsyssel and Djursland but the source situation unfortunately makes a comparison between the *snekke* place-names and the re-sources suitable for shipbuilding impossible.

Several of the *snekke* place-names form part of compound names where the second element refers to a hilly area, for example Snekke*bjerg,* Snekke*dal* and Snäcke*hög* (fig. 57).[56] Viewed in relation to the demonstrated connection be-tween the hilly landscapes and the occurrence of closed-canopy woodland habitats,[57] this is notable, because the *snekke* place-names are thus grouped in areas where the resources suit-able for shipbuilding could probably be felled. In other cases, the *snekke* place-names occur in connection with words that refer to an area with cultivated land, for example Snekke*ager,* Snekke*tofter* or Snekke*skifte.* Perhaps these place-names refer to agrarian production of raw materials reserved for other ship-related crafts, for example flax for making sailcloths or hemp for the production of ropes?[58]

There are several examples – historical as well as present-day – where place-names have arisen by virtue of the resource growing in the area.[59] Fundamentally, a place-name is an expression of a past community's naming practice in relation to one or more experienced aspects of the land-scape, including the utilisation of resources.[60]

To sum up, it seems likely that several of the *snekke* place-names arose because of the occur-rence of wood resources suitable for shipbuild-ing, which raises the question of why the re-sources of the area are singled out as suitable for a specific type of production.

Regulated woodland management

The provincial laws of the High Middle Ages speak of ownership and usufruct of woodlands. There is a clear distinction between common woodlands and privately-owned woodlands, and only in special cases, for example when a carriage axle was broken, was it permissible to fell the necessary resources in another man's forest. While it is difficult to determine how much woodland was privately owned in the 11th century, it must be considered likely that parts of the woodland areas were in private hands.[61] The woodland resources were used in connec-tion with more or less all tasks in 11th-century communities, so the privately owned forests are unlikely to have been so numerous that a short-age of common forest was a general problem.[62] Annette Hoff's analyses of the written sources of the High Middle Ages suggest that wood-lands were only directly fenced-in in a few cases,[63] which in turn would have made it dif-ficult to protect the private woodlands. It should be mentioned, however, that ditches, ramparts, boulders, roads, streams and de-barked trees were used to demarcate the various woodland areas,[64] and that place-names such as Hindsgavl[65] near Middelfart on Funen indi-cate that woodlands were fenced-in in the High Middle Ages.[66]

It is evident from the Swedish provincial laws that the use of some of the resources of the common woodlands were subject to special regulations. For example, the illegal debarking or felling of mast-bearing trees was punished considerably more severely than if a non-mast-bearing tree was debarked or felled illegally, presumably because the sustenance for the many mast-fed pigs was to be protected.[67] Some of the woodland resources were in other words more highly valued than others, and the communities of the High Middle Ages tried to

55. Dam 2015: 142–165.
56. Holmberg & Skamby Madsen 1998: 210.
57. See chapter IV, section: Woodland composition and stracture, for a more detailed account.
58. This will not be further investigated in the present context. But reference may be made to Ravn 2017.
59. Ulriksen 1998: 76; Møller 2012; Godal 2012.
60. Albris 2014.
61. Hybel and Poulsen 2007: 5.
62. Hoff 1997: 286–287.
63. The Swedish landscape laws mention fencing in a few cases, see Hoff 1997: 286.
64. Hoff 1997: 286.
65. *Hægnæthscogh,* i.e. fenced-in wood.
66. Hybel and Poulsen 2007: 4.
67. Hoff 1997: 263.

regulate the use of the woodland resources. In the Danish communities of the 11th century, where wood was used as a raw material in connection with more or less all production, the wood resources suitable for shipbuilding had to be protected if the trees were to reach the necessary dimensions. In particular, the major construction works such as the building of estates and halls[68] as well as bridges,[69] stockades[70] and fortifications[71] would have required wood resources in volumes very similar to those needed for shipbuilding. The high consumption of wood resources for construction work in the 11th century and hence the need for regulated woodland management can in fact be observed in written as well as archaeological sources elsewhere in northern Europe, for example in Ireland,[72] and is probably related to the increasing urbanisation of the time. Woodland management in this context does not mean that the trees of a woodland landscape were planted regularly in quantified and cultivated tree cultures, but that attempts were made to protect the trees in a wooded area, for example against livestock, and that felling and cutting in the area was regulated – in both cases to ensure the continued presence of existing suitable wood resources and the potential regeneration of suitable wood resources.[73]

In the Danish realm of the Late Viking Age, where ownership and usufruct were not always clearly defined,[74] special rights to particular resources would have been problematic to enforce for a central power. A decentralised social understanding of the importance of protecting the resources that were indispensable in a specific production context would therefore have been necessary. A common, locally rooted understanding of the need to protect special resources may have been the reason why areas with resources particularly well suited for shipbuilding were designated as such – often using *snekke* place-names.

The extent to which the common understanding was established through direct orders or in consultation between rulers and their subjects cannot be clarified. Finally, it is possible that the protected, named trees were subject to taboos if they were used for anything but the assigned purposes. A protection of tree resources by using taboo – some trees were considered sacred – can be read in Irish law texts *Bretha Comaithchesa* and *Bechbretha* from the 9th or 10th centuries.[75] An ethnographic parallel to such protection of tree resources has been documented by Béat Arnold in connection with his studies of boatbuilding among East African tribes (*nikhula, kapepe* and *muterere).*[76]

One example of locally-based exploitation of resources can be read in the written sources *Rectitudines singularum personarum* and *Be sceadwisan gerefan* from 11th-century England.[77] These describe, indeed in great detail, how an estate at the time was to be managed, and which duties and rights the individuals involved in its management had. Duties and rights are for example described for the thane, the free tenant, the cottager, the peasant, the beekeeper, the swineherd, the sower, the cheese-wright, the steward, the forester and the messenger, as well as the ox and cow herd, the shepherd and the goatherd. In addition, they describe the provisions for men and women in the service of the manor and – in detail – how a prudent reeve should manage a manor.[78]

Other Viking-Age written accounts on how to conduct proper woodland management can be found in the Irish law texts *Crith Gablach, Bretha Comaithchesa* and *Bechbretha* from the 9th or 10th centuries.[79]

Whether the management of the contemporary southern Scandinavian estates was just as regulated, and whether a similar organisational structure was possible, cannot be determined clearly on the basis of the sources presently available. However, it does seem evident that duties and rights also applied to those involved in the agriculture and forestry of Viking-Age Scandinavia.

68. Jørgensen, L. 2008; Jessen 2015: 198.
69. Schou Jørgensen 1997.
70. Jessen 2015.
71. Hellmuth Andersen 1998.
72. E.g. O'Sullivan 1994: 676; Murphy and Potterton 2010: 360; Lyons 2014: 453.
73. For more on this use of the term woodland management see Rackham 2003: 21; Jessen 2015: 200–201.
74. Fritzbøger 2004: 69–93; Jessen 2015: 202–203.
75. Kelly 2000: 387.
76. Arnold 2015.
77. *Rectitudines singularum personarum* [Lund 2015a]; *Be sceadwisan gerefan* [Lund 2015b].
78. *Rectitudines singularum personarum* [Lund 2015a]; *Be sceadwisan gerefan* [Lund 2015b].
79. Kelly 2000: 379–390.

V. Maritime warfare

In war, armed force is used. Through the practice of war, called warfare, the end is to make the opponent defenceless in order to achieve the purpose of the war, to impose one's will.[1] The 'will' is not determined in a military context. War is therefore to be viewed as an expression of an underlying purpose, which may be politically, ideologically or economically determined. Often, the purpose is defined on the basis of a combination of political, ideological and economic aspects,[2] and the actual effort to achieve the purpose often leads to a redistribution, exchange and transformation of material and non-material values, for example resources, technologies, knowledge and ideologies.[3]

The connection between the military ends of the war and the political, ideological and economic purposes means that warfare is closely related to the fundamental structures, values and norms of the belligerents.[4] This relation is dynamic and dialectical and can be described in terms of a doctrine – that is, the way in which war is perceived and the approach to how war is waged.

A fundamental discourse in research on military history is how the concept of 'war' is to be defined. And – let it be said at once – there is no consensus.[5] Can an isolated raid with economic enrichment as its purpose be regarded as a war? Or is it rather an armed conflict or perhaps an isolated instance of violence? Most researchers agree that 'war' cannot be used to describe an isolated armed conflict or act of violence;[6] on the contrary, several related armed conflicts are viewed cumulatively as defining a war. However, can an armed conflict or an act of violence at all be regarded as isolated? In several cases the individual raids of the Viking Age prompted the victims to mobilise defensive measures,[7] sometimes locally, at other times regionally or supra-regionally,[8] in order to protect themselves against a repetition of the violent attack. The question is thus how many offensive and defensive features must be present before the armed conflicts can, as a whole, be described as a war.

Another discussion in the discourse is how many warriors must participate in the armed conflicts before they can be described as a war,[9] and whether wars are only waged between states and kingdoms – that is at the societal level, or whether armed conflict between two or more parties is a more suitable definition of the concept of war.[10]

Whichever definitions of war are emphasised, it is at any rate clear that war is a special form of violence,[11] but at the same time that an unambiguous understanding of the concept of war is not possible. For this very reason it is necessary to clarify the meaning that the term 'war' has in a specific context. In this book the term 'war' is only used in combination with other words such as warfare and war fleet. In these contexts, war is understood as armed conflicts between two or more parties in recognition of the fact that the sources for the military actions of the Late Viking Age make it difficult to determine whether a specific military operation was an isolated event or part of a larger military campaign. The practice of armed conflict is called warfare and in some cases military operations, and since the focus in this book is on the maritime, it is the maritime aspects of the practice of conflict that are analysed. 'War fleet' is used as a term for a collection of vessels involved in armed conflict.

1. Clausewitz [1832]1986: 32–33.
2. Clausewitz [1832]1986: 23 & 29–30; Wright 1965: 74–80.
3. Lystrup Nielsen 1985: 58.
4. Hedenstierna-Jonson 2006: 22–39.
5. See Turney-High [1949]1991; Wright 1965: 8–13, 423–437 & 689–700; Schjødt 2003; Bossen 2006 for a clarification of the issues.
6. 'See for example Lystrup Nielsen 1985: 55-56; Clausewitz [1832]1986: 35-36; Højrup 2002: 198; Schjødt 2003.
7. Williams 2008: 198–199.
8. An example that can be mentioned is the Anglo-Saxon Chronicle's mention of Alfred the Great's defensive measures against the Scandinavian raids of the time. See *Anglo-Saxon Chronicle, the Parker Chronicle* (A), 895, 897 [Garmonsway 1953: 89–91].
9. Wright 1965: 8–21 & 688–689; Bossen 2006: 91.
10. Schjødt 2003: 94–102; Bossen 2006: 91.
11. Dennen 1981.

Fleet size

One of the most comprehensive attempts to clarify the size of the Danish war fleet is Rikke Malmros' article from 1988.[12] Through statistical calculations, Malmros tries to arrive at a probable estimate of the number of ships in the fleet during the later part of the Viking Age and the High Middle Ages. The point of departure is to be found in the military regulations of the Nordic provincial laws and in selected skaldic poems. Malmros estimates that the number of Danish warships in the Late Viking Age and the early High Middle Ages was between 600 and 800, each with 40 or 42 rowers.[13]

There are several doubtful factors in Malmros' analysis, some of which are noted by Malmros herself.[14] Firstly, the factual reliability of the provincial laws and the other sources used – the *Gesta Danorum* of Saxo Grammaticus and the *Gesta Hammaburgensis Ecclesiae Pontificum* of Adam of Bremen – has been cast in doubt. Secondly, there are several rationally based roundings-up and -down and other choices in connection with the calculations that are not necessarily – but may be – problematic.[15] For example, the standardised ship size for 40 or 42 rowers cannot be demonstrated by the archaeological evidence, from which the diversity of ship sizes and types is clear.[16] However, despite these problematic factors, Malmros' proposal for the size of war fleets in the later part of the Viking Age is backed up by several archaeologists.[17]

Operational fleets

One important factor in the discussion of the sizes of the war fleets is that the written sources for the fleets of the Late Viking Age[18] are unlikely to state the total fleet strength of a magnate or king, but rather the sizes of operational war fleets used in connection with one or more military operations. Nor, in my opinion, can the military regulations of the provincial laws of the High Middle Ages be used to indicate the total fleet strength of a magnate or king. Even if the stated mobilisation figures are taken at face value, this does not mean that the stated number of warriors and vessels was the total fleet strength of a powerful man. A magnate or king may have had other ways of mobilising ships and warriors, for example through his *hird*, through alliances with other magnates or kings, or by paying for the services of the warriors.

This book thus does not deal with the size or character of the total war fleet of the 11th century in Denmark, but with the widely differing operational war fleets which were active in connection with specific military operations during the hundred years analysed.

Judging from the inscriptions on rune stones, and skaldic poems, the number of vessels engaged in warfare varied greatly. Local and regional disputes between magnates are mentioned. In one specific example, 11 ships participated on one side, while the opponent's fleet consisted of five ships.[19] In other far more extensive military actions one side is said to have respectively 71, 180, 360 or as many as 720 participating ships. However, as Judith Jesch emphasises, these figures should be treated with caution, since exaggeration is a common feature of skaldic poetry.[20]

A second source which describes the military expeditions of Scandinavian magnates and kings is the *Anglo-Saxon Chronicle*. According to the entries in the annals, the war fleets in the late 9th century and most of the 10th century usually consisted of 10–20 ships, while the war fleets in the late 10th century and into the 11th century consisted of a larger number of ships, – that is, between 20 and 60.[21]

Towards the end of the 10th century and at the beginning of the 11th century, the Anglo-Saxon Chronicle describes several large fleet operations. In 994, it is entered that Anlaf[22] and Swein[23] appeared at the head of a war fleet of 94 ships. The expedition targeted London, but there the attacking forces met so much resistance that they withdrew and subsequently harried the coasts of Essex, Kent, Sussex and Hampshire.[24]

12. Malmros 1988.
13. Malmros 1988: 35.
14. Malmros 1988: 34.
15. Malmros 1988: 33–35.
16. Crumlin-Pedersen 1988: 153; Crumlin-Pedersen 1997a: 192.
17. Crumlin-Pedersen 1996b: 188–189; Klassen 2010: 311–312.
18. For example skaldic poems, see Jesch 2001: 187–203; and the Anglo-Saxon Chronicle, see *Anglo-Saxon Chronicle* [Garmonsway 1953].
19. Jesch 2001: 206.
20. Jesch 2001: 206.
21. *Anglo-Saxon Chronicle, the Laud Chronicle*, 885, 897, 981, 1028 & 1040 [Garmonsway 1953: 79, 91, 125, 157 & 163].
22. Olav Tryggvason.
23. Svend Tveskæg / Sweyn Forkbeard.
24. *Anglo-Saxon Chronicle, the Laud Chronicle*, 994 [Garmonsway 1953: 129].

A war fleet of even larger size – 160 ships – was led by Canute[25] in 1016. It was in connection with this campaign that he conquered England.[26] Fifty years later we read that King Harald[27] attacked England with a war fleet consisting of 300 ships, and again in 1068 or 1069, a war fleet consisting of 240 or 300 ships is mentioned, this time under the leadership of three of Svend Estridsen's sons, his brother Jarl Osbern and perhaps Jarl Thurkil.[28]

In 1962, Peter H. Sawyer pointed out that the sizes of the largest war fleets were always stated in round figures, and he therefore doubted their accuracy. Sawyer thought that the numbers of ships in the war fleets were exaggerated and that no magnates or kings could procure war fleets of several hundred ships with several thousand men on board.[29] Against this Nicholas P. Brooks remarked in 1979 that in several cases there was matching information on the sizes of particular war fleets in independent Anglo-Saxon, Irish and Frankish sources, which gives the stated war fleet sizes greater credibility.[30]

In relation to the general view of the social organisation of the Viking Age, it appears correct when Peter H. Sawyer points out that no magnate or king alone could muster a war fleet of several hundred ships.[31] On the other hand, associations of magnates and a king could muster war fleets of several hundred ships. At the same time, a critical approach to the 11th-century written sources' statements of war fleet sizes is necessary, for, as Sawyer noted more than 50 years ago, it is suspicious that the war fleets are always described in round figures – there are never 256 or 143 ships, but 160, 240 or 300 ships.[32]

A unique written source, known as *the ship list of William the Conqueror* provides insight into the sizes of the large northern European war fleets of the 11th century. The time and place of the writing of the ship list is disputed.[33] In an article from 1988, Elisabeth M.C. van Houts argues systematically and convincingly that the ship list was a written down in Normandy between 1067 and ca 1072, and later, presum-

ably in the High Middle Ages, the text was copied and incorporated as part of Battle Abbey's documentation of William's conquest of England.[34] The ship list states how many ships and knights the magnates and bishops participating in the Conquest contributed. The total fleet is described as consisting of 776 ships, but as early as around a hundred years after the drawing-up of the ship list and on throughout the Middle Ages there are diverging statements about the size of the fleet. This has led to discussions among present-day researchers concerning the factual size of William the Conqueror's war fleet in 1066.[35] Irrespective of the diverging statements and interpretations, it must be considered reasonably likely that in 11th-century northern Europe, it was possible in special cases to muster war fleets consisting of between 700 and 800 ships.

There is also an archaeological source that can inform us of a probable number of ships participating in some of the military sea transports of the 11th century: the Fribrødre Å site. In a comprehensive analysis of the traces of the ship-related activities at the site, Lutz Klassen arrives at the conclusion that more than a hundred ships were fitted out over a short period of years for military campaigns in the second half of the 11th century, probably targeted at the Abodrites in the southwestern Baltic area.[36]

It is impossible to attain certainty about the precise sizes of the operational war fleets of the 11th century, but it is evident that they varied in terms of size and ship types. The great diversity means that we can assume that the war fleets were organised in different ways, and that the resource basis of the various fleets was not the same.

Fleet composition

It seems reasonable to assume that many of the ship types of the Viking Age were used in connection with military sea transport. However, sailing tests and trial voyages with reconstructed boats and ships[37] suggest that logboats and

25. Knud – later Canute the Great.
26. *Anglo-Saxon Chronicle, the Laud Chronicle,* 1016 [Garmonsway 1953: 146].
27. Harald Hårderåde / Harald Hardrada.
28. *Anglo-Saxon Chronicle, the Laud Chronicle,* 1066, 1068, 1069 [Garmonsway 1953: 197, 202]; *Anglo-Saxon Chronicle, the Worcester Chronicle,* 1068 [Garmonsway 1953: 204].
29. Sawyer 1962 [1971]: 117–128.
30. Brooks 1979: 1–20.
31. Sawyer 1962 [1971]: 117–128.
32. Sawyer 1962 [1971]: 117–128.
33. For a survey of the discussions see Houts 1988.
34. Houts 1988.
35. See Gillmore 1985; Houts 1988.
36. Klassen 2010: 349–351 & 354.
37. See section: The ships at sea, for a more detailed account.

the smallest plank-built vessels were of such limited seaworthiness that they must be assessed as generally unsuitable in a military context. Nor do logboats and the smallest plank-built vessels appear to be mentioned in the skaldic poems, which deal with the naval operation of the 11th century,[38] which suggests that the vessel types were not used for warfare. However, military history mentions special situations where all available vessels were used in connection with military sea transport. An example that can be given is the military sea transport of Prussian forces between 28th and 29th June in 1864. The transport of some 2500 men took place on board boats and rafts across Alssund to Arnkil on Als.[39] Other examples are when a band of Algerian pirates used small boats in 1631 as landing craft in an amphibious raid on Baltimore in Ireland[40] and when Teutonic Knights campaigned against the Lithuanians in 1393 using logboats.[41] Finally it should be mentioned that for the year 862 the annals of St. Bertin speak of military sea transport on small ships,[42] that the magnate Ohthere in the late 9th century mention raids conducted by the Cwenas people on the Northmen using small and very light boats[43], and that small ships are mentioned as used in connection with the military operations of Scandinavian Viking-Age warriors on what are now the Ukrainian and Russian rivers.[44]

Thus, we cannot preclude the possibility that logboats and small plank-built vessels were used for military purposes in special situations in the 11th century, but these must be treated as exceptions, which means that logboats and the smallest of the plank-built vessels will not be analysed further in the following.

The fleet from Fribrødre Å

The ship-related activities at the Fribrødre Å site have been interpreted as evidence of the fitting-out of more than a hundred ships over a short period of years prior to military campaigns in the second half of the 11th century.[45] Lutz Klassen's analyses show that small, medi-

um-sized and large cargo and personnel carriers participated in military sea transport – even boats can be demonstrated.[46] However, it is Klassen's assessment that the boats should not be interpreted as part of the demonstrated war fleet, but as local transport vessels used in connection with the shipbuilding-related activities at the site.[47] The same probably applies to the small cargo ships whose limited seaworthiness, one can reasonably assume, made them unsuitable for military transport on the open sea.[48]

At least 19 and at most 38 of the many vessels can be typed. Of these, the medium-sized and large ships make up at least 14 and at most 28. On the basis of this, the relative ship-type composition of the fitted-out war fleet can be estimated as ca three times more personnel carriers than cargo ships (fig. 60), approximately as many medium-sized and large personnel carriers (fig. 61), and as many medium-sized and large cargo ships (fig. 62).[49]

It should be noted that the estimated ship-type composition must be seen in the context of the military operation of which the war fleet was a part. If Lutz Klassen's historical interpretation of the activities at the site[50] is correct, the aim of fitting out the many ships was to affect a short sea voyage with a large number of warriors and supplies. For such a military sea transport, both medium-sized and large cargo ships as well as personnel carriers would have been suited.

Written evidence of ship types involved in military operations

The Skaldic tradition of using kennings[51] means that the names given to ship types include *skip, herskip, kaupskip, hlægiskip, skeid, snekkja, dreki, knörr, beit, fura, eik, eikikjolr, naðr, ormr, borð, flaust, kjoll, langskip, far, ferja, súð, karfi* and *bátr*.[52] It is clear that these kennings are based partly on the raw materials of which the vessels were built, partly on the constructional or characteristic qualities assigned to the vessels described. In the following, the most frequently

38. Jesch 2001: 135.
39. Buk-Swienty 2010: 88–111.
40. McCarthy 2013.
41. Ossowski 2010: 193.
42. Albrectsen 1981: 42.
43. Bately 2007: 46–47.
44. Hjardar & Vike 2014: 350; Sorokin 2015.
45. Klassen 2010: 349–351 & 354.
46. Klassen 2010: 116–119.
47. Klassen 2010: 121.
48. See chapter V, section: The ships at sea, for a more detailed account.
49. Klassen 2010: 116–119.
50. See above.
51. Poetic synonyms.
52. Jesch 2001: 120–136; Malmros 2010: 89–90.

	Medium-sized and large personnel carriers	Medium-sized and large cargo ships
Min. no. of ships	10	4
Max. no. of ships	22	6

	Medium-sized personnel carriers	Large personnel carriers
Min. no. of ships	4	6
Max. no. of ships	11	11

	Medium-sized cargo ships	Large cargo ships
Min. no. of ships	2	2
Max. no. of ships	3	3

used names of ships deployed for warfare will be analysed.

The term *skeið* is used almost exclusively of ships involved in warfare. Only in two cases is the term used in a non-military context. *Skeið* is used at least 49 times in the skaldic poems and in two or three runic inscriptions. The prominence of the military contexts in which the term is used prompts Judith Jesch to interpret *skeið* as a ship involved in warfare,[53] and Rikke Malmros and Ole Crumlin-Pedersen both agree. Crumlin-Pedersen adds that a *skeið* was probably a particular ship type,[54] while Malmros exclusively interprets the various names of ships involved in warfare as synonyms for the basis term *skeið*.[55]

One of these other names for ships involved in warfare is *snekkja*. This is used in eight verses, but not at all in runic inscriptions.[56] In the research literature and among maritime researchers the difference between a *snekkja* and a *skeið* is often described as based on size:[57] a *snekkja* as a smaller ship than a *skeið*. This sup-

position comes from the work of Hjalmar Falk, but Judith Jesch points out that Falk supported his interpretation with descriptions taken from the prose literature, which may be problematic to use to describe aspects of the Viking Age. On the other hand a verse in the skaldic poem *Þofinnsdrápa* seems to indicate just this: a difference in size between the two ship types.[58]

As stated by Jesch, it is also possible that the use by the skalds of the name *snekkja* has the aim of describing a war fleet consisting of various ship types without distinguishing so carefully between the morphological features of the ships.[59] Ole Crumlin-Pedersen describes the difference between a *snekkja* and a *skeið* thus: "Skeið seems to have been the most common name for longships in Scandinavia, and it is also known in English sources, whereas the more mundane ships were probably called snekkja in their home countries and in some cases in England and Normandy as well".[60] However, Eldar Heide takes the view that the written sources, skaldic poems as well as prose

53. Jesch 2001: 123–126.
54. Crumlin-Pedersen 2010: 90–91.
55. Malmros 2010: 89–92.
56. Jesch 2001: 126–127.
57. Crumlin-Pedersen & Olsen 2002: 315; Klassen 2011.
58. Falk 1912: 102; Jesch 2001: 126–127.
59. Jesch 2001: 126–127.
60. Crumlin-Pedersen 2010: 91.

literature, suggest that the name *snekkja* gradually replaced the term *skeið* in the course of the 11th century. Whether this means that one ship type gradually superseded another, or it is simply a different way of naming the same ship type, is not clear.[61]

Christer Westerdahl arrives at the conclusion that *snekkja* was mainly used in the written sources in the period 1100–1400 – although the designation is used in a few places in skaldic poems which should probably be dated to the 11th century[62] – and that *snekkja* meant a warship.[63] Narve Bjørgo pointed out in 1965 that in Håkon Håkonsson's Saga *snekkja* was also used of ships that transported passengers – not just anyone, but the social elite – in a non-military context.[64] However, Håkon Håkonsson's Saga was written down in and speaks of events in the 13th century, and it is therefore possible that the name *snekkja* in the saga was different from the understanding of the term in the 11th century. However, Westerdahl's specific interpretation of *snekkja* as a warship becomes less likely. Lutz Klassen instead proposes that a *snekkja* was a ship under the command of the king and was used for both military and civilian sea transport.[65]

No definitive explanation of the meaning of the *snekkja* concept in the 11th century can be derived from the present source basis. It seems certain that in the 11th century *snekkja* was a term for a ship that was used for warfare, but the size of the ship and its other dimensions as well as who commanded it, and whether it was only used for military purposes, cannot be determined.

In seven verses in the skaldic poems, ships involved in warfare are called *dreki*. Hjalmar Falk and Nicholas Andrew Martin Rodger think the term was used to describe the largest warships.[66] Judith Jesch and Ole Crumlin-Pedersen also interpret *dreki* as a designation for a warship but not necessarily one of the largest warships of the time. The name may come from the fact that some vessels had stems with dragon symbolism.[67]

Another ship name that must be mentioned is *knörr*. It is used both on rune stones and in the skaldic poems. In the 10th century, *knörr* is used exclusively of ships involved in warfare. During the course of the 11th century, the term was used in both military and civilian contexts.[68] The latter fact prompts Judith Jesch to conclude that the term simply means a ship.[69] Ole Crumlin-Pedersen has proposed that the changing use of the term should be viewed in the context of the ship specialisation briefly described in the introduction to this book. In this interpretation, in the 10th century and possibly also before then, *knörr* was used of a ship type constructed for transporting both crew and cargo, while during the course of the 11th century, as an element in the ship specialisation, the word gradually came to mean a specialised and large cargo ship.[70]

As pointed out by Anton Englert, it is only with Saxo Grammaticus, that is, in the second half of the 12th century, that a written source explicitly mentions the use of cargo ships in connection with military sea transport,[71] which does not mean, however, that cargo ships were not used in military contexts before then. Saxo Grammaticus does not single out the use of cargo ships in military contexts as something new,[72] and that other northern European 11th-century war fleets also consisted of many different ship types and sizes has been indicated by several researchers in connection with the discussions of William the Conqueror's great war fleet.[73]

Finally, the likely ship-type composition at the Fribrødre Å site must be mentioned as an archaeological source indicating that cargo ships were used for military sea transport in the 11th century.[74]

The ships at sea

In the following, the military use of the personnel carriers and cargo ships will be investigated. The manoeuvrability of the various ship types and sizes and their average travelling speeds will

61. Heide 2012.
62. See above.
63. Westerdahl 2002: 173–175.
64. Bjørgo 1965: 19.
65. Klassen 2010: 314–335.
66. Falk 1912: 107; Rodger 1995: 395.
67. Jesch 2001: 127; Crumlin-Pedersen 2010: 90–91.
68. Jesch 2001: 128–130; Crumlin-Pedersen & Olsen 2002: 313 & 324–325; Westerdahl 2002: 176; Malmros 2010: 93.
69. Jesch 2001: 130.
70. Crumlin-Pedersen & Olsen 2002: 313 & 324–325.
71. Englert 2015: 53–54.
72. Saxo Grammaticus: Book 16, 4,5 & 5,3 [Friis-Jensen & Zeeberg 2005: 523 & 527].
73. Gillmor 1985; Houts 1988.
74. See above.

Ship-type	Recon-struction	Area of use	Boat speed under favourable conditions measured in relation to the ground below. Measured in knots	Distance made good under favourable conditions, measured in nautical miles a day	Distance made good under unfavourable conditions, measured in nautical miles a day	References
Small, medium-sized cargo ship	Roar Ege	Coastal waters (under favoura-ble conditions also open sea)	Under oars: 2.0-3.2; Under sail: ca 8.5	67-110	35-53	Crumlin-Pedersen & Vinner 1993: 21-28; Vinner 1997b: 259-271
Large, medium-sized cargo ship	Ottar	Open sea	Under oars: - Under sail: ca 8.9	67-110	35-53	Englert 2006: 35-42; Englert 2012: 269-277
Medium-sized personnel carrier	Helge Ask	Coastal waters (under favoura-ble conditions also open sea)	Under oars: 4.7-6 Under sail: ca 9.2	101-127	44-75	Appendix 2; Crumlin-Pedersen & Vinner 1993: 24-28
Large personnel carrier	Sea Stallion from Glendal-ough	Open sea	Under oars: 4-4.5 Under sail: ca 13	94-159	40-95	Nielsen 2011: 59-82; Nielsen 2012a: 266-268; Englert 2012: 269-277

Fig. 63. The manoeu-vring qualities, seawor-thiness and travel speed of various ship types and sizes. Table: The author, Viking Ship Museum in Roskilde.

be analysed, and the seamanship and communication on board the different ship types will be discussed.

The personnel carriers were particularly suitable for transporting a large number of warriors, and the ships could be propelled both by sail and oars. The medium-sized cargo ships could only with difficulty – and the large cargo ships not at all – be propelled with oars, while the high cargo capacity of the cargo ships made them particularly suitable for transporting large quantities of supplies and other military equipment, and on short voyages also large numbers of warriors.

The speed at which warriors, supplies and other military equipment could be transported was of great importance to the military operations of the time. The manoeuvrability and seaworthiness of the ships were directly related to where and when the military sea transports could take place. In order to analyse the manoeuvrability, seaworthiness and travelling

speeds, it is necessary to make full-scale reconstructions of Viking-Age ships, and subsequently use these reconstructions as platforms for experimental archaeological sea trials.[75] The trials can be divided into sailing tests and trial voyages. In sailing tests, selected sailing properties are analysed in specific situations, using the ships' different means of propulsion.[76] In trial voyages a ship's sailing performance is analysed over an extended period, permitting an estimate of how long a specific voyage took for the original ship.[77] Moreover, the trial voyages give us an understanding of social conditions on board and seamanship in general.[78]

In relation to military sea transport and seaborne warfare, it has been particularly relevant to analyse sailing qualities and travel speeds for the medium-sized and large cargo ships as well as medium-sized and large personnel carriers. The result of this analysis is shown in figure 63. In the following these results will be compared and discussed.

75. Ravn et al. 2011: 241–246.
76. Englert 2006: 35.
77. Englert 2006: 36.
78. Englert & Ossowski 2009: 257–270; Ravn 2013: 157–160.

Only the large medium-sized and large cargo ships and the large personnel carriers were true seagoing ships. The smaller medium-sized cargo ships and the medium-sized personnel carriers may have participated in military transports on the open sea, but experimental archaeological sailing tests have shown that this probably involved considerable risks.[79]

The smaller medium-sized and small vessels must therefore mainly be viewed as seaworthy in connection with military transport in sheltered waters, that is, in the inner Danish waters, to some extent in the Baltic and in coastal sailing in general.

In connection with the analysis of the sailing qualities of the ships it is necessary to distinguish between boat speed on the one hand and travel speed on the other. Travel speed is to be understood as the speed at which a crew can sail from one specific harbour to another specific harbour,[80] while boat speed is either measured in relation to the surrounding water or the ground below. Speed through the water, known as 'way', is measured 'by the log', while 'ground speed', i.e. speed over the sea bed, is measured with the Global Positioning System.[81] Relatively large differences between way and ground speed can occur because of current, so one must state which type of speed measurement has been used if different measurements are to be compared.[82] In figure 63, ground speed is used for a comparative analysis of the maximum speed achieved with the various reconstructions.[83] This involves a potential source of error, since the data have not been gathered at the same time and place, which means among other things that wind and current conditions were not the same. Nevertheless, the measurements give an indication of the speed potentials over short stretches among different ship types and sizes from the 11th century.

Travel speed should be used when the average duration of a voyage has been analysed,[84] and the speed measurement can be converted to 'distance made good',[85] which is measured in nautical miles. The travel speed is usually slower than the boat speed, which is due to wind, current, drift and steering errors.[86] Finally, it is necessary to distinguish between time spent at sea from starting point to destination, and the total time from starting point to destination. The total time includes harbour activities[87] and waiting for favourable winds and suitable sailing conditions in general.[88]

The draughts and hull forms of the different ship types make it likely that the medium-sized and large personnel carriers were particularly suitable for amphibious military operations. The personnel carriers could land on beaches, after which warriors, supplies and other military equipment could be landed. If a withdrawal became necessary, the ships could quickly be launched again. Experiments with the Skuldelev 5 reconstruction *Helge Ask* make it seem likely that a launch followed by vigorous rowing, even in a moderate onshore wind, can take the ship to a safe distance from all the ranged weapons used at the time within about 15 minutes.[89] The personnel carriers have a higher potential speed than the cargo ships, and in unfavourable wind conditions the personnel carriers could exploit their great rowing power to achieve remarkable speeds quickly over short stretches (fig. 63). In connection with a quick retreat it should be pointed out that medium-sized personnel carrier under oar appear to have been the fastest ship type over short stretches, while large personnel carriers – over short stretches and in good sailing conditions – have the highest potential speed with the sail as propulsion (fig. 63).

The large medium-sized and the large cargo ships, as a result of hull form and draught, would have been problematic to beach, and their limited or absent rowing power and thus their dependence on propulsion by sail in favourable wind, would have made them unsuitable for hit-and-run attacks.[90] The medium-sized and large cargo ships were, however, particularly suitable as carriers of military supplies, and sometimes large cargo ships were also used for massive deployments of warriors.[91]

79. Crumlin-Pedersen & Vinner 1993: 23–29.
80. Englert 2011: 102; Englert 2012: 269.
81. Often abbreviated GPS.
82. Englert 2006: 35; Villumsen & Raben 2010: 41.
83. This under favourable sailing conditions and over short stretches.
84. Englert 2011: 102.
85. Often abbreviated DMG.
86. Vinner 1997a: 239; Englert 2011: 102.
87. For example unloading and loading.
88. Englert 2012: 269 & 276.
89. Crumlin-Pedersen & Vinner 1993: 27.
90. Englert 2015: 53.
91. See chapter V, section: The fleet from Fribrødre Å; Englert 2015: 53–54.

As regards military sea transport over long distances, it should be noted that when sailing close-hauled, the cargo ships have a higher boat speed than the personnel carriers, which is primarily due to the different hull forms of the two ship types.[92] However, the personnel carriers, thanks to their considerable rowing power, can compensate for this and thus achieve a faster travel speed (fig. 63). In both favourable and unfavourable sailing conditions the potential speed of the personnel carriers was thus considerably higher than that of the cargo ships (fig. 63).

Moreover, the travel speed of a fleet is considerably lower than the travel speed of a single ship, since ships in a war fleet must adapt their manoeuvres and speed to one another in order to remain a unified force.[93]

About 30 nautical miles in 24 hours is considered a conservative estimate for the average distance made good by a war fleet in unfavourable conditions, while in favourable conditions a war fleet could cover at least 60 nautical miles per 24 hours.[94] At such speeds a war fleet could sail in favourable conditions from Vordingborg to Rügen and land warriors in less than 24 hours, which makes it clear how advantageous it was to conduct military transports by sea rather than by land.[95]

Ship and crew

On a fully-manned Viking-Age personnel carrier there was not much room. The very limited space and the dimensions of the ship – long and narrow – as well as the military context in which the ship was primarily used, created special working conditions, and thus special requirements for organisation and communication.

Several texts from the High Middle Ages, including the Norwegian legal text *Gulatingslovi*,[96] speak in detail of the organisation on board the military ships – most of which were presumably personnel carriers. It is evident from the texts that discipline and a hierarchical order prevailed on board the warships of the High Middle Ages. However, the texts can be criticised for being rooted in the reality of the High Middle Ages and therefore only partially or not at all able to provide knowledge of the use of ships for warfare in the Viking Age.

Nor can traditional analyses of the archaeological material contribute significantly to our knowledge of communication and organisation on board the personnel carriers of the Viking Age. It is difficult to understand the challenges the seaman faced aboard a personnel carrier in the Viking Age, but crewing the ship finds reconstructed in full size makes it possible to analyse and discuss the written and archaeological sources about the maritime activities of Viking-Age people with new inspiration.

In 2004, the Viking Ship Museum in Roskilde launched a full-scale reconstruction of the Viking-Age personnel carrier, Skuldelev 2. The 30 m long ship was named *The Sea Stallion from Glendalough*, and has since been used for numerous sailing tests and trial voyages in both Danish and international waters.[97] How the crews of the personnel carriers in the Viking Age were organised is unclear, but we can assume that a crew of 60 men involved in a military operation must have had a well-defined organisational and command structure.[98] Communication on board a ship like *The Sea Stallion from Glendalough* mainly takes place internally among the crew members with whom one shares common practice – that is, in a community of practice. Tasks should as far as possible be performed without much internal verbal communication, because talking and shouting internally will make it difficult to hear orders from the skipper or other commanding officers on board. Gradually, as experience of the tasks on board is built up among the ship's crew, practical chores will be performed with a minimum of verbal communication. Such a community of practice, when it functions well, will only need an order issued by the skipper; the rest of the work will be done independently by the crew.[99]

92. Crumlin-Pedersen & Vinner 1993: 27–29.
93. Gillmor 1985: 128.
94. Personal communication from Anton Englert. Anton Englert is a PhD and archaeologist specialising in maritime archaeology.
95. Albrethsen 1997: 211.
96. *Gulatingslovi* [Robberstad 1952: 268–284].
97. Nielsen 2011 & 2012.
98. Englert *et al.* 2013: 57.
99. Ravn 2013.

Although the crew in the forebody, midship and afterbody have their own practical chores to perform, which makes sense in itself, it is always clear that the ship is a totality, which can only function if all its parts work together. The crew on board are constantly reminded of this through practice. All tasks are both determined by, and are prerequisites of, the performance of other tasks. Often, it is necessary for the skipper to give an order to the whole crew or a part of the crew, which is not in the immediate vicinity of the skipper. During sailing, strong winds or the position of the sail may make this communication difficult, and especially in the forebody an order from the skipper, who will usually be on the afterdeck, will be impossible to hear.[100]

The skipper primarily has his position on the afterdeck, mainly because this position offers the best overview of the sailing.[101] However, at the same time the aft positioning means that the skipper is dependent on the – in the forebody positioned – lookout's observations, since the sail and other things may limit or block the skipper's view. In critical situations, the observations of the lookout must reach the skipper as quickly as possible, which again may be difficult because of wind or the position of the sail.

On *the Sea Stallion from Glendalough*, and on board the smaller personnel carrier *Helge Ask*,[102] the communication problems are partly solved by using a middleman placed amidships by the mast. In concentrated form, the middleman passes on the orders of the skipper by shouting to the crew amidships and fore. The middleman also functions as a channel for the statements or observations of the crew amidships and fore to the skipper.[103]

One can assume that wind, weather and the position of the sail during sailing would also have affected communication on board the Viking-Age personnel carriers. It may have been necessary to limit, or in extreme cases to forbid verbal communication among the crew, if orders from the skipper were to be heard and obeyed. This accords well with the fact that the personnel carriers were mainly used in a military context where being able to hear, understand and obey an order was of great importance to the fighting power of the whole unit.

The crews on board the Viking-Age personnel carriers were probably experienced seamen who had since childhood acquired their knowledge of seamanship and boat-handling.[104] The need for internal verbal communication in connection with ordinary tasks would therefore probably have been minimal. Nevertheless we must assume that communication over longer distances – for example from afterbody to forebody or vice versa – was also necessary on board the personnel carriers of the Viking Age, but whether the Viking-Age crews also used a middleman can only be suggested – not proven. The shouting middleman is only one of several possible solutions to a communication problem. Other solutions, for example involving non-verbal signals, may also have been used. It should be noted, however, that the Bayeux Tapestry's depictions of the military sea transport prior to the Battle of Hastings in 1066 show people whose function on board can be interpreted as that of the above-mentioned middleman.[105]

Altogether, the experiences gained during the trial voyages demonstrates that the large crew and the limited space on board the long, narrow personnel carriers would have made special demands on working conditions, organisation and communication. Crew and ship would have been involved in a dialectical interaction where the design of the ship formed the organisation and communication of the crew. If the large crews on board the long, narrow ships were to function efficiently it was necessary to have a well-defined organisational structure and a clear chain of command, which are very much also values aspired to today by smoothly functioning fighting units in connection with military operations. The conditions on board helped to mould the crew into a unit whose individual members understood and obeyed orders, functioned as a single collective

100. Ravn 2013.
101. Personal communication from the ship reconstructor Vibeke Bischoff, who has in several cases functioned as skipper on board *The Sea Stallion from Glendalough*.
102. *Helge Ask* was reconstructed after the Skuldelev 5 ship find. It is 17.3 m long and 2.5 m wide.
103. For example the statement: "tack is fast!" or observations made by the lookout.
104. Ravn 2012a.
105. Ravn 2014: 254–255; Ravn 2016.

unit, knew their places and functions in practice, gave one another courage and protected one another.[106] A similarly intense collective formation is often seen among warriors – in prehistoric,[107] historical[108] and present-day contexts.[109] Furthermore, it is notable that the inscriptions of the rune stones[110] and the skaldic poems[111] make it clear that courage, valour and loyalty were also aspired to and valued among the people of the Viking Age – and especially among the warriors of the time. It is furthermore clear that a strong sense of solidarity among the warriors excisted.[112] The strong bonds can be seen expressed on rune stones and in skaldic poems, which use terms like *félagi* and *drengr* (fig. 64). Both terms have a conceptual content referring to brothers-in-arms – that is, a group of warriors whose common practice bonds them closely together socially.[113] One important point is, therefore, that practice on board personnel carriers helped to forge strong, smoothly functioning units. The self-commanding military units expressed in a ship's crew could adapt to the dynamic and dialectical process of war, where uncertainty, lack of clarity and chaos forces ongoing re-evaluation and adaptation. The warriors within the framework of the ship's collectivity, gained both an identity and a meaning from their practice. In various learning processes, knowledge of seamanship and the art of war was developed and passed on. On board the personnel carrier, the seaman became a crew-member and the warrior was incorporated in the fighting unit.

Amphibious warfare

Judging from the written sources of the Viking Age, both Frankish annals and the Anglo-Saxon Chronicle, the offensive part of the Scandinavian warfare of the time was based on avoiding a direct confrontation with the opponent's military forces.[114] Surprise attacks and a quick retreat were preferred instead.[115] Another type

of offensive military operations that was practised can be exemplified by the fitting-out activities indicated at the Fribrødre Å site, prior to a military sea transport from Falster to a landing place in the southwestern Baltic area,[116] and by William the Conqueror's cross-channel operation in 1066.[117]

In connection with both types of offensive operations a fast, efficient transport and landing of warriors and supplies would have been essential, but in the latter type of attack, in which many warriors and large amounts of supplies and other military equipment were to be transported over short stretches of sea and landed in a suitable place, the possibility of a quick retreat was probably not part of the operational plan.

The transport and landing of warriors, horses and supplies can be described as amphibious military operations, and the operations were the precondition of both the hit-and-run attacks and the massive deployment of troops.[118] At the same time, the landing was extremely vulnerable to resistance from a well-prepared enemy.[119] It is therefore likely that a given area was reconnoitred prior to an attack in order to find places suitable for landing, in terms of both terrain and the positioning of enemy forces. Alternatively, the landing may have taken place where allies were in control, or informants with local knowledge may have been used to gather information and intelligence.[120]

As described above, personnel carriers would have been suitable for beaching and then landing warriors, supplies and other military equipment. However, landing would have been more difficult from the large cargo ships. Perhaps the personnel carriers functioned as temporary landing stages, as suggested in the *Saga of the Joms-vikings* from the High Middle Ages?[121] Perhaps transported planks were used to make temporary landing stages (fig. 65)? Or perhaps the large cargo ships anchored out in deeper water, after which crew, supplies and other military equipment were reloaded on to more suitable landing vessels?

106. Englert *et al.* 2013: 57; Damgård-Sørensen in prep.
107. Hedenstierna-Jonson 2006: 27–28.
108. Remarque [1928] 2014: 29.
109. Brødsgaard Larsen 2009: 41–45.
110. Such as the Sjörup Stone, DR 279, Jacobsen & Moltke 1942: 332–334 and the Hällestad 1 Stone, DR 295, Jacobsen & Moltke 1942: 349–350.
111. Jesch 2001: 216–222.
112. Varenius 1998: 8; Jesch 2001: 180–186 & 216; Hedenstierna-Jonson 2006: 26–30.
113. Wimmer 1908: viii; Jesch 2001: 225, 231, 235 & 255.
114. Albrectsen 1981; Abels 1997: 257–258.
115. Griffith 1995: 114–117; Williams 2008: 197.
116. Klassen 2010: 339 & 343–351.
117. Houts 1988; Rud 2008: 95–99.
118. Jesch 2001: 178; Rose 2002: 25.
119. Griffith 1995: 79–80.
120. Gillmor 1985: 124.
121. *Jomsvikingernes Saga*: paragraph 26, pages 97–98.

Fig. 64. Left: Hedeby 1 rune stone, with the inscription "Þórulfr raised this stone, Sveinn's retainer, in memory of Eiríkr, his partner (félagi), who died when 'drengjar' besieged Hedeby; and he was a 'captain', a very good 'drengr'". Right: Århus 4 rune stone, with the inscription "Gunnulfr and Eygautr/Auðgautr and Áslakr and Hrólfr raised this stone in memory of Fúl, their partner (félagi), who died when kings fought". Both inscriptions use the term 'félagi' and the Hedeby 1 rune stone also uses the term 'drengr'. Both terms refer to the close-knit relations among fellow warriors – comrades-in-arms. After Jacobsen & Moltke 1942: Atlas 1-2 & 180-181 and the website www.runer.ku.dk

Battles at sea

Besides the amphibious military operations, military sea transports were also conducted with a view to bringing war fleets to a sea battle. The skaldic poems speak of at least 11 sea battles.[122] The descriptions of the sea battles follow a pattern that can be divided into several phases, but it is difficult to tell whether the phased procedure represents the true course of a sea battle, or is more the result of stylistic choices in the recitation of the poems.

According to the skaldic poems sea battles did not arise spontaneously. Sea battles were well-prepared events. It appears that the time and place for a sea battle were agreed between the opponents[123] and that battles took place in sheltered waters and fair weather.[124]

Several sea battles were probably planned and agreed events, but it should be noted that the intention of skaldic poems was mainly to praise the deeds of a magnate or king, so an idealised course of events may well have been invented. As an extension of this, the highly stylised verbal exchanges between the leaders of the opposing war fleets can be taken as a narrative device used by the skalds in the recitation of the poems.

122. Jesch 2002: 58.
123. Jesch 2002: 58–59 & 63.
124. Rose 2002: 25.

Before the actual hostilities, the military leaders would try to instil courage in their warriors, and the tactics they intended to use would be announced to the warriors.[125] After this, the ships of the fleet would be manoeuvred into close order so they could be tied together[126] and thus create platforms on which the subsequent close combat could take place.[127]

In this connection, the saga of Sverri Sigurdsson should be mentioned.[128] It was written down in the time between the end of the 12th and the beginning of the 13th century.[129] In the saga, Sverri orders his men – as an exception – not to tie the ships together.[130] When Sverri calls the tying-together of the ships an old, familiar preparation for the close combat, this supports the interpretation of its use in connection with the seaborne warfare of the 11th century (fig. 66).

After the ships were tied together, the opposing fleets were brought together, and with the boarding of the enemy's ships there followed a phase with close combat.[131] The close combat is often described as introduced by an advance phase in which the opponents used various kinds of ranged weaponry[132] against each other.[133] In this context, it is interesting that in the 12th strake in the bow of Skuldelev 1 there is a plank fragment with a conical hole that was probably made by an arrowhead (fig. 67).[134]

According to the skaldic poems, the close combat ended when a ship had been 'cleared' of enemies. In this way, a conquered ship could join the war fleet of the victor. Besides the capturing of ships, the skaldic poems mention that weapons, shields, chain mail and helmets as well as other war booty were shared out among the warriors of the winning party.[135]

125. Jesch 2002: 60.
126. *Tengja.*
127. Jesch 2002: 60.
128. Who lived at the end of the 12th century.
129. Hauksson 2007: V-LXXXI.
130. *Sverris Saga*, chap. 88 [Hauksson 2007: 135–138].
131. Jesch 2002: 60–62.
132. Stones, arrows and spears.
133. Rose 2002: 24.
134. Crumlin-Pedersen & Olsen 2002: 108 & 137.
135. Jesch 2002: 62–63.

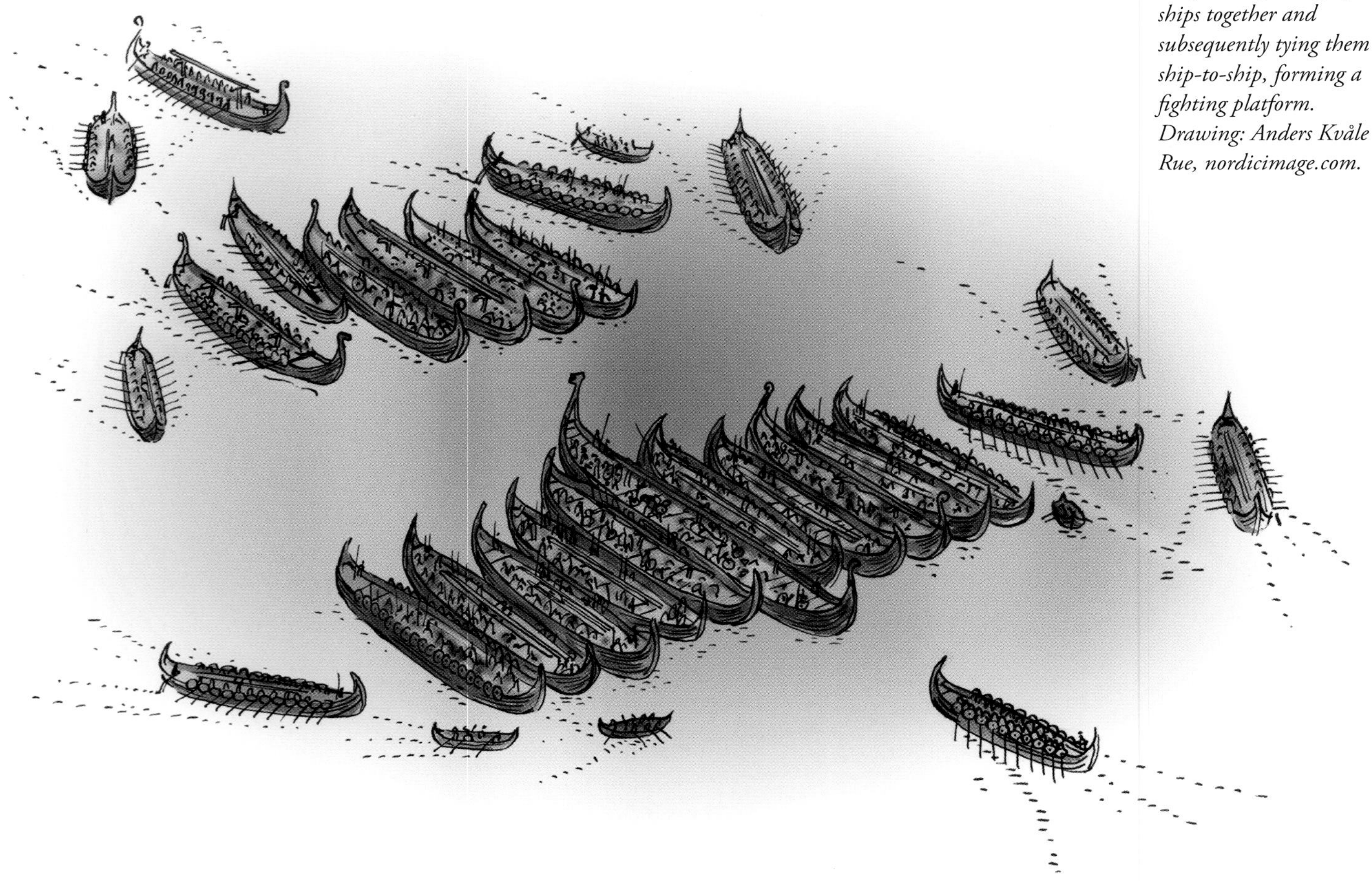

Fig. 66. Artist's impression of two opposing fleets in the process of bringing ships together and subsequently tying them ship-to-ship, forming a fighting platform. Drawing: Anders Kvåle Rue, nordicimage.com.

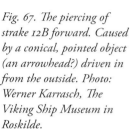

Fig. 67. The piercing of strake 12B forward. Caused by a conical, pointed object (an arrowhead?) driven in from the outside. Photo: Werner Karrasch, The Viking Ship Museum in Roskilde.

One specific operational tactic that was probably used in connection with an attack by a fleet on a town or another war fleet was to use fire-ships. If flammable materials were stacked on board a ship and then set on fire, the burning ship could drift with the wind towards the intended target. The successful use of a fire-ship could burn down enemy structures or break up the disposition of the opponent's war fleet – sailing or anchored. The use of such a fire-ship is mentioned by Saxo Grammaticus in his description of the attack by Absalon and Esbern Snare on the town of Wolgast.[136] However, Esbern's fire-ship hit a stake that was hidden under the water and burned up without reaching its target.[137] It is possible that Hedeby 1 was used as such a fire-ship in an attack on Hedeby at the end of the 10th century or at the beginning of the 11th century.[138]

Logistical aspects

In all military operations, logistical aspects, including the securing of the lines of supply and the ability to transport warriors, would have been extremely important.[139] Extensive preparations were made before a military sea

136. *Urbs Walogustum.*
137. Saxo Grammaticus: Book 16, 6,4 [Friis-Jensen & Zeeberg 2005: 533].
138. Crumlin-Pedersen 1997b: 94–95. See however Kalmring 2010: 330–331 for a different interpretation of the traces of fire on Hedeby 1's ship components.
139. Randsborg 1998: 173.
140. Gillmor 1985: 124.
141. Jesch 2001: 171–173.
142. Englert *et al.* 2013: 57.
143. Englert *et al.* 2013: 57.

transport.[140] These aspects are rarely mentioned in skaldic poems.[141] The provincial laws of the High Middle Ages, on the other hand, describe the equipping of the ships of the war fleet; but these sources are problematic to use in an analysis of the war fleets of the 11th century because of their dubious value as regards the maritime warfare of the Viking Age. It is more productive to use the results gained from trial voyages with reconstructed ships from the time. It must at the same time be pointed out that these results can be criticised for being related more to present-day researchers' experience of conditions on board than to the Late Viking-Age crews, which means that in a scientific context the results must exclusively be viewed as indicative.

The limited space on board the personnel carriers means that a fully-manned ship could only bring provisions for a number of days, and hardly for a week.[142] In addition to this, the limited space on board made it difficult for the crew to sleep during long voyages, which may have affected the crew's ability to handle the ship and to wage war.[143]

By contrast, the conditions on board cargo ships for a small crew would have made it possible to have an almost unlimited amount of provisions on board, while still making it possible for those not on watch to rest and sleep enough to engage in long voyages.[144] However, it should be added that if a cargo ship is used to transport a large group of warriors or horses, the same problems as described above for a fully-manned personnel carrier will arise.

During a military sea transport that lasted several days, the cargo ships of the war fleet would be able to supply the crew on board the personnel carriers with drink and provisions, but if the warriors had to be landed or participate in a sea battle in a reasonably rested condition, the experimental trial voyages suggest that attempts would have been made to limit the time at sea as much as possible. Waiting for favourable wind and weather conditions and going ashore as required to rest, sleep and take on drink and provision could have limited the time at sea.[145] However, such an 'amphibious method' of sailing would have lengthened the military transports and made it difficult to use the element of surprise which was important to the warfare of the time.

The expected length of a military campaign would have been matched to the amount of supplies taken. A military operation consisting of a short sea transport, raids and the subsequent sea transport of warriors and war booty would not have required large quantities of supplies. On the other hand, lengthier military operations would have necessitated various methods of procuring drink, provisions and other necessities of life.[146]

While the small war fleets could probably procure drink and provisions by living off the land – that is, raiding for the necessary resources[147] – the warriors on board the ships in a medium-sized and large war fleets would have been extremely dependent on a well-conceived and well-executed plan for the procurement of supplies and other equipment.[148]

Medium-sized and large war fleets could raid large centres for provisions[149] and afterwards take the booty to a camp.[150] The archaeologically excavated Viking-Age camps in England[151] show that such camps were constructed by establishing earthworks and entrenchments.[152]

Alternatively, the war fleet could be divided into smaller units so that, as small war fleets, they could *live off the land*.[153] Such a division of a Scandinavian war fleet into smaller sections is described in the *annals of St. Bertin*[154] in France for the years 861 and 862.[155] Another method was probably to set up camps in areas where the relations with the local population were less antagonistic.[156]

144. Englert & Ossowski 2009: 264–266.
145. Englert 2012: 276.
146. Williams 2008: 198–199.
147. Griffith 1995: 113.
148. Griffith 1995: 114–115; Williams 2008: 198–199.
149. For example, agrarian and urban settlements, and other places where supplies were stored.
150. Williams 2008: 198–199.
151. For a survey of known Viking-Age camps in England and Ireland (*Longphorts*), see Williams 2008: 198.
152. Abels 1997: 258.
153. Griffith 1995: 113–114.
154. *Annales Bertiniani*; see Albrectsen 1981: 27–61.
155. Albrectsen 1981: 42–44.
156. Griffith 1995: 115.

VI. Conclusions

Every single ship in the war fleets of the Late Viking Age was a unique product of craftsmanship. All ship parts were selected and dressed to a particular ship. It is thus unlikely that drawings and templates were used. The uniform conceptual understanding and methodological and technical choices suggest that the shipbuilding of the age was based on a technology with conservative basic principles and a measuring system where the ship parts were dimensioned in relation to one another. However, it must also be emphasised that the basic principles and the system of relative measurements were exclusively guidelines for the boatbuilders of the time. In several cases, markings on ship parts show that the final positioning in the hull of the ship as well as the design of the individual ship parts did not always follow the planned pattern. It is thus probable that ongoing adjustment of the existing guidelines was at the core of the shipbuilding of the age.

Alongside the conservative conceptual understanding and uniform methodological and technical practices, regional and local differences are recognisable. This dialectic may be due to the fact that the manpower for the shipbuilding was basically decentrally organised in local collectivities, but at the same time that the construction supervisors belonged to other collectivities, families or kinship groups with special shipbuilding expertise, whose practice perpetuated the fundamental principles of Nordic shipbuilding across the local differences.

As suggested in the resource analyses of Late Viking-Age shipbuilding, large parts of the work could be carried out by a non-specialised workforce. At the same time, we can assume that individuals with specialised knowledge and skills also participated in the construction work. Some of these specialised boatbuilders had a knowledge of the system of relative measurement and rules-of-thumb that could be used as guidelines in the monitoring of the form of the ships, the selection of the suitable resources and the final establishment of the dimensions of the ship parts. In addition, sail-making and getting the whole rig to function optimally in relation to the hull were probably dealt with by specialised craftsmen. Finally, it is possible that the technically most difficult details of the ships were executed by specialists.[1]

Another result of the analysis is that the degree of advance planning with sub-goals as well as the coordination of the working processes and tasks increased proportionally with the size of the ship types, but at the same time, that several of the raw materials and primary products could be procured and produced as part of other work in the various collectivities of the community. The total construction period could therefore be shortened considerably, and the total time consumption must therefore be understood in a context where the work was probably spread over the year – or years – and distributed over several individuals and collectivities. Charcoal-burning, tar-making, sailcloth production, as well as the felling, splitting, rough-dressing of raw materials and their transport to the building site are examples of such production, and these processes could take place alongside other ongoing tasks in the village collectivities. If the magnate, as part of the obligations entailed by the relationship between ruler and subjects, could demand products, the labour burden as well as the resource consumption would have been spread geographically and across time, but within the local or regional context defined by the magnate's domain.

1. For example the carving of the so-called stepped stem and tongued scarfs.

The raw materials were carefully selected: particular iron qualities were probably used in different parts of the vessels, and the quality of the sailcloth was probably matched to the size of the sail. Oak was mainly used as a wood resource, but alder, ash, maple, pine and in a few cases, beech, was also used. Treenails were made of many different woods, and the method of making the treenails was mainly determined by the wood chosen. In addition, the trees were selected on the basis of their growth: the straight, high-boled trees were used to make keels, keelsons, planks, stringers, masts and yards, while the crooked, low-boled trees as well as branches and roots were used to make frame parts and stems. The forms and species of trees seem to have been equally important in the choice of suitable resources. The analysis also shows that the plank-built ships – large and small – were built with differing timber qualities, which underscores the fact that access to suitable resources was not the same for all. In order to make wood tar, pine and perhaps to a lesser extent birch were used, while charcoal was mainly made from deciduous trees, probably oak. Within this book's field of investigation, iron was made of bog ore, and in addition usable iron and finished objects were imported and used for shipbuilding and outfitting. To make the sails, wool and possibly linen were used. The standing and running rigging were mainly made of lime bast, and the caulking material of spun or unspun wool. However, the relatively uniform impression presented by the range of raw materials may be due to preservation conditions.

To achieve the desired qualities and properties in the raw materials, several resources were consciously manipulated, for example by coppicing and debarking trees to make them into suitable resources for a specific type of production such as charcoal, treenails and wood-tar production. Some resources were reserved for shipbuilding, and several *snekke* place-names should probably be viewed as an indication of this. Since ownership and usufruct were probably not clearly defined entities in the late part

of the Viking Age, it would by all indications have been problematic to enforce special rights to particular resources. The protection of the reserved resources would have been locally rooted and managed by local magnates and their subjects, both of whom had an interest in building and maintaining the ships that were important to the community.

Moreover, the book's analyses of the resource areas and the manpower necessary to build and maintain the war fleets make it seem likely that a single magnate or king would have been able to fund and control a minor war fleet, while it seems unlikely that the resource area and manpower needed to build and maintain a large war fleet could be managed and exploited by a single magnate or king. The large war fleets were only possible in the context of associations of the smaller war fleets of powerful men.

Another conclusion that can be drawn is that the war fleets of the time were of widely differing sizes and vessel type compositions. Some war fleets consisted only of a handful of ships, while others comprised several hundred. The character of the organisational problems, especially the logistical ones, would therefore have varied greatly. In this context, is should be emphasised that the sources for the understanding of the war fleets of the Late Viking Age do not specify the overall fleet strength of a magnate or king, but the size of an operational war fleet used for a specific military operation. This book has thus not analysed the total fleet strength of 11th century Denmark, but that of some of the widely differing operational war fleets that were active in specific military operations in the late part of the Viking Age.

At sea, a small war fleet could more easily become a unified force, and the procurement of provisions and other necessities could be supplemented by raiding. For the largest war fleets, it would have been far more difficult to remain a unified force during sailing, and it was probably a massive challenge to maintain the necessary supplies. With regard to this issue it is important to stress the various military ways and means of the time. The core aim of late

Viking-Age maritime warfare was to use ships to attack quickly and unexpectedly and with great precision. Experimental archaeological trial voyages clearly show that sea transport was by far the quickest and most efficient way of conducting troop movements.

In some cases, this could be followed by a quick withdrawal, and by using such hit-and-run attacks the Scandinavian war fleets were able to carry out successful military operations. The attackers needed ships which, independently of favourable winds, could ensure a successful, quick withdrawal. For this, personnel carriers were particularly well suited, since they could be propelled quickly and precisely by both sail and oars.

Other maritime military operations tried to deploy massive numbers of warriors quickly and unexpectedly and with great precision, and in these cases a quick withdrawal was not part of the operational deployment of the military resources. The medium-sized and large cargo ships, which were exclusively propelled by sail, and thus highly dependent on favourable winds, could therefore also be used.

The special working conditions on board the personnel carriers necessitated a well-defined organisational structure and clear lines of command. Being able to understand and obey an order, to function and know one's function in a collectivity, to endure, and to instill courage in one another, and finally to protect one another, were highly-prized values in ship-handling and seamanship as well as in battle. The conditions and practice on board the personnel carriers therefore helped to support the cohesiveness of the military organisation of the time.

Summary

Viking-Age War Fleets. Shipbuilding, resource management and maritime warfare in 11th-century Denmark

In the Scandinavian societies of the Viking Age, the ship was omnipresent. Politically, ideologically and economically the ship played a central role, and in the military operations, which are the subject of this book, the ship and its armed crew were the fundamental means of achieving military goals. This publication deals with the organisational, resource-related and operational aspects of the building and use of ships for warfare in 11th-century Denmark.

The first chapter gives an account of methodological choices and the geographical and chronological framework of the investigation. This is followed by a brief presentation of the analysed ship finds, which leads into chapter II of the book, in which Late Viking-Age shipbuilding is examined. Many different crafts were involved in the building of ships: the knowledge and skills of the boatbuilder, the tar-burner, the blacksmith, the weaver, the sailmaker and the ropemaker are analysed and discussed, all with a starting point in experimental archaeology's potential for indicating the operational and dynamic processes of various crafts of the past. The detailed analyses suggest that shipbuilding of the time was based partly on guidelines consisting of basic principles and a measuring system, where the dimensions of the ship parts were determined relative to one another, and partly by ongoing adaptation of the individual ship parts and their positioning in the hull of the ship. Alongside the relatively conservative basic principles, regional and local differences are clear. This can be interpreted as evidence that the workforce for shipbuilding was fundamentally decentrally organised, while at the same time, people with particular shipbuilding expertise supervised the construction work. These specialists formed communities that maintained the fundamental principles of Nordic shipbuilding despite the degree of local variation.

Chapter III begins with an analysis of the evidence for the choice of tree species and material qualities connected with shipbuilding in the Late Viking Age, as reflected by the ship finds. Subsequently, the Viking Ship Museum's many years of experimental archaeological reconstruction of ship finds forms the empirical basis for detailed analyses of how many raw materials and how much manpower were procured in order to build and use the different ship types of the Late Viking Age. It seems likely that the degree of advance planning increased proportionally with the sizes of the ship types, but also that several of the raw materials and primary products could be procured and manufactured in the course of the year or over several years. The total construction period could therefore be shortened considerably.

The chapter ends with an indication of the resource areas and manpower necessary to build and maintain both small and medium-sized fleets, and the larger war fleets. On this basis, it can be concluded that the large war fleets of the time, consisting of several hundred ships, were only possible as a result of associations of the smaller war fleets of powerful men.

Chapter IV discusses woodland management in the later part of the Viking Age. The point of departure is an analysis of the character and species composition of the woodlands of the period. It is shown that resources could be reserved for shipbuilding, and that this is partly expressed by the *snekke* place-names of the time. By means of both deliberate manipulation and reservation of special resources, efforts were made to secure the resources necessary for shipbuilding.

Chapter V show that a variety of ship types and sizes were used for military sea transports during the period in question, and that the war fleets had widely different sizes. Some war fleets consisted of a handful of ships, while others consisted of several hundred. This diversity means that the war fleets were organised in various ways and that both size and ship-type composition were fundamentally determined by the purpose of the military operation, what was transported, the available resources, the distance from the destination, the duration of the transport and the waters where the transport took place. Each Viking-Age war fleet was therefore unique.

In general, the intentions of the military sea transports of the time can be divided into two groups, one consisting of hit-and-run attacks in which the personnel carriers would preferably have been used for fast transports as well as the landing of warriors, who could then unexpectedly and with great precision attack an unprepared opponent. Such expeditions tried to avoid a direct confrontation with the opponent's battle-ready forces, and it might therefore be necessary to make a quick withdrawal. For this, the personnel carriers were especially well suited, since they could be propelled quickly and precisely by both sail and oars and were thus relatively independent of favourable winds. The second group consists of military operations whose purpose was the transport and landing of large combat forces, large amounts of supplies and other military equipment in order to gain direct military control of an area. In such operations, the swift, unexpected and efficient transport of warriors was also of great importance, while a quick withdrawal was only relevant in the event of a military defeat. Consequently, the cargo ships and their large transport capacity were used to transport warriors, horses and supplies even though the cargo ships, which were exclusively propelled by sails, were dependent on favourable winds. Chapter V also analyses the sea battles of the time, in which the ships were used

as platforms on which close combat could take place, and how the necessary supplies for the combatants could be procured.

Finally, chapter V investigates the special working conditions on board the personnel carriers and it is concluded that a well-defined organisational structure and clear lines of command were necessary if the crews on board the long, narrow ships were to be able to understand and obey orders and to function as a collective unit. Along with courage, endurance and solidarity, these were the fundamental values in connection with boat-handling and seamanship as well as warfare. The conditions and practice on board the personnel carriers thus helped to support the cohesiveness of the military organisations of the time.

Chapter VI states the conclusions of the investigation as regards the war fleets of the Late Viking Age. The main points in the book are:

- Each ship was a unique product of craftsmanship in which a combination of laid-down guidelines and ongoing adaptation was at the core of shipbuilding practice.
- The raw materials for the shipbuilding were carefully selected, but at the same time access to the most suitable resources was not the same for all.
- In order to attain the desired raw material qualities and properties, resources were manipulated, for example by coppicing and debarking, and some resources were reserved for shipbuilding.
- The sizes and ship-type compositions of the war fleets varied greatly. The primary determining factors were: 1) the purpose of the military sea transport; 2) what was transported; 3) the available resources; 4) the distance from the destination; 5) the duration of the transport; and 6) the waters in which the transport took place.

- The sizes of the necessary resource areas and the manpower necessary to build and maintain different sizes of war fleets make it seem likely that a single king or magnate could manage the construction and use of a small war fleet, while the large war fleets were only possible as a result of associations of the smaller war fleets of powerful men.

- Experimental archaeological sailing tests and trial voyages show that sea transport was the fastest and most efficient way of conducting troop movements, and for the characteristic hit-and-run attacks of the time, the personnel carriers were especially well suited.
- Finally, the conditions and practice on board the personnel carriers helped to ensure the cohesiveness of the military organisations of the time.

Resumé på dansk

Vikingetidens krigsflåder. Skibsbygning, ressourcekontrol og maritime krigsførelse i det 11. århundredes Danmark

I de skandinaviske vikingetidssamfund var skibet allestedsnærværende. Både politisk, ideologisk og økonomisk havde skibet en central rolle, og i datidens militære operationer, som er emnet for denne bog, var skib og bevæbnet mandskab grundlæggende midler til at opnå militære mål. Bogen udforsker ressourcemæssige, organisatoriske og operationelle aspekter i forbindelse med bygning og brug af skibe anvendt til krigsførelse i det 11. århundredes Danmark.

Første kapitel redegør for metodiske valg samt undersøgelsens geografiske og kronologiske afgrænsning. Herefter følger en kort præsentation af de analyserede skibsfund, der leder til bogens kapitel II, hvor skibsbygningen i den sene vikingetid analyseres. Mange forskellige håndværkere var involveret i bygningen af skibene: bådebyggere, tjærebrændere, smede, vævere, sejlmagere og reblæggere. Deres viden og kunnen bliver analyseret og diskuteret med et udgangspunkt i den eksperimentelle arkæologis mulighed for at sandsynliggøre forskellige fortidige håndværks operationelle og dynamiske processer. Analyserne viser, at datidens skibsbygning var baseret på dels retningslinjer bestående af grundprincipper og et målesystem, hvor fartøjsdelenes dimensioner var bestemt i forhold til hinanden, dels en løbende tilpasning af de enkelte skibsdele og deres placering i skibets skrog. Samtidig med de relativt ensartede grundprincipper er regionale og lokale forskelle tydelige. Dette kan tolkes som et vidnesbyrd om, at arbejdskraften til skibsbygningen grundlæggende var decentralt organiseret, samtidig med at særligt skibsbygningskyndige ledte byggerierne. Disse specialister dannede fællesskaber, der vedligeholdt den nordiske skibsbygnings grundlæggende principper på tværs af de lokale forskelle.

Kapitel III indledes med en analyse af skibsfundenes udsagn vedrørende valg af træarter og materialekvaliteter i forbindelse med den sene vikingetids skibsbygning. Efterfølgende danner Vikingeskibsmuseets mangeårige eksperimentalarkæologiske rekonstruktionsprojekter af skibsfund det empiriske grundlag for detaljerede analyser af hvor mange råmaterialer og hvor megen arbejdskraft, der blev tilvejebragt for at kunne bygge og bruge den sene vikingetids forskellige skibstyper. Det kan sandsynliggøres, at graden af forudgående planlægning stiger proportionalt med størrelsen på skibstyperne, men ligeledes at flere råmaterialer og grundprodukter kunne tilvejebringes og fremstilles i løbet af året eller over flere år. Den sammenhængende byggeperiode kunne derfor afkortes betydeligt.

Kapitlet afsluttes med en sandsynliggørelse af de nødvendige ressourceområder og den nødvendige arbejdskraft til at bygge og vedligeholde dels små og mellemstore, dels store krigsflåder. På dette grundlag kan det konkluderes, at datidens store krigsflåder, bestående af flere hundrede skibe, udelukkende var mulige gennem sammenslutninger af mægtige mænds mindre krigsflåder.

I kapitel IV drøftes skovdrift i den sene del af vikingetiden. Udgangspunktet er en analyse af datidens trælandskabers karakter og artssammensætning. Det bliver sandsynliggjort, at ressourcer blev reserveret til skibsbygning, og at dette kommer delvist til udtryk gennem de i datiden givne snekkestednavnene. Gennem både bevidst manipulation og reservation af særlige ressourcer, blev de nødvendige ressourcer til skibsbygningen søgt sikret.

Kapitel V fremhæver, at forskellige fartøjstyper blev anvendt til datidens militære søtransporter samt tillige, at krigsflåderne havde vidt forskellige størrelser. Nogle krigsflåder bestod af en håndfuld skibe, mens andre bestod af flere hundrede. Diversiteten betyder, at krigsflåderne var organiseret forskelligt, og at både størrelse og fartøjstypesammensætningen grundlæggende var betinget af: målet med den militære operation, det, der blev transporteret, de tilgængelige ressourcer, afstanden til målet, transportens varighed og de farvande, hvor transporten fandt sted. Derfor var hver vikingetidskrigsflåde unik.

Den militære hensigt med datidens militære søtransporter kan generelt set inddeles i to grupper. En bestående af *hit and run attacks*, hvor fortrinsvis mandskabsskibene blev anvendt til hurtige transporter samt landsætninger af krigsfolk, der uventet og med stor præcision efterfølgende kunne angribe en uforberedt modpart. Sådanne togter søgte at undgå en direkte konfrontation med modpartens kampklare styrker, og derfor kunne det blive nødvendigt med en hastig retræte. Til dette var mandskabsskibet særligt egnet idet, det kunne fremdrives hurtigt og præcist via såvel sejl som årer, og dermed var relativt uafhængig af gunstig vind. Den anden gruppe består af militære operationer, hvor hensigten var transport og landsætning af talrige krigsfolk og store mængder af tros for herved at opnå direkte militær kontrol over et område. I sådanne operationer var en hurtig, uventet og effektiv transport af krigsfolk også af stor betydning, men en hastig tilbagetrækning var kun relevant i tilfælde af et militært nederlag. Følgelig kunne lastskibene og deres store transportkapacitet udnyttes til transport af såvel krigsfolk og heste som tros, også selvom lastskibene, der udelukkende var fremdrevet via sejl, var afhængige af gunstig vind. I kapitel V analyseres desuden datidens søslag, hvor skibene blev udnyttet som platforme, hvorpå nærkampe kunne udkæmpes, samt hvordan krigsfolkenes nødvendige forsyninger blev tilvejebragt.

Endelig undersøger kapitel V de særlige arbejdsforhold om bord på mandskabsskibene. Og det konkluderes, at en veldefineret organisation og klare kommandostrukturer var nødvendige for at mandskabet om bord på de lange og smalle skibe skulle kunne forstå og adlyde en ordre samt fungere og kende sin funktion i ét fællesskab. Sammen med mod, udholdenhed og sammenhold udgjorde disse egenskaber grundlæggende værdier i forbindelse med såvel bådhåndtering og sømandsskab som krigsførelse. Vilkårene og praksis om bord på mandskabsskibene bidrog således til at understøtte datidens militære organisations sammenhængskraft.

Kapitel VI indeholder undersøgelsens konklusioner vedrørende den sene vikingetids krigsflåder. Bogens hovedpointer er:

• Hvert skib var et unikt håndværksprodukt, hvor en kombination af udstukne retningslinjer og en løbende tilpasning var kernen i skibsbygningen.

• Råmaterialerne til skibsbygningen var nøje udvalgte, men samtidig var adgangen til de bedst egnede ressourcer ikke lige for alle.

• For at kunne opnå de ønskede råmaterialekvaliteter og egenskaber blev ressourcer manipuleret gennem for eksempel stævningsdrift og afbarkning, og enkelte ressourcer blev reserveret til skibsbygning.

• Krigsflådernes størrelser og fartøjstypesammensætningen i flåderne var vidt forskellige. De primært bestemmende faktorer var: 1) målet med den militære søtransport, 2) det, der blev transporteret, 3) de tilgængelige ressourcer, 4) afstanden til målet, 5) transportens varighed samt 6) de farvande, hvor transporten fandt sted.

• Størrelsen på de nødvendige ressourceområder og den nødvendige arbejdskraft til at bygge og vedligeholde forskellige størrelser af krigsflåder sandsynliggør, at en enkelt konge eller stormand kunne varetage bygning og brug af en mindre krigsflåde, mens de store krigsflåder udelukkende var mulige i kraft af sammenslutninger af mægtige mænds mindre krigsflåder.

- De eksperimentalarkæologiske testsejladser og forsøgsrejser viser, at søtransport var datidens hurtigste og mest effektive måde at foretage troppebevægelser på, og til de for datiden karakteristiske *hit and run attacks* var mandskabsskibene særdeles egnede.

- Endelig bidrog vilkårene og praksis om bord på mandskabsskibene til at understøtte datidens militære organisations sammenhængskraft.

Terminology

The ship-related technical terms used in the book have their origin in the terminological apparatus used by the National Museum's Research Centre for Maritime Archaeology in Roskilde (NMF), which is today internationally accepted. The committee behind the systematisation of the terminology consisted of Vibeke Bischoff, Ole Crumlin-Pedersen, Anton Englert and Fred Hocker. Below it is exclusively the terms relevant to this book that are defined. A complete glossary for the ship technology can be seen at the Viking Ship Museum in Roskilde.

English terms	Danish terms	German terms	Definition
Abaft	Agter for	Achter, Hinter	Preposition; lying farther aft.
Abeam	Tværskibs	Querab, Dwars	Adverb; lying outside the hull and directly to one side. When the point was abeam, the captain decided to tack.
After	Agter	Achter-, Hinter-	Adjective; pertaining to something toward the stern. The after hatchway is smaller.
Afterbody	Agterskib	Achterschiff (n), Hinterschiff (n)	The part of the hull abaft the midship section.
After stem	Agterstævn	Achtersteven (m)	Stem at the stern of a double-ended vessel of traditional Nordic construction.
Afterdeck	Agterdæk	Achterdeck (n)	Small deck in the stern.
Ahead	Forude	Voraus	Adverb; lying outside the vessel and in front of it. Another ship could be seen ahead.
Amidships	Midtskibs	Mittschiffs	Adverb; the point at the middle of the ship's length. The main hatch is normally found amidships.
Batten	Revle, liste	Stab (m)	A light strip of wood fastened over a seam, either inside or outside. Heavier than the lath in sintel technique.
Beam	Bjælke	Balken (m), Decksbalken (m)	Transverse timber, usually relatively straight and strongly fastened to the sides of the hull, providing significant strength to the structure. May be used to support a deck.
Beam	Største bredde	größte Breite (f)	The maximum breadth of the hull, to the outside of the structural timbers of the hull.

English terms	Danish terms	German terms	Definition
Before	Foran	Vor	Preposition; lying closer to the bow. The anchor windlass is usually found before the foremast.
Bilge	Bund, Flak	Boden (m), Flach (n)	That part of the bottom of a ship on either side of the keel which approaches nearer to a horizontal than a vertical direction. The transition towards the sides is called the turn of the bilge accordingly.
Biti	Bite	Bite (f)	(From Old Norse) In traditional Nordic construction, the lowest beam in a framing unit, directly above the heads of each of the floor timbers and fastened to the sides by standing knees.
Bitt	Pullert	Poller (m)	Device for belaying a line, consisting of a vertical post set in the deck or caprail.
Boltrope	Ligtov	Liektau (n)	A length of line sewn into the edge of a sail to reinforce it.
Bottom	Bund	Boden (m)	The part of the ship's hull below the waterline, especially the part from the turn of the bilge and below.
Bowline	Bugline, Boline	Buline (f)	Line running from the luff of a square sail forward, to help keep the luff stiff and at a proper angle of attack to the wind.
Breast-hook	Bovbånd	Bugband (n), Heckband (n, if used aft)	Transverse internal timber at the bow, across the centreline, reinforcing the bow against spreading. Performs same function as a transom timber at the stern. In double-ended ships there can be breast-hooks at the stern as well.
Bulkhead	Skot	Schott (n)	Transverse partition dividing the interior of the hull into separate spaces.
Cargo capacity	Lasteevne	Tragfähigkeit (f)	Estimated maximum amount of cargo (measured in weight) that a vessel can carry and still remain seaworthy.
Caulking cove	Kalfatringsrille	Kalfatnut (f)	A groove in the land of a clinker seam, into which inlaid caulking is placed.
Clinker, Clinker-built	Klinkbygget	Geklinkert, Klinkergebaut, In Klinkerbauweise	Shell-based shipbuilding method characterised by overlapping planks, usually fastened together.
Crooked timbers	Krumtræ, Krumtømmer	Krummholz (n)	Naturally curved wood used for correspondingly curved components in a vessel.
Deck	Dæk, Dæksplanker	Deck (n)	Planking over the beams to provide a working surface and in late medieval and modern vessels to keep water out of the ship.

English terms	Danish terms	German terms	Definition
Displacement	Deplacement	Verdrängung (f)	The weight of the water/fluid displaced by the vessel. The displacement is equal to the weight of the vessel. The weight of the vessel comprises hull, rigging, cargo, personnel, supplies and other necessities.
Draught	Dybgang	Tiefgang (m)	The distance from the load waterline to the bottom of the hull, the minimum depth of water needed for the hull to float.
Driven caulking	Slået kalfatring	Eingetriebene Kalfaterung (f)	Caulking forced into the seams, usually by striking a specially shaped iron with a hammer.
Expanded log-boat	Udspændt stammebåd	Geweitete Einbaum	A vessel based on a single hollowed-out and expanded (by heating) tree trunk (a log). The expanded shape is maintained by inserting thwarts and ribs. In some cases planks are added along both sides.
Floor	Bund	Boden (m)	The part of the ship's bottom below the turn of the bilge.
Floor timber	Bundstok	Bodenwrange (f), Bodenstück (n), Lieger (m)	Central frame element that crosses the keel at the lowest point in the section, over the floor.
Flush-laid	Kravellagt	Karweelgeplankt, Bündig gelegt	Planks laid edge-to-edge, so that the finished surface is smooth, rather than stepped.
Fore-	For-	Vor-	Adjective, usually attached to the word modified; pertaining to the area toward the bow. The foremast is shorter in schooners.
Forebody	Forskib	Vorschiff (n)	The part of the hull before the midship section.
Fore stem	Forstævn	Vorsteven (m)	Stem at the bow of a double-ended vessel of traditional Nordic construction.
Forward	Forude	Vorn	Adverb; in the direction of the bow. The anchors are usually kept far forward.
Frame	Spant	Spant (n)	A transverse timber or group of connected / related timbers against the inner surface of the planking, providing the hull with substantial strength and stiffness.
Frame spacing	Spantafstand	Spantabstand (m)	Distance from the centre of one frame to the next.
Freeboard	Fribord	Freibord (m)	The distance from the waterline to the top of the ship's side at its lowest point.
Futtock	Oplænger	Auflanger (m)	Frame element against one side of the hull, associated with a floor timber, to which it may or may not be fastened. A frame may be made up of a number of overlapping futtocks.

English terms	Danish terms	German terms	Definition
Hood-end	Bordhals	Plankenende (n)	End of a strake, where it attaches to the keel, stem, sternpost, or stem-wing.
Hook scarf	Hagelask	Hakenlasche (f)	Scarf with a stepped table arranged so that the assembled joint resists tensile force.
Horizontal scarf	Horisontalt skar eller lask	Horizontale Schäftung (f), Horizontale Lasche (f)	Scarf in which the table is more or less horizontal.
Hull	skrog	Rumpf	The structural body of the ship, not including the rig.
Inlaid caulking	Indlagt kalfatring	Eingelegte Kalfaterung (f)	Caulking laid into the seams of a clinker-built boat during assembly of the planks rather than driven in after assembly.
Intermediate or Side frame	Mellemspant	Zwischenspant (n)	Independent frame element against the side of the hull, spaced midway between the main frames.
Keel	Køl	Kiel (m)	Longitudinal centreline timber providing substantial strength and resistance to leeway. When it is possible a keel is described as either a rabbeted keel or a 'winged' keel with a T- or Y-shaped cross section midship.
Keelson	Kølsvin	Kielschwein (n)	Centreline timber on top of the frames, distributing the weight of the mast, often a long timber giving increased longitudinal strength and stiffness to the hull.
Knee	Knæ	Knie (n)	L-shaped timber in which the grain follows (at least approximately) the sweep of the timber, typically used to reinforce the angular joint between two other timbers, such as the keel and sternpost.
Land	Land	Landung (f), Lannung (f)	The area or surface where two planks or strakes overlap in clinker technique.
Lath	Liste	Sintelrute (f), Kalfatleiste (f)	A light batten of wood, laid over the caulking to protect it, and held in place by sewing or iron staples, clamps or sintels.
Length over all	Længde overalt	Länge (f) über alles	The length from the forward face of the stem/fore stem to the after face of the sternpost/after stem. This does not include any decorative finials on the posts.
Limber hole	Spygat	Nüstergatt (n)	Notch or opening on the underside of the frames to allow water to circulate through the bilge and reach the pump or bailing well.
Logboat	Stammebåd	Einbaum (m)	A vessel based on a single hollowed out tree trunk (a log).

English terms	Danish terms	German terms	Definition
Lot	Lot	Lot (n)	(From Old Norse) An intermediate curved timber between the stem and keel.
Mast-fish or Mast partner	Mastefisk	Mastfischung (f)	Longitudinal internal timber resting on the beams, acting as support for the mast.
Mast step	Mastespor	Mastspur (f)	Mortise or cavity in the keelson or other timber into which the heel of the mast is stepped.
Meginhufr	Meginhufr	Meginhufr (m)	(From Old Norse) A heavy strake, descended from the heavy sheer strake of earlier Nordic craft (such as the Nydam vessels), normally found at the upper end of the floor timbers.
Midship	Midtskibs-	Mittschiffs-	Adjective; pertaining to things located amidships. The midship cleat was used to belay the fall of the running shroud.
Midship section	Middelspant	Hauptspant (n)	The transverse section at the widest point in the hull. It may or may not be in the middle of the length.
Moulding	Profil, Pynteprofil	Zierprofil (n)	A decorative profile in the edge of a plank or timber, typically made with a shaped scraper, a typical feature of Viking construction.
Oar	Åre	Riemen (m)	Long shaft with a broad blade at one end for propelling a boat. The oar bears on a thole or rowlock to transfer energy to the hull.
Oar grommet	Hamlebånd	Riemenband (m)	A ring of flexible material attached to the thole or keipe and through which the oar is passed. The grommet helps to keep the oar at the right gearing or the oar can bear against it when backing water.
Oar hole, Oar port	Årehul	Riemenpforte (f)	A hole in the side of the hull through which an oar is inserted. The edge of the oar hole usually acts as the pivot point for the oar.
Plank	Bordplanke, Planke	Planke (f)	A single board of the planking.
Plank-built vessel	Plankebygget fartøj	Planken-fahrzeug (n)	A vessel based on a shell composed of a keel and planks.
Planking	Bordlægning, Klædning	Beplankung (f), Außenhaut (f)	Collectively, the planks fastened to the outer surface of the frames.
Port	Bagbord	Backbord (n)	Having to do with the left side of the ship.
Rabbet or Rebate	Spunding	Sponung (f)	Longitudinal groove cut into the side of the keel/keel plank or stem/sternpost to receive the edge or hooding ends of the planking.

English terms	Danish terms	German terms	Definition
Radially cleft	Spejlkløvet	Radial gespalten	Components produced by splitting the log along the medullary rays, producing wedge-sectioned pieces of great strength and stability.
Reef point	Rebbånd	Reffbändsel (n)	Short length of line fixed on or through a sail to allow the power portion of the sail to be tied up and sail area thus reduced in heavier weather.
Rig	Rigning,	Rigg (n), Takelage (f), Takelung (f)	The spars, sails and rigging as a unit.
Rigging	Tovværk, Rigning. Stående og løbende rig	Takelage (f). Stehendes und laufendes Gut (n)	All of the ropes and blocks etc. used to support the spars and sails and control them.
Rivet	Klinknagle	Klinkernagel (m), Niet (m, when finished)	Nail driven through two elements and then clenched or peened over a rove.
Rocker	Kølbugt	Kielsprung (m), Kielbucht (f)	The upward curving of the ends of the keel or keel plank, relative to its centre. The adjective form is rockered.
Room	Spantrum, Rum	Spantraum (m)	The longitudinal space between two frame units.
Rove	Klinkplade	Nietplatte (f)	Small, pierced metal plate over which the point of a rivet/clinker nail is clenched or peened.
Rowlock	Åretol, Årefæste	Dolle (f)	Fitting at the side of the hull to serve as the pivot point for an oar and to help keep it in place. Keipar/åretoller, oar holes, and thole pins are all forms of rowlock.
Rudder	Ror	Ruder (n)	Device for steering a vessel, operates by turning in the water and generating either lift or drag in a lateral direction.
Rudder frame	Rorspant	Ruderspant (n)	In vessels with side rudders, the frame that supports the rudder, normally heavier or bulkhead-like.
Scarf	Skar	Schäftung (f) or Lasche (f)	Joint between two long timbers aligned on approximately the same axis.

English terms	Danish terms	German terms	Definition
Seam	Samling	Naht (f), Plankennaht (f)	The joint between the edges of two planks.
Shank	Stilk	Schaft (m)	The shaft of a rivet or spike.
Sheer	Spring	Sprung (m), Decksprung (m)	The upper edge of the ship's side, as well as its curvature.
Shelf clamp	Bjælkevæger, Bitevæger (under the biti)	Balkweger (m)	Clamp on which the ends of beams rest.
Shell-based	Skalbaseret	Schalengebaut, In Schalenbauweise	Shipbuilding methods characterised by planks, directly fastened together.
Shroud	Vant	Want (f)	Ropes providing sideways support for the mast.
Side rudder	Sideror	Seitenruder (n)	Rudder mounted on the side of the hull, typically toward the stern. On northern European craft before ca 1200 it is the most common type of steering device, mounted on the starboard quarter.
Skeleton-based	Skeletbaseret	skelettgebaut	Shipbuilding methods in which the internal elements of framing and longitudinal reinforcement are the primary elements in the design, assembly or final structure.
Spike	Spiger	Spieker (m)	An iron fastening with a flattened head and a tapered shank. A spike is driven blind rather than through.
Square rig	Råsejlsrig	Rahtakelung (f)	Sail arrangement in which the sail or majority of sails are suspended from horizontal yards across the mast.
Square sail	Råsejl	Rahsegel (n)	Sail suspended from a yard, i.e. a horizontally rigged spar.
Stanchion	Støtte	Stütze (f)	Turned or carved post supporting a beam.
Starboard	Styrbord	Steuerbord (n)	Having to do with the right side of the ship.
Stay	Stag	Stag (n)	Ropes providing lengthways support for the mast.
Stem	Stævn	Steven (f)	Centreline timber at either end of the hull of a double-ended vessel, to which the hooding ends of the planking are attached.
Stem-wing	Stævnfløj	Stevenflügel (m)	Extension of the inboard edge of a stem amidships in order to provide a landing for the hooding ends of the strakes.

English terms	Danish terms	German terms	Definition
Stepped stem	Trappestævn	Treppensteven (m)	Type of winged stem in which the wings have individual steps for the hooding ends.
Stern	Agterskib, Hæk	Heck (n)	The after part of the ship, particularly the after end and its structure.
Stocks	Bedding	Helling (f), Helgen (n)	Heavy timbers laid on or driven into the ground on which a ship is built, to provide a stable base for the keel or bottom during construction.
Strake	Bordgang, Rang	Gang (m), Plankengang (m)	A continuous run of planking, one plank in width and consisting lengthwise of one or more planks.
Stringer	Væger	Weger (m), Stringer (m)	Longitudinal internal timber providing strength to the structure, usually attached directly to the inner surface of the planking.
Table	Anlægsflade	Kontaktfläche (f), Auflage-fläche (f)	The primary mating surface of a scarf, usually at a slight angle to the axis of the joined timbers.
Tangentially cleft	Plankløvet, Tangentielt kløvet	Tangential gespalten	Of a log split in half and with the round sides split or hewn off to produce a small number of wide planks.
Thwart	Tofte	Ducht (f)	Light beam or plank intended to act as a seat for rowers or paddlers. May or may not be rigidly fastened to the rest of the hull structure.
Tongue scarf	Tungeskar	Schäftung mit Zunge (f)	Plank scarf with the outer half tapering in width to a narrow tip.
Treenail	Trænagle	Holznagel (m)	Wooden fastening of relatively constant cross-section, usually used to fasten major structural elements together.
Trim (1)	Trimme	Trimmen	To adjust the ballast of the vessel to achieve proper draught without list and with the proper amount of drag.
Trim (2)	Trimme	Trimmen	To adjust the set of a sail so that it fills and draws well, and so that it imparts forward motion to the vessel as efficiently as possible.
Turn of the bilge	Kimming	Kimm (f)	The area where the more or less horizontal part of a ship's bottom (the floor) meets the more vertical portion of the side, in a conventional round-bottomed hull.

English terms	Danish terms	German terms	Definition
Vertical scarf	Vertikalt skar eller lask	vertikale Schäftung (f), vertikale Lasche (f)	Scarf in which the table is vertical.
Wale	Barkholt	Bergholz (n)	Heavy strake providing longitudinal strength and stiffness to the sides.
Waterline	Vandlinje	Wasserlinie (f)	A hypothetical line on the hull surface, defined by a horizontal plane's intersection with the hull. This plane is normally oriented parallel to the load waterline or to the keel. Shown in the half-breadth view.
Wedge	Kile	Keil (m)	Small slip or peg of wood driven into the end of a treenail to spread it and prevent it from being withdrawn.
Winged stem	Fløjstævn	Flügelsteven (m)	A stem in which the inboard edges are extended amidships in a wing or series of steps to provide the landings for the hooding ends. Typically found in Nordic clinker construction.

References

Abels, R. 1997: English logistics and military administration, 871–1066. The impact of the Viking wars. In A. Nørgård Jørgensen & B. L. Clausen (eds.): *Military Aspects of Scandinavian Society in a European Perspective, AD 1–1300. Papers from an International Research Seminar at the Danish National Museum, Copenhagen, 2–4 May 1996*, 257–265. Copenhagen.

Aistrup, M. S. 1979: Jernankeret fra Ribe. Beskrivelse af ankeret før konservering. *Nationalmuseets Arbejdsmark 1979*, 157–161.

Albris, S. L. 2014: Tolkninger med tolkninger på – udfordringer ved arbejde på tværs af arkæologi og stednavneforskning. *Arkæologisk Forum 31*, 26–31.

Albrectsen, E. 1981: *Vikingerne i Franken. Skriftlige Kilder fra det 9. Århundrede.* Odense.

Albrethsen, S.E. 1997: Logistical problems in Iron Age warfare. In A. Nørgård Jørgensen & B.L. Clausen (eds.): *Military Aspects of Scandinavian Society in a European Perspective, AD 1–1300. Papers from an International Research Seminar at the Danish National Museum, Copenhagen, 2–4 May 1996*, 210–219. Copenhagen.

Andersen, B. & Andersen, E. [1989] 2007: *Råsejlet – Dragens Vinge.* Roskilde.

Andersen, E. 1995: Square sails of wool. In O. Olsen, J. Skamby Madsen & F. Rieck (eds.): *Shipshape – Essays for Ole Crumlin-Pedersen*, 249–270. Roskilde.

Andersen, E. 1997a: Rekonstruktion af rig. In E. Andersen, O. Crumlin-Pedersen, S. Vadstrup & M. Vinner: *Roar Ege. Skuldelev 3 skibet som arkæologisk eksperiment*, 175–207. Roskilde.

Andersen, E. 1997b: *Roar Eges* sejl. In E. Andersen, O. Crumlin-Pedersen, S. Vadstrup & M. Vinner: *Roar Ege. Skuldelev 3 skibet som arkæologisk eksperiment*, 209–222. Roskilde.

Andersen, E. 1997c: Grundlaget. In E. Andersen, O. Crumlin-Pedersen, S. Vadstrup & M. Vinner, *Roar Ege. Skuldelev 3 skibet som arkæologisk eksperiment*, 15–34. Roskilde.

Andersen, E. 2009: Rekonstruktion af uldsejl. In M. Ravn (ed.): *Et uldsejl til* Oselven. *Arbejdsrapport om fremstillingen af et uldsejl til en traditionel vestnorsk båd*, 4–14. Roskilde.

Andersen, E. & Bischoff, V. 2016: Vikingeskibsmuseets sejlforskning: råsejl af uld og plantefibre i vikingetiden. In M. Ravn, L. Gebauer Thomsen, H. Lyngstrøm & E. Andersson Strand (eds.), *Vikingetidens Sejl, 137–160*. Arkæologiske Skrifter. Copenhagen & Roskilde

Andersen, E. & Bjøru, F. 2000: *Tilskæring og syning af uldsejlet.* Upubliceret rapport omhandlende fremstillingen af *Ottars* uldsejl. Roskilde.

Andersen, E., Milland, J. & Myhre, E. 1989: *Uldsejl i 1000 år.* Roskilde.

Andersen, E., Crumlin-Pedersen, O., Vadstrup, S. & Vinner, M. 1997: *Roar Ege. Skuldelev 3 skibet som arkæologisk eksperiment.* Roskilde.

Andersen, S. Th., Aaby, B. & Odgaard, B. V. 1983: Environment and Man. Current Studies in Vegetational History at the Geological Survey of Denmark. *Journal of Danish Archaeology 2*, 184–196.

Andersson, E. 2000: Textilproduktion i Löddeköpinge – endast för husbehov? In F. Svanberg & B. Söderberg (eds.): *Porten till Skåne. Löddeköpinge under järnålder och medeltid*, 158–187. Malmö.

Andrus, C.D. & Menard, H.W. 1980: *Principles of a Resource/Reserve Classification For Minerals.* Geological Survey Circular 831. Arlington.

Anglo-Saxon Chronicle. Translated with an introduction by G.N. Garmonsway in 1953. London & New York.

Arnold, B. 2015: Bark-canoes of East Africa: typology and construction techniques. Paper presented at the symposium: *International Symposium on Boat and Ship Archaeology 14. Baltic and beyond. Change and continuity in shipbuilding.* National Maritime Museum in Gdansk, Poland, 21–25 September.

Arup, E. 1914: Leding og ledingsskat i det 13. aarhundrede. *Historisk Tidsskrift 8* (5), 141–237.

Austrheim, G., Asheim, L.-J., Bjarnason, G., Feilberg, J. Fosaa, A.M., Holand, Ø., Høegh, K., Jónsdóttir, I.S., Magnússon, B., Mortensen, L.E., Mysterud, A., Olsen, E., Skonhoft, A., Steinheim, G. & Thórhallsdóttir, A. G. 2008: *Sheep grazing in the North-Atlantic region – A long term perspective on management, resource economy and ecology.* Rapport zoologisk serie 2008, 3. Trondheim.

Bach Nielsen, L. 2005: En vikingeboplads ved Højby. *Fynske Minder 2005*, 113–129.

Barbré, H. & Thomsen, R. 1983: Rekonstruktionsversuche zur frühgeschichtlichen Eisengewinnung. *Offa, 40*, 153–155.

Barrett, J., Hall, A., Johnstone, C., Kenward, H., O'Connor, T. & Achby, S. 2007: Interpreting the Plant and Animal Remains from Viking-age Kaupang. In D. Skre (ed.): *Kaupang in Skiringssal*, 283–319. Århus.

Bartholin, T. S. 1976: Dendrokronologiske og vedanatomiske undersøgelser af træfundene. In A.W. Mårtensson (ed.): *Uppgrävt förflutet för PKbanken i Lund. En investering i arkeologi*, 145–169. Lund.

Bartholin, T. S. 1998: *Dendrokronologiske undersøgelser af Vrag 1 og 6 fra Skuldelev-fundet.* NNU rapport 15. Copenhagen.

Bastrup-Birk, A., Riis-Nielsen, T., Kehlet Hansen, J. & Rune, F. 2008: Biologisk diversitet. In T. Nord-Larsen, V. Kvist Johannsen, B. Bilde Jørgensen & A. Bastrup-Birk (eds.): *Skove og plantager 2006*, 87–105. Copenhagen.

Bately, J. 2007: Text and translation: the three parts of the known world and the geography of Europe north of the Danube according to Orosius' *Historiae* and its Old English version. In J. Bately & A. Englert (eds.): *Ohthere's Voyages. A late 9th-century account of voyages along the coasts of Norway and Denmark and its cultural context*, 40–50. Maritime Culture of the North 1. Roskilde.

Bately, J. 2009: Wulfstan's voyage and his description of *Estland*: the text and the language of the text. In A. Englert & A. Trakadas (eds.): *Wulfstan's Voyage. The Baltic Sea region in the early Viking Age as seen from shipboard*, 14–28. Maritime Culture of the North 2. Roskilde.

Be sceadwisan gerefan. Oversat til dansk af Niels Lund i 2015a. In T. Christensen 2015: *Lejre bag myten – de arkæologiske udgravninger*, 241–242. Højbjerg.

Beck, A.S. 2004: Eksperimentel arkæologi i en post-processuel tid? In A. Beck, H.N. Frederiksen, L. Harvig, C. Juel, K. Langsted, T. Rasmussen & G. B. Ravnholt (eds.): *Kystkultur – aktuel arkæologi i Norden*, 117–122. Kontaktstencil 44. Copenhagen.

Beck, A. S. 2011: Working in the Borderland of Experimental Archaeology. On Theoretical Perspectives in Recent Experimental Work. In B. Petersson & L.E. Narmo (eds.): *Experimental Archaeology. Between Enlightenment and Experience*, 167–194. Acta Archaeologica Lundensia Series in 8°, No 62. Lund.

Behre, K.-E. 1983: *Ernährung und Umwelt der wikingerzeitlichen Siedlung Haithabu. Die Ergebnisse der Untersuchungen der Pflanzenreste*. Die Ausgrabungen in Haithabu, Achter Band. Neumünster.

Bencard, M. 1979: Jernankeret fra Ribe. Fundforhold. *Nationalmuseets Arbejdsmark* 1979, 156–157.

Bender Jørgensen, L. 1992: *North European Textiles until AD 1000*. Århus.

Bender Jørgensen, L. 2012: The introduction of sails to Scandinavia: Raw materials, labour and land. In R. Berge, M.E. Jasinski & K. Sognnes (eds.): *N-TAG TEN. Proceedings of the 10th Nordic TAG conference at Stiklestad, Norway 2009*, 173–181. BAR International Series 2399. Oxford.

Berglund, B. E. (ed.). 1991: *The cultural landscape during 6000 years in southern Sweden – the Ystad Project*. Ecological Bulletins No. 41. Copenhagen.

Berglund, B. E. 1991: Landscape, land use, and vegetation. In B. E. Berglund (ed.): *The cultural landscape during 6000 years in southern Sweden – the Ystad Project*, 82–83. Ecological Bulletins No. 41. Copenhagen.

Berglund, B.E., Larsson, L., Lewan, N., Gunilla, E., Olsson, A. & Skansjö, S. 1991: 6. Ecological and social factors behind the landscape changes. In B.E. Berglund (ed.): *The cultural landscape during 6000 years in southern Sweden – the Ystad Project*, 424–445. Ecological Bulletins No. 41. Copenhagen.

Bill, J. 1994: Iron Nails in Iron Age and Medieval Ship-building. In C. Westerdahl (ed.): *Crossroads in Ancient Shipbuilding. Proceedings of the Sixth International Symposium on Boat and Ship Archaeology, Roskilde 1991*, 55–63. Oxbow Monograph 40. Oxford.

Bill, J. 1997: *Small Scale Seafaring in Danish Waters AD 1000–1600*. Unpublished PhD dissertation. Copenhagen.

Bill, J. 2006a: *Beretning for udgravning af skibsvrag "Roskilde 2" fra ældre middelalder, udført af museumsinspektør Hanne Marie Myrhøj for Roskilde Museum og Nationalmuseets Marinarkæologiske Undersøgelser i december 1996 og januar 1997*. NMU 1469. Roskilde Havn. Roskilde.

Bill, J. 2006b: *Beretning for udgravning af skibsvrag "Roskilde 3" fra tidlig middelalder, udført af arkitekt, MA Morten Gøthche for Roskilde Museum og Nationalmuseets Marinarkæologiske Undersøgelser 25.2–4.3 1997*. NMU 1479 Roskilde Havn. Roskilde.

Bill, J. 2007a: *Beretning for udgravning af skibsvrag "Roskilde 5" fra tidlig middelalder, udført af arkitekt, MA Morten Gøthche for Roskilde Museum og Nationalmuseets Marinarkæologiske Undersøgelser 5.3.– 23.9.1997*. NMU 1481. Roskilde Havn. Roskilde.

Bill, J. 2007b: *Beretning for udgravning af skibsvrag "Roskilde 6" fra sen vikingetid/tidlig middelalder, udført af arkitekt, MA Morten Gøthche for Roskilde Museum og Nationalmuseets Marinarkæologiske Undersøgelser 12.3–24.9.1997*. NMU 1482 Roskilde Havn. Roskilde.

Bill, J. 2007c: *Beretning for udgravning af skibsvrag "Roskilde 9" fra tidlig middelalder, udført af arkitekt, MA Morten Gøthche for Nationalmuseets Marinarkæologiske Undersøgelser 11.9.–19.9.1997*. NMU 1534 Roskilde Havn. Roskilde.

Bill, J. 2009: Piracy and naval organisation in the Baltic Sea in the 9th century: some security considerations concerning Wulfstan's voyage. In A. Englert & A. Trakadas (eds.): *Wulfstan's Voyage. The Baltic Sea region in the early Viking Age as seen from shipboard*, 343–353. Maritime Culture of the North, 2. Roskilde.

Bill, J. 2010: Viking Age ships and seafaring in the west. In I.S. Klæsøe (ed.): *Viking Trade and Settlement in Continental Western Europe*, 19–42. Copenhagen.

Bill, J. & Daly, A. 2012: The plundering of the ship graves from Oseberg and Gokstad: an example of power politics? *Antiquity* 86, 808–824.

Bill, J., Gøthche, M. & Myrhøj, H.M. 1998: Nordeuropas største skibsfund. Ni vrag fra vikingetid og middelalder under museumsøen i Roskilde. *Nationalmuseets Arbejdsmark* 1998, 136–158.

Bill, J., Gøthche, M. & Myrhøj, H.M. 2000: Roskildeskibene. In T. Christensen & M. Andersen (eds.): *Civitas Roscald – fra byens begyndelse*, 211–259. Roskilde.

Bill, J., Nielsen, S., Andersen, E. & Damgård-Sørensen, T. 2007: *Velkommen ombord! Havhingsten fra Glendalough. Et genskabt langskib fra vikingetiden*. Roskilde.

Bill, J., Poulsen, B., Rieck, F. & Ventegodt, O. 1997: *Fra stammebåd til skib. Dansk Søfarts Historie*, bind 1. Copenhagen.

Binford, L.R. 1962: Archaeology as Anthropology. *American Antiquity* 28 (2), 217–225.

Birkedahl Christensen, P. & Johansen, E. 1992: En handelsplads fra yngre jernalder og vikingetid ved Sebbersund. *Aarbøger for Nordisk Oldkyndighed og Historie* 1991, 199–229.

Bischoff, V. 2016: Vikingetidens sejl – form og proportion. In M. Ravn, L. Gebauer Thomsen, H. Lyngstrøm & E. Andersson Strand (eds.), *Vikingetidens Sejl*, 97–118. Arkæologiske Skrifter. Copenhagen & Roskilde.

Bischoff, V. & Jensen, K. 2001: Ladby II. The Ship. In A.C. Sørensen: *Ladby. A Danish Ship-Grave from the Viking Age*, 183–248. Ships and Boats of the North 3. Roskilde.

Bischoff, V., Englert, A., Nielsen, S., & Ravn, M. 2014: From Ship-Find to Sea-Going Reconstruction. Experimental Maritime Archaeology at the Viking Ship Museum in Roskilde. In J.R. Flores & R. P. Paardekooper (eds.): *Experiments Past. Histories of Experimental Archaeology*, 233–247. Leiden.

Bjørgo, N. 1965: Skipstypar i norrøne samtidssoger. *Sjøfartshistorisk årbok* 1965: 7–20.

Blakelock, E., Martinón-Torres, M., Veldhuijzen, H.A & Young, T. 2009: Slag inclusions in iron objects and the quest for provenance: an experiment and a case study. *Journal of Archaeological Science* 36: 1745–1757.

Bolton, T. 2009: *The Empire of Cnut the Great. Conquest and the Consolidation of Power in Northern Europe in Early Eleventh Century.* Leiden & Boston.

Bonde, N. 1984: Dendrokronologiske undersøgelser på skibstømmer fra Fribrødre Å på Falster. *Hikuin* 10, 275–278.

Bonde, N. 1998: *Dendrokronologisk undersøgelse af skibsvrag i 'Peberrenden' i Roskilde Fjord, ud for Skuldelev. Vrag 3: 'det lille handelsskib'.* NNU rapport 44b. Copenhagen.

Bonde, N. 1999: *Dendrokronologisk undersøgelse af skibsvrag i 'Peberrenden' i Roskilde Fjord, ud for Skuldelev. Vrag 2: 'det store krigsskib'.* NNU rapport 32. Copenhagen.

Bonde, N. 2010: *Dendrokronologisk undersøgelse af prøver fra historisk skibsvrag (vrag 6) fundet i 'Roskilde gl. havn'.* NNU rapport, 3. Copenhagen.

Bonde, N. & Stylegar, F.-A. 2011: Roskilde 6 – et langskib fra Norge. Proveniens og alder. *Kuml* 2011, 247–262.

Borg, J., Gustafsson, M. & Sjölin, M. 2000: *The story of the Viking-age ship from Äskekärr.* Gothenburg.

Bossen, C. 2006: War as Practice, Power and Processor: A Framework for the Analysis of War and Social Structural Change. In T. Otto, H. Thrane & H. Vandkilde (eds.): *Warfare and society. Archaeological and Social Anthropological Perspectives*, 89–102. Aarhus.

Brattli, T. & Johnsen, H. 1991: Noen kritiske kommentarer til den eksperimentelle arkeologien. In E. Backman & C. Fredriksson (eds.): *Experimentell Arkeologi. Rapport från Kontaktseminaret i Hällnäs, Västerbotten 8–14. Oktober 1989*, 49–52. Kontaktstencil 33. Umeå.

Breuning-Madsen, H., Balstrøm, T., Greve, M.H. & Jensen, N.H. 2013a: Jordbundsudvikling i danske landskaber. *Geoviden* 2013 (4), 2–5.

Breuning-Madsen, H., Bird, K.L., Elberling, B. & Lei, E.,B. 2013b: Jordbunden som landskabsdannende faktor. *Geoviden* 2013 (4), 6–8.

Brink, S. 2007: Geography, toponymy and political organization in early Scandinavia. I: J. Bately & A. Englert (eds.): *Ohthere's Voyages. A late 9ᵗʰ-century account of voyages along the coasts of Norway and Denmark and its cultural context*, 66–73. Roskilde.

Brink, S. 2012: *Vikingarnas slavar. Den nordiska trälldomen under yngre järnålder och äldsta medeltid.* Stockholm.

Brooks, N.P. 1979: England in the Ninth Century: The Crucible of Defeat. *Transactions of the Royal Historical Society* 29, 1–20.

Brorson Christensen, B. 1981: Landskabet ved Vorbasse. In R. Egevang, C. Ejlers, B. Friis, O. Højrup & E. Munksgaard (eds.): *Det skabende menneske, bind 1. Kultur-historiske skitser tilegnet P. V. Glob 20. februar 1981*, 102–111. Copenhagen.

Brødsgaard Larsen, M. 2009: *Krigerkultur eller managementkultur. Fastholdelse i forsvaret – en undersøgelse af stampersonellets arbejdsvilkår.* Rapport fra Dansk Institut for Militære Studier. Copenhagen.

Brøgger, A.W. & Shetelig, H. 1951: *The Viking Ships.* Oslo.

Bråthen, A. 1998: Datering av skeppet Äskekärr 1. *GASTen* 22, 13–15.

Buchwald, V. 1991: Jernfremstilling i Danmark i Middelalderen – lidt om bondeovne og kloder. *Aarbøger for nordisk Oldkyndighed og Historie* 1991, 265–286.

Buchwald, V. 1996: *Rapport 14.03.1996.* In Nationalmuseets rapportarkiv 080106, sb 6. Unpublished report. Copenhagen.

Buchwald, V. 2005: *Iron and steel in ancient times.* Historisk-filosofiske Skrifter 29. Copenhagen.

Buchwald, V. 2008: *Iron, steel and cast iron before Bessemer. The slag-analytical method and the role of carbon and phosphorus.* Historisk-filosofiske Skrifter 32. Copenhagen.

Buk-Swienty, T. 2010: *Dommedag Als. 29. Juni 1864. Kampen for Danmarks eksistens.* Copenhagen.

Carpenter, S. 1995: Nye funn. *Spor – fortidsnytt fra midt-norge* 1995 (2), 44–45.

Christensen, A.E. 1938: Danmarks Befolkning og Bebyggelse i Middelalderen. In A. Schück (ed.): *Befolkning i Middelalderen, Nordisk kultur II*, 1–57. Copenhagen.

Christensen, A.E. 1979: Gokstadskipets dekorative utstyr. *Universitetets Oldsaksamling 150 år. Jubilæumsårbok*, 145–149.

Christensen, A.E. 1985: Boat finds from Bryggen. In A. Hagen, K. Helle & A. Herteig (eds.): *The Bryggen Papers. Main series 1*, 47–280. Bergen, Oslo, Stavanger & Tromsø.

Christensen, A. E. 1995: Båtbygging, naturgitt desentralisering av et vigtig håndverk. In H. Gjøstein Resi (ed.): *Produksjon og samfunn. Om erverv, spesialisering og bosetning i Norden i 1. årtusen e. Kr. Beretning fra 2. nordiske jernaldersymposium på Granavolden Gjæstgiveri 7.–10. mai 1992*, 123–130. Varia 30. Oslo.

Christensen, A.E. 1996a: Trenagler – en vigtig sammenføyningsdetalj. *Marinarkæologisk nyhedsbrev fra Roskilde* 7, 20–21.

Christensen, A.E. 1996b: Proto-Viking, Viking and Norse Craft. In R. Gardiner & A.E. Christensen (eds.): *The earliest Ships. The Evolution of Boats into Ships*, 72–88. London.

Christensen, C.A. 1965a: Landvärn (Danmark). In J. Brøndsted, L.R. Jacobsen, G. Rona, J. Danstrup & A. Karker (eds.): *Kulturhistorisk leksikon for nordisk middelalder. Fra vikingetid til reformationstid, bind 10*, 305–308. Copenhagen.

Christensen, C.A. 1965b: Leidang (Danmark). In J. Brøndsted, L.R. Jacobsen, G. Rona, J. Danstrup & A. Karker (eds.): *Kulturhistorisk leksikon for nordisk middelalder. Fra vikingetid til reformationstid, bind 10*, 443–450. Copenhagen.

Christensen, T. 1993: Lejre Beyond Legend – The Archaeological Evidence. *Journal of Danish Archaeology* 10, 163–185.

Christensen, C. & Fischer Mortensen, M. 2010: Fribrødre Å – Palaeoecological investigations. In J. Skamby-Madsen & L. Klassen: *Fribrødre Å. A late 11th century ship-handling site on Falster*, 25–60. Århus.

Christie, O.H., Alfsen, B.E. & Rosenqvist, A.M. 1979: Opprinnelsen til nagler og spiker fra vikingtidsbåter funnet i Sørnorge. In O.H.J. Christie, B.E. Alfsen & A.M. Rosenqvist (eds.): *Universitetets Oldsaksamling 150 år, jubileums-årbok*, 173–180. Oslo.

Clausewitz, C., von [1832] 1986: *Om krig.* Bind I–III. Oversat og redigeret af Nils Berg. Copenhagen.

Coles, J. 1979: *Experimental Archaeology.* London/New York.

Contamine, Ph. 1996: *War in the Middle Ages.* Oxford & Cambridge.

Cooke, B. & Christiansen, C. 1999: Laboratory analyses at UMIST: Textiles of Seafaring – summary of Test Results. Unpublished report. Roskilde.

Cottrell, J.E., Munro, R. C., Tabbener, H.E., Gillies, A.C.M., Forrest, G.I., Deans, J.D. & Lowe, A.J. 2002: Distribution of chloroplast DNA variation in British oaks (Quercus robur and Q. petraea): the influence of postglacial colonisation and human management. *Forest Ecology and Management* 156, 181–195.

Crumlin-Pedersen, O. 1981: Viking shipbuilding and seamanship. In H. Bekker-Nielsen, P. Foote & O. Olsen (eds.): *Proceedings of the Eighth Viking Congress, Århus 24–31 August 1977*, 271–286. Odense.

Crumlin-Pedersen, O. 1984: Fotevik. De marinarkæologiske undersøgelser 1981 og 1982. In C. Bunte (ed.): *Pugna Forensis-? Arkeologiska undersökningar kring Foteviken, Skåne 1981–83*, 7–68. Malmö.

Crumlin-Pedersen, O. 1985: *Roar Ege af Roskilde – bygget 1982–84 i Roskilde – en nøjagtig kopi af et handelsskib fra vikingetiden.* An Unpublished manuscript for a brochure. Findes i Vikingeskibsmuseets arkiv vedrørende *Roar Ege*. Roskilde.

Crumlin-Pedersen, O. 1986: Aspects of Wood Technology in Medieval Shipbuilding. In O. Crumlin-Pedersen & M. Vinner (eds.): *Sailing into the Past. Proceedings of the International Seminar on Replicas of Ancient and medieval Vessels, Roskilde, 1984*, 138–149. Roskilde.

Crumlin-Pedersen, O. 1988: Gensyn med Skuldelev 5 – et ledingsskib? In Aa. Andersen (ed.): *Festskrift til Olaf Olsen på 60-års dagen den 7. juni 1988*, 137–156. Copenhagen.

Crumlin-Pedersen, O. 1996a: Studiet af det maritime kulturlandskab. In O. Crumlin-Pedersen, E. Porsmose & H. Thrane (eds.): *Atlas over Fyns kyst i jernalder, vikingetid og middelalder*, 10–20. Odense.

Crumlin-Pedersen, O. 1996b: Kystforsvaret. In O. Crumlin-Pedersen, E. Porsmose & H. Thrane (eds.): *Atlas over Fyns kyst i jernalder, vikingetid og middelalder*, 182–193. Odense.

Crumlin-Pedersen, O. 1997a: Large and small warships of the North. In A. Nørgård Jørgensen & B. L. Clausen (eds.): *Military Aspects of Scandinavian Society in a European Perspective, AD 1–1300. Papers from an International Research Seminar at the Danish National Museum, Copenhagen, 2–4 May 1996*, 184–194. Copenhagen.

Crumlin-Pedersen, O. 1997b: *Viking-Age Ships and Shipbuilding in Hedeby/Haithabu and Schleswig.* Ships & Boats of the North 2. Schleswig & Roskilde.

Crumlin-Pedersen, O. 1999a: Ships as indicators of trade in Northern Europe. In J. Bill & B. L. Clausen (eds.): *Maritime Topography and the Medieval Town. Papers from the 5th International Conference on Waterfront Archaeology in Copenhagen, 14–16 May 1998*, 11–20. Publications from the National Museum. Studies in archaeology & history 4. Copenhagen.

Crumlin-Pedersen, O. 2004: Nordic Clinker Construction. In F.M. Hocker & C.A. Ward (eds.): *The Philosophy of Shipbuilding. Conceptual approaches to the Study of Wooden Ships*, 37–63. Texas.

Crumlin-Pedersen, O. 2010: *Archaeology and the Sea in Scandinavia and Britain. A personal account.* Maritime Culture of the North 3. Roskilde.

Crumlin-Pedersen, O. 2012: Ikon eller realitet? Om 'sandhedsværdien' af vikingetidens skibsbilleder. *Aarbøger for Nordisk Oldkyndighed og Historie 2010*, 163–172.

Crumlin-Pedersen, O. & Olsen, O. (ed.) 2002: *The Skuldelev Ships I. Topography, History, Conservation and Display.* Ships and Boats of the North 4.1. Roskilde.

Crumlin-Pedersen, O. & Vinner, M. 1993: Roar og Helge af Roskilde – om at bygge og sejle med vikingeskibe. *Nationalmuseets Arbejdsmark 1993*, 11–29.

Daly, A. 1999: *Dendrokronologisk undersøgelse af skibsvrag, "Roskilde 3", fra Roskilde gamle havneområde.* NNU rapport, 33. Copenhagen.

Daly, A. 2007: *Timber, Trade and Tree-rings. A dendrochronological analysis of structural oak timber in Northern Europe, c. AD 1000 to c. AD 1650.* Unpublished Ph.D. thesis. University of Southern Denmark.

Daly, A. 2012: Skovens tilstand, med fokus på vikingetiden – årringsdata. Paper presented at the seminar: *Skoven som ressource. Et seminar omhandlende tømmer til skibsbygning i vikingetiden*, the Viking Ship Museum in Roskilde, Denmark, November 1.

Dam, P. 2009: Skovenes udbredelse før landboreformerne. *Landbohistorisk Tidsskrift 2009* (1), 51–88.

Dam, P. 2015: *Bebyggelser og stednavnetyper.* Navnestudier nr. 44. Copenhagen.

Damgård-Sørensen, T. in prep.: *Thoroughbred of the Sea. The Sea Stallion from Glendalough. Trial Voyage with a Longship.* Roskilde.

Damgård-Sørensen, T. & Sørensen A.C. (eds.) unpublished.: *The Skuldelev Ships II.* Manuscript archive. Viking Ship Museum. Rosk

Damgård-Sørensen, T., Nielsen, S. & Andersen, E. 2004: Fuldblod på havet. In N. Lund (ed.), *Beretning fra toogtyvende tværfaglige Vikingesymposium*, 5–50. Højbjerg.

Damgård-Sørensen, T., Christensen, C. & Busch, M. 2007: *Årsberetning 2006.* Roskilde.

Dennen, J.M.G., van der 1981: On War: Concepts, Definitions, Research Data – A Literature Revies and Biliography. *UNESCO Yearbook on Peace and Conflict Studies 1980*, 128–189.

Dobat, A.S. 2009: The state and the strangers: the role of external forces in a process of state formation in Viking Age south Scandinavia (ca. AD 900–1050). *Viking and medieval Scandinavia 5*, 65–104.

Egenberg, I. M. 1997: Kiln-Produced Tar. In W. Brzezinski & W. Piotrowski (eds.): *Proceedings of the First International Symposium on Wood Tar and Pitch*, 141–148. Warszawa.

Ejstrud, B. & Thomsen, B. 2012: *Hørrens rejse fra mark til mand. Forsøg på Ribe VikingeCenter.* Esbjerg.

Ejstrud, B., Andresen, S., Appel, A., Gjerlevsen, S. & Thomsen, B. 2011: *From Flax to Linen. Experiments with flax at Ribe Viking Centre.* Esbjerg.

Eldjarn, G. & Godal, J. 1988: *Nordlandsbåten og Åfjordsbåten. Bind 1. Båten i bruk. Segling, roing, fisking og vedlikehald.* Lesja.

Elsner, H. 1992: *Wikinger Museum Haithabu: Et portræt af en tidlig by.* Neumünster.

Englert, A. 2000: *Large Cargo Vessels in Danish Waters. AD 1000–1250.* Dissertation zur Erlangung des Doktorgrades der Philosophischen Fakultät der Christian-Albrechts-Universität zu Kiel. Roskilde & Kiel.

Englert, A. 2004: Naves Magnae – Den professionelle søhandels fartøjer. Store lastskibe i danske farvande 1000–1250 som vidnesbyrd om søhandelens professionalisering forud for hansetiden. In P. Carelli, L. Hermanson & H. Sanders (eds.): *Ett Annat 1100-Tal. Individ, kollektiv och kulturella mönster i medeltidens Danmark*, 111–119. Gothenburg & Stockholm.

Englert, A. 2006: Trial voyages as a method of experimental archaeology: The aspect of speed. In L. Blue, F. Hocker & A. Englert (eds.): *Connected by the Sea*, 35–42. Proceedings of the Tenth International Symposium on Boat and Ship Archaeology, Roskilde 2003. Oxford.

Englert, A. 2011: Rejsehastighed over Kattegat og Skagerrak i vikingetiden. In L. Appel & K. Langsted (eds.): *Ressourcer og Kultur-kontakter. Arkæologi rundt om Sagerrak og Kattegat*, 101–113. Kulturhistoriske skrifter fra Nordsjælland 1. Gilleleje.

Englert, A. 2012: Travel Speed in the Viking Age: Results of Trial Voyages with Reconstructed Ship Finds. In N. Günsenin (ed.): *Between Continents. Proceedings of the Twelfth Symposium on Boat and Ship Archaeology, Istanbul 2009*, 269–277. Istanbul.

Englert, A. 2015: *Large Cargo Ships in Danish Waters 1000–1250. Evidence of specialised merchant seafaring prior to the Hanseatic Period*. Ships and Boats of the North 7. Roskilde.

Englert, A. & Ossowski, W. 2009: Sailing in Wulfstan's wake: the 2004 trial voyage Hedeby-Gdansk with the Skuldelev 1 reconstruction, *Ottar*. In A. Englert & A. Trakadas (eds.): *Wulfstan's Voyage. The Baltic Sea region in the early Viking Age as seen from shipboard*, 257–270. Maritime Culture of the North 2. Roskilde.

Englert, A., Nielsen, S. & Ravn, M., 2013: Vikingetidens langskib og eksperimentel arkæologi. In M. Blom, M. Boritz, M. Broen, M. Danielsen, K.-J. Hemmersam, M. Kramm & C. Vollmond (eds.): *Vinkler på Vikingetiden*, 44–58. Copenhagen.

Erslev, K. S. A. [1898] 1972: *Valdemarerenes Storhedstid. Studier og Omrids*. Copenhagen.

Fabech, C. 1993: Skåne – et kulturelt og geografisk grænseland. *Tor, Tidskrift för arkeologi* 25: 201–245.

Falk, H. 1912: Altnordisches Seewesen. *Wörter und Sachen* 4, 1–122.

Falk, H. [1912] 1995: *Fornnordisk Sjöfart*. Oversat af Bo Varenius. Skärhamn.

Fentz, M. 1998: En hørskjorte fra 1000-årene. In J. Hjermind, M. Iversen & H. Krongaard Kristensen (eds.): *Viborg Søndersø 1000–1300. Byarkæologiske undersøgelser 1981 og 1984–85*, 249–266. Jysk Arkæologisk Selskabs Skrifter XXXIV. Århus.

Fentz, M. 1999: Dragter. In E. Roesdahl (ed.): *Dagligliv i Danmarks middelalder – en arkæologisk kulturhistorie*, 151–171. Århus.

Feveile, C. 2010: Landskabet omkring Ribe. In S., B. Christensen (ed.): *Ribe Bys Historie 1. 710–1520*, 20–25. Esbjerg.

Finderup, T. 2006a: *Værktøj*. Unpublished report. Roskilde.

Finderup, T. 2006b: History written in tool marks. In L. Blue, F. Hocker & A. Englert (eds.): *Connected by the Sea*, 21–26. Proceedings of the Tenth International Symposium on Boat and Ship Archaeology, Roskilde 2003. Oxford.

Flor, J. R. 2005: Positivisme. In F. Collin & S. Køppe (eds.): *Humanistisk Videnskabsteori*, 61–96. Copenhagen.

Forseth, L. 2003: Maktsentra og forskjeller mellom Østfold og Vestfold under jernalderen: en kildekritisk undersøkelse baseret på de arkeologiske funnene og fornminnene. In J.V. Sigurðsson & P.G. Norseng (eds.): *Over grenser. Østfold og Viken i yngre jernalder og middelalder*, 31–69. Oslo.

Frandsen, L.B. 2013: Hvad var vikingerne i Henne bange for? In H. S. Lyngstrøm & L.G. Thomsen (eds.): *Vikingetid i Danmark. tekster skrevet til Jørgen Poulsen i anledning af den eksperimentelle og formidlende arkæologi, som Vikingelandsbyen i Albertslund har praktiseret og udviklet fra 1992 til 2012*, 165–168. Copenhagen.

Frederiksen, Aa. 2009: *Nagler, værktøj og ankre. Arbejdsrapport, fra 2001, omhandlende planlægning, arbejdsgang og perspektiver i forbindelse med rekonstruktion af jerngenstande til Vikingeskibsmuseet i Roskilde*. Roskilde.

Fritzbøger, B. 2004: *A Windfall for the Magnates. The Development of Woodland Ownership in Denmark c. 1150–1830*. Odense.

Fritzbøger, B. 2011: Retrospective landscape analysis: Horns and Voldborg districts c. AD 1150–1850. In L. Boye (ed.): *The Iron Age on Zealand. Status and Perspectives*, 41–50. Copenhagen.

Frost, T. 1985: *From Tree to Sea. The building of a wooden steam drifter*. Suffolk.

Geijer, A. 1972: *Ur textilkonstens historia*. Lund.

Gelting, M. H. 1999: Det komparative perspektiv i dansk højmiddelalderforskning. Om Familia og familie, Lið, leding og landeværn. *Historisk Tidsskrift* 99, 146–188.

Gelting, M.H. 2007: The kingdom of Denmark. In N. Berend (ed.), *Christianization and the rise of Christian monarchy. Scandinavia, Central Europe and Rus' c. 900–1200*, 73–120. New York.

Gelting, M.H. 2012: Lund, Dalby og Bornholm: Politik og mission i biskop Eginos tid. In S. Borgehammar & J. Wienberg (eds.): *Locus celebris: Dalby kyrka, kloster och gård*, 101–111. Gothenburg/Stockholm.

Gillmor, C.M. 1985: Naval logistics of the cross-channel operation, 1066. *Anglo-Norman Studies* VII, 105–131.

Glastrup, J. 2010: Tjærebrænding i Finland – og limning af jernalderpotteskår i Ringe. *Nationalmuseets Arbejdsmark* 2010, 150–159.

Godal, J.B. 1990: Measurements, Figures and Formulas for the Interpretation of Western Norwegian Boats and Viking Ships. *Acta Borealia* 7 (2), 56–80.

Godal, J.B. 1994: Maritime archaeology beneath church roofs. In C. Westerdahl (ed.): *Crossroads in Ancient Shipbuilding. Proceedings of the Sixth International Symposium on Boat and Ship Archaeology, Roskilde 1991*, 271–278. Oxbow Monograph 40. Oxford.

Godal, J.B. 2012: Fin furuskog og lys. Paper presented at the seminar: *Skoven som ressource. Et seminar omhandlende tømmer til skibsbygning i vikingetiden*, the Viking Ship Museum in Roskilde, Denmark, November 1.

Grieg, S. 1928: Kongsgaarden. In A.W. Brøgger, H. Falk & Haa. Schetelig (eds.): *Osebergfundet*, bind 2, 1–286. Oslo.

Griffith, P. 1995: *The Viking Art of War*. London & Pennsylvania.

Gulatingslovi. Umsett frå gamalnorsk av Knut Robberstad i 1952. Norrøne Bokverk, 33. Oslo.

Gøgsig Jakobsen, J.G. & Dam, P. 2009: Nordvestsjællands kystbebyggelse fra vikingetid til ca. 1700. Årbog for kulturhistorien i Nordvestsjælland 2009, 11–45. Holbæk.

Haarnagel, W. 1979: *Die Grabung Feddersen Wierde. Metthode, Hausbau, Siedlungs- und Wirtschaftsformen sowie Sozialstruktur*. Wiesbaden.

Hald, M. 1950: *Olddanske tekstiler. Komparative tekstil- og dragthistoriske studier paa grundlag af mosefund og gravfund fra jernalderen*. Nordiske Fortidsminder 5. Copenhagen.

Hardt, N. 2003: Jernalderens og vikingetidens landbrug. In L.S. Madsen & O. Madsen (eds.): *Det Sønderjyske Landbrugs Historie. Jernalder, Vikingetid og middelalder*, 17–122. Haderslev.

Hasslöf, O. 1966: Sources of maritime history and methods of research. *Mariner's Mirror* 2, 127–144.

Hauksson, þ. 2007: Introduktion til Sverris saga. In J. Kristjánsson & þ. I. Gudjónsson (eds.): *Íslenzk Fornri, bind XXX, V-LXXXI*. Reykjavík.

Hedenstierna-Jonson, C. 2006: *The Birka Warrior. The material culture of a martial society*. Stockholm.

Heide, E. 2006: Låge og breie segl, likevel? Vurdert særleg ut frå seglkrympingsmåtar, etymologi og norrøne skriftlege kjelder. In T. Arisholm, K. Paasche & T.L. Wahl (eds.): *Klink og seil – festskrift til Arne Emil Christensen*, 165–174. Oslo.

Heide, E. 2012: Early Viking Age ship types and their terms. Paper presented at the seminar: The 13th International Symposium on Boat and Ship Archaeology, Amsterdam: Dutch Maritime Museum, 9th October.

Heide, V. 2006: Låge og breie segl, likevel? Ulike strategier for å kombinere framdrift med segl og årer. In T. Arisholm, K. Paasche & T.L. Wahl (eds.): *Klink og seil – festskrift til Arne Emil Christensen*, 175–185. Oslo.

Hellmuth Andersen, H. 1998: *Danevirke og kovirke. Arkæologiske undersøgelser 1861–1993*. Moesgård Museums skrifter. Højbjerg.

Hermanson, L. 2000: *Släkt, vänner och makt. En studie av elitens politiska kultur i 1100-talets Danmark*. Gothenburg.

Hill, J. N. & Gunn, J. 1977: Introducing the Individual in Prehistory. In J.N. Hill & J. Gunn (eds.): *The Individual in Prehistory. Studies of Variability in Style in Prehistoric Technologies*, 1–12. New York, San Francisco & London.

Hjardar, K. & Vike, V. 2014: *Vikinger i krig*. Aarhus.

Hjelm Petersen, A. 2012: *Kalfatringer fra Roskilde Havn*. Unpublished kandidat-dissertation. Copenhagen.

Hjulström, B., Isaksson, S. & Hennius, A. 2006: Organic geochemical evidence for pine tar production in Middle Eastern Sweden during the Roman Iron Age. *Journal of Archaeological Science* 33, 283–294.

Hoff, A. 1997: *Lov og Landskab. Landskabslovenes bidrag til forståelsen af landbrugs- og landskabsudviklingen i Danmark ca. 900–1250*. Århus.

Holm, P. forthcoming: Manning and Paying the Hiberno-Norse Dublin Fleet. In E. Purcell, P. MacCotter, J. Nyhan & J. Sheehan (eds.): *Clerics, Kings and Vikings. Essays on medieval Ireland*. Dublin.

Holmberg, B. & Skamby Madsen, J. 1998: Da kom en snekke… Havnepladser fra 1000- og 1100-tallet? *Kuml* 1997–98, 197–225.

Houts, E.M.C. van 1988: The ship list of William the Conqueror. *Anglo-Norman Studies* X, 159–183.

Howard, I. 2003: *Swein Forkbeard's Invasions and the Danish Conquest of England 991–1017*. Woodbridge.

Humbla, Ph. 1934: Båtfyndet vid Äskekärr. I: Ph. Humbla & H. Thomasson, Äskekärrsbåten, 1–21. Gothenburg.

Hutchinson, G. 1994: *Medieval Ships and Shipping*. Rutherford, Madison, Teaneck.

Hvid, C. & Ravn, M. 2016: Barkning og smøring af sejl – praktiske erfaringer samt refleksion over vikingetidens imprægnering af sejldug. In M. Ravn, L. Gebauer Thomsen, H. Lyngstrøm & E. Andersson Strand (eds.), *Vikingetidens Sejl*, 173–187. Arkæologiske Skrifter. Copenhagen & Roskilde.

Hybel, N. & Poulsen, B. 2007: *The Danish Resources c. 1000–1550. Growth and Recession*. Leiden & Boston.

Hägg, I. 1984: *Die Textilfunde aus dem Hafen von Haithabu*. Berichte über die Ausgrabungen in Haithabu Bericht 20. Neumünster.

Høgseth, H.B. 2013: The language of craftsmanship. In M. L. S. Sørensen & K. Rebay-Salisbury (eds.): *Embodied Knowledge. Perspectives on belief and technology*, 95–105. Oxford and Oakville.

Højrup, O. 1966: *Landbokvinden. Rok og kærne. Grovbrød og vadmel*. Copenhagen.

Højrup, T. 2002: *Dannelsens dialektik. Etnologiske udfordringer til det glemte folk*. Copenhagen.

Højrup, T. 2003: *State, Culture and Life-Modes. The Foundation of Life-Mode Analysis*. Aldershot & Burlington.

Haarnagel, W. 1979: *Die Grabung Feddersen Wierde. Methode, Hausbau, Siedlungs- und Wirtschafts-formen sowie Sozialstruktur*. Wiesbaden.

Haasum, S. 1989: *Svensk Marinarkeologi*. Arkeographica 3. Stockholm.

Ihlen, C. 1932: *Tjærebrenning i mile*. Oslo.

Indruszewski, G. 2004: *Man, Ship, Landscape. Ships and Seafaring in the Oder Mouth Area AD 400–1400. A case-study of an ideological context*. Studies in Archaeology & History Vol. 9. Copenhagen.

Indruszewski, G., Nilsson, M. & Wazny, T. 2006: The ships that connected the people and the people that commuted by ships: The western Baltic case-study. In L. Blue, F. Hocker & A. Englert (eds.): *Connected by the Sea*, 177–186. Proceedings of the Tenth International Symposium on Boat and Ship Archaeology, Roskilde 2003. Oxford.

Ingesman, P. 1999: Middelalderen – en introduktion. In P. Ingesman, U. Kjær, P.K. Madsen & J. Vellev (eds.): *Middelalderens Danmark. Kultur og samfund fra trosskifte til reformation*, 8–15. Copenhagen.

Ingstad, A. S. 1992a: Tekstilene i Osebergskibet. In A.E. Christensen, A.S. Ingstad, B. Myhre (eds.): *Osebergdronningens Grav. Vår arkeologiske nasjonalskatt i nytt lys*, 176–220. Oslo.

Ingstad, A. S. 1992b: Hva har tekstilene vært brugt til? In A.E. Christensen, A.S. Ingstad, B. Myhre (eds.): *Osebergdronningens Grav. Vår arkeologiske nasjonalskatt i nytt lys*, 209–223. Oslo.

Ingvardson, G.T. 2013: Alene i Østersøen? Bornholm i vikingetiden. In H.S. Lyngstrøm & L.G. Thomsen (eds.): *Vikingetid i Danmark. Tekster skrevet til Jørgen Poulsen i anledning af den eksperimentelle og formidlende arkæologi, som Vikingelandsbyen i Albertslund har praktiseret og udviklet fra 1992 til 2012*, 187–190. Copenhagen.

Jacobsen, L. & Moltke, E. 1942: *Danmarks runeindskrifter, Text & Atlas*. København.

Jahn, F. H. 1825: *Krigsvæsenet i Middelalderen, Norden især Danmarks Krigsvæsen i Middelalderen*. Copenhagen.

Jahnke, C. 2015: The Baltic Trade. In D.J. Harrald (ed.): *A companion to the Hanseatic League*, 194–240. Brill's Companions to European History, Vol. 8. Leiden.

Jakobsson, C. 2003: *Ett vikingaskeppsbygge. Äskekärrsskeppet – 934, Vidfamne – 1994. En rekonstruktion*. Gothenburg.

Jensen, H. 2002: *Trænagler. Materiale, antal tidsforbrug, mateialeforbrug, håndværker etc.* Unpublished report. Roskilde.

Jensen, J. 2004: *Danmarks Oldtid. Yngre jernalder og Vikingetid 400–1050 e.Kr.* Copenhagen.

Jensen, K. 1999: *Documentation and Analysis of Ancient Ships.* Centre for Maritime Archaeology & Department of Naval Architecture and Offshore Engineering. Lyngby.

Jensen, S. 1991: *Ribes Vikinger.* Ribe.

Jesch, J. 2001: *Ships and Men in the Late Viking Age. The Vocabulary of Runic Inscriptions and Skaldic Verse.* Woodbrigde.

Jesch, J. 2002: Sea-battles in skaldic poetry. In A. Nørgård Jørgensen, J. Pind, L. Jørgensen & B. Clausen (eds.): *Maritime Warfare in Northern Europe. Technology, organization, logistics and administration 500 BC – 1500 AD. Papers from an International Research Seminar at the Danish national museum, Copenhagen, 3–5 May 2000,* 57–64. Publications from the National Museum. Studies in archaeology & History 6. Copenhagen.

Jespersen, K. 1986: *Infra-Rød Spektroskopi.* Roskilde.

Jessen, M.D. 2015: Stave, stolper og Skagerrak – spørgsmål om ressourcer og arkitektur under Harald Blåtand. In A. Pedersen & S.M. Sindbæk (eds.): *Et fælles hav – Skagerrak og Kattegat i vikingetiden,* 188–209. Seminar på Nationalmuseet, Copenhagen, 19.–20. September 2012. Copenhagen.

Jessen, C. & Stylegar, F.-A. 2012: Ødegården Sosteli i Åseral fra romertid til vikingtid. *Viking,* 2012, 131–144.

Johannsen, V. K., Nord-Larsen, T., Riis-Nielsen, T, Suadicani, K. Jørgensen, B.B. 2013: *Skove og plantager 2012.* Institut for Geovidenskab og Naturforvaltning, Københavns Universitet. Frederiksberg.

Johnson, L.L. 1978: A History of Flint-Knapping Experimentation, 1838–1976. *Current Anthropology* 19 (2), 337–372.

Jomsvikingernes Saga. Oversættelse, indledning og noter ved Helle Degnbol og Helle Jensen i 1978. Copenhagen.

Jouttijärvi, A. 1996: Forhistoriske "højovne" – forsøg med oldtidens jernudvinding. In M. Meldgaard & M. Rasmussen (eds.): *Arkæologiske eksperimenter i Lejre,* 81–88. Copenhagen.

Jöns, H. 1997: *Frühe Eisengewinnung in Joldelund, Kr. Nordfriesland. Ein Beitrag zur Siedlungs- und Technikgeschichte Schleswig-Holsteins. Teil 1: Einführung, Naturraum, Prospektionsmethoden und archäologische Untersuchungen.* Bonn.

Jönsson, E. 2003: *Pollenanalytisk studie av råhumusprofiler från Säröhalvön i norra Halland.* Unpublished student report in geology at Lunds Universitet 167. Lund.

Jørgensen, B. 2008: *Danske stednavne.* Copenhagen.

Jørgensen, L. 2008: Manor, Cult and Market at Lake Tissø. In S. Brink & N.Price (eds.): *The Viking World,* 77–82. London & New York.

Jørgensen, S. 1989: Mosegeologiske og pollenanalytiske Undersøgelser ved Pine Mølle-Dæmningen (1973) og Trelleborg (1975). *Aarbøger for Nordisk Oldkyndighed og Historie* 1989, 60–81.

Kalmring, S. 2005: Ein Snekke-name in Wagrien? Snikrode und sein umland. *Archäologisches korrespondenzblatt* 35, 263–272.

Kalmring, S. 2010: *Der Hafen von Haithabu.* Neumünster.

Karlsson, S. 2000: Kan medeltida järnhantering i norra Skåne spåras med hjälp av pollenanalys. In A. Ödman (ed.): *Järn. Wittsjöskog-konferensen 1999,* 125–149. Institute of Archaeology. Report Series 75. Lund.

Kastholm, O. T. 2009: De gotlandske billedsten og rekonstruktion af vikingetidens sejl. *Aarbøger for Nordisk Oldkyndighed og Historie* 2005, 99–159.

Kastholm, O.T. 2016: Sejlform og skibstype – tradition og fornyelse. In M. Ravn, L. Gebauer Thomsen, H. Lyngstrøm & E. Andersson Strand (eds.), *Vikingetidens Sejl, 119–136.* Arkæologiske Skrifter. Copenhagen & Roskilde.

Kelly, F. 2000: *Early Irish Farming. A study based mainly on the law-texts of the 7th and 8th centuries AD.* Dublin.

Klassen, L. 2010: The finds and their interpretation. In *Fribrødre Å. A late 11th century ship-handling site on Falster,* 61–465. Århus.

Klassen, L. 2011: Fribrødre Å på Falster. Aktiviteter med skibe i 1000-tallet og deres historiske kontekst. Paper presented at the seminar: *Vikingeskibsmuseets Venneforenings foredrag,* the Viking Ship Museum in Roskilde, Denmark, March 24.

Kloster, R. 1972: Håndverksbygden og bygdehåndverkeren. In S. Svensson (ed.): *Nordisk folkkonst,* 126–143. Lund.

Kolstrup, E. 2009: Vegetational and environmental history during the Holocene in the Esbjerg area, west Jutland, Denmark. *Vegetation history and archaeobotany* 18, 351–369.

Kristjánsson, L. 1982: Íslenzkir Sjávarhættir, bind II. Reykjavík.

Körber-Grohne, U. 1977: Botanische Untersuchungen des Tauwerks der frühmittelalterlichen Siedlung Haithabu und Hinweise zur Unterscheidung einheimischer Gehölzbaste. *Berichte über die Ausgrabungen in Haithabu* 11, 64–111. Neumünster.

Larsen, A.-C. (ed.) 1994: *Kongehallen fra Lejre – et rekonstruktionsprojekt.* International workshop 25.–27. November 1993 på Historisk-Arkæologisk Forsøgscenter, Lejre, om rekonstruktionen af vikingehallen fra Gl. Lejre og et vikingetidsmiljø. Lejre.

Laur, W. 1992: *Historisches Ortsnamen-Lexikon von Schleswig-Holstein.* Neumünster.

Lave, J. & Wenger, E. 1991: *Situated Learning. Legitimate Peripheral Participation.* Cambridge.

Lemonnier, P. 1980: *Les salines de l'Quest. Logique technique, logique sociale.* Paris.

Leroi-Gourhan, A. 1965: *Le Geste et la Parole II. La Memoire et les Rytmes.* Paris.

Lightfoot, A. & Aarø, M. 1998: *Registrering av Ullseil.* Unpublished report. Roskilde.

Lihammer, A. 2007: *Bortom riksbildningen. Människor, landskap och makt I sydöstra Skandinavien.* Lund Studies in Historical Archaeology 7. Lund.

Lund, N. 1991: Denemearc, tanmarkar but and tanmarka ala. In I. Wood & N. Lund (eds): *Peoples and Places in Northern Europe 500–1600,* 161–169. Woodbridge.

Lund, N. 1996: *Lið, leding og landeværn. Hær og samfund i Danmark i ældre middelalder.* Roskilde.

Lund, N. 2003: Naval Power in the Viking Age and in high medieval Denmark. In J.B. Hattendorf & R.W. Unger (eds.): *War at Sea in the Middle Ages and the Renaissance,* 25–34. Woodbridge.

Lundström, P. 1981: *De kommo vida… Vikingars hamn vid Paviken på Gotland.* Stockholm.

Lüdtke, H. 1987: Die Keramik von Hollingstedt. *Berichte über die Ausgrabungen in Haithabu* 25, 9–82. Neumünster.

Lyngstrøm, H.S. 2002: *Myremalmens mestre. Ved jernalderbondens ovn og esse.* Forsøg med fortiden 8°. Lejre.

Lyngstrøm, H.S. 2008: *Dansk Jern. En kulturhistorisk analyse af fremstilling, fordeling og forbrug.* Nordiske Fortidsminder, Serie C, bind 5. Copenhagen.

Lyngstrøm, H. S. 2011a: Iron from Zealandic bog iron ore. In L. Boye (ed): *The Iron Age on Zealand. Status and Perspectives,* 139–145. Copenhagen.

Lyngstrøm, H.S. 2011b: Vestjyske jernalderbønders råstofudnyttelse. Myremalmen mellem landskab og bebyggelse. In N.A. Møller, S.S. Qvistgaard & S. Frydenlund Jensen (eds.): *Nyt fra Vestfronten. Nord- og vestjyske bebyggelser fra ældre jernalder,* 113–121. Beretning fra et colloquium i Ribe 2010. Arkæologiske Skrifter 10. Copenhagen.

Lyngstrøm, H.S. 2012: På sporet af en god historie – Robert Thomsen, stålværket i Varde og det gamle jern. *Opdatering, Årbog for Museet for Varde By og Omegn og Ringkøbing-Skjern Museum* 2011, 169–175. Skjern.

Lyngstrøm, H.S. 2013a: Mellem formidling og forskning – jern, jernudvinding og BBC2 på Herning Museum. *Museum Midtjylland. Midtjyske fortællinger* 2012, 135–143.

Lyngstrøm, H.S. 2013b: Slaggeaftapningsovne i Danmark, udgravninger og forsøg. In B. Rundberget, J.H. Larsen & T.H. Borse Haraldsen (eds.): *Ovnskronologi og ovnstypologi i den nordiske jernvinna,* 119–133. Seminar i Kittilbu, 16.–18. juni 2009. Oppland.

Lyngstrøm, H.S. 2015: *En meget mærkelig mand. Jernforskeren Robert Thomsen.* Aarhus.

Lyons, S. 2014: Wood use, management and local woodland. In M. F. Hurley & C. Brett (eds.): *Archaeological Excavations at South Main Street 2003–2005,* 448–470. Cork.

Lystrup Nielsen, H.-E. 1985: Krig. In B. Heurlin & B. Nørretranders (eds.): *Veje til fred. Håndbog i sikkerhed og nedrustning,* 54–68. Copenhagen.

McCarthy, B. 2013: *Pirates of Baltimore. From the Middle Ages to the Seventeenth Century.* Baltimore.

McGrail, S. 1987: *Ancient boats in NW Europe. The archaeology of water transport to AD 1500.* London.

Magnus, O. 1998a: *Tovværk i vikingetid og Middelalder.* Unpublished report. Roskilde.

Magnus, O. 1998b: 5.12. Tovværk. In J. Hjermind, M. Iversen & H. Krongaard Kristensen (eds.): *Viborg Søndersø 1000–1300. Byarkæologiske undersøgelser 1981 og 1984–85,* 271–275. Viborg Stiftsmuseums skriftrække 2. Jysk Arkæologisk Selskabs Skrifter XXXIV. Aarhus.

Magnus, O. 1999: *Projekt træbast.* Unpublished report. Roskilde.

Magnus, O. 2006: Reconstruction of rope for the copy of Skuldelev 2: Rope in the Viking Period. In L. Blue, F. Hocker & A. Englert (eds.): *Connected by the Sea,* 27–34. Proceedings of the Tenth International Symposium on Boat and Ship Archaeology, Roskilde 2003. Oxford.

Magnus, O. 2008: *Sif Ege. Lindebastprojekt.* Unpublished report. Frederiksund.

Malmros, R. 1988: Den danske ledingsflådes størrelse. In P. Enemark, P. Ingesman & J.V. Jensen (eds.): *Kongemagt og samfund i middelalderen. Festskrift til Erik Ulsig på 60-årsdagen 13. februar 1988,* 19–39. Århus.

Malmros, R. 2010: *Vikingernes syn på militær og samfund. Belyst gennem skjaldenes fyrstedigtning.* Århus.

Mannering, U. 1996: Oldtidens brændenældeklæde. Forsøg med fremstilling af brændenældegarn. I: M. Meldgaard & M. Rasmussen (eds.): *Arkæologiske eksperimenter i Lejre,* 73–80. Copenhagen.

Marsden, P. 1994: *Ships of the Port of London. First to eleventh centuries AD.* London.

Martens, I. 1995: Deltidsspesialist og utkantbonde. Presentasjon av et forskningsprosjekt. In H.G. Resi (ed.): *Produksjon og samfunn. Om erverv, spesialisering og bosetning i Norden i 1. årtusen e. Kr. Beretning fra 2. nordiske jernaldersymposium på Granavolden Gjæstgiveri 7.–10. mai 1992,* 175–181. Varia 30. Oslo.

Mikkelsen, V.M. 1949: *Præstø Fjord. The Development of the Post-Glacial Vegetation and a Contribution to the History of the Baltic Sea.* Copenhagen.

Miller, H. 1889: *My School and Schoolmasters or the Story of My Education.* Edinburgh.

Moltesen, P. 1988: *Skovtræernes ved og dets anvendelse.* Copenhagen.

Murphy, M. & Potterton, M. 2010: *The Dublin region in the Middle Ages: Settlement, land-use and economy.* Dublin.

Myking, T., Hertzberg, A. & Skrøppa, T. 2005: History, manufacture and properties of lime bast cordage in northern Europe. *Forestry* 78 (1), 65–71.

Myrhøj, H.M. 2005: Skibstømmer. In M. Svart Kristiansen (ed): *Tårnby. Gård og landsby gennem 1000 år,* 343–347. Jysk Arkæologisk Selskabs Skrifter 54. Højbjerg.

Müller, S. 1884: Mindre Bidrag til den forhistoriske Archæologis Methode II. Den archæologiske Sammenligning som Grundlag for Slutning og Hypothese. *Aarbøger for nordisk Oldkyndighed og Historie* 1884, 183–203.

Møller, P.F. 1992: Naturskov i Danmark. In K. Olesen (ed.): *Dansk Jagt- og Skovbrugsmuseum 1942–1992,* 49–64. Hørsholm.

Møller, P. F. 2012: Egen og skoven i Vikingetiden. Paper presented at the seminar: *Skoven som ressource. Et seminar omhandlende tømmer til skibsbygning i vikingetiden,* the Viking Ship Museum in Roskilde, Denmark, November 1.

Møller Hansen, K. & Høier, H. 2000: Næs – en vikingetidsbebyggelse med hørproduktion. *Kuml* 2000, 59–89.

Möller-Wiering, S. 1997: Appendix I. Fibre analysis of caulking materials found at Hedeby and Schleswig. In O. Crumlin-Pedersen (ed.): *Viking-Age Ships and Shipbuilding in Hedeby/Haithabu and Schleswig,* 304–305. Ships & Boats of the North 2. Schleswig & Roskilde.

Möller-Wiering, S. 2002: *Segeltuch und Emballage. Textilien im mittelalterlichen Warentransport auf Nord- und Ostsee.* Rahden.

Nicklasson, P. 2001: *Strävsamma bönder och sturska stormän. Stafsinge och Halland från bronsålder till medeltid.* Acta Archaeologica Lundensia, Series in 8°, No. 35. Stockholm.

Nielsen, J. N. 2002: *Sebbersund. Handel, håndværk og kristendom ved Limfjorden.* Aalborg.

Nielsen, S. 2002: *Fremstilling af milebrændt tjære i Finland. En tjæremile i Latiiva, juni 2002.* Unpublished report. Roskilde

Nielsen, S. 2003: *Havknarren.* Unpublished report. Roskilde.

Nielsen, S. 2011: The *Sea Stallion from Glendalough*: Reconstructing a Viking-Age longship. In K. Staubermann (ed.): *Reconstructions: Recreating Science and Technology of the Past,* 59–82. Edinburgh.

Nielsen, S. 2012: Skibet og skoven – skibstypers afhængighed af tilgængelige ressourcer. Paper presented at the seminar: *Skoven som ressource. Et seminar omhandlende tømmer til skibsbygning i vikingetiden*, the Viking Ship Museum in Roskilde, Denmark, November 1.

Nielsen, S. 2013a: Hvor mange timer går der på et langskib? In H.S. Lyngstrøm & L.G. Thomsen (eds.): *Vikingetid i Danmark. Tekster skrevet til Jørgen Poulsen i anledning af den eksperimentelle og formidlende arkæologi, som Vikingelandsbyen i Albertslund har praktiseret og udviklet fra 1992 til 2012*, 141–144. Copenhagen.

Nielsen, S. 2013b: Hvor mange timer går der på et langskib? Paper presented at the seminar: *Vikingeskibsmuseets Venneforenings foredrag*, the Viking Ship Museum in Roskilde, Denmark, April 18.

Nielsen, V. 1993: *Jernalderens Pløjning. Store Vildmose*. Hjørring.

Nilsson, T. 1964: Standardpollendiagramme und C14-datierungen aus dem Ageröds Mosse im Mitteleren Schonen. *Lunds Universitets Årsskrift* 59 (7), 1–52. Lund.

Nyberg, G.G. 1984: Eine Schaftrolle aus Haithabu als Teil eines Trittwebstuhls mit waagerecht gespannter Kette. In C. Radtke (ed.): *Berichte über die Ausgrabungen in Haithabu* 19, 145–150. Neumünster.

Nýlen, E. 1986: The *Krampmacken* Project. In O. Crumlin-Pedersen & M. Vinner (eds.): *Sailing into the Past. Proceedings of the International Seminar on Replicas of Ancient and Medieval Vessels, Roskilde, 1984*, 104–113. Roskilde.

Nørgård, A. 2009a: *Vævning af sejldugsprøver på opstadvæv. Udført på Vikingeskibsmuseet i Roskilde i 1999*. Roskilde.

Nørgård, A. 2009b: *Oselvens uldsejl*. In M. Ravn (ed.): *Et uldsejl til Oselven. Arbejdsrapport om fremstillingen af et uldsejl til en traditionel vestnorsk båd*, 15–60. Roskilde.

Nørgård, A. 2016: Store og små sejl – tidsforbrug ved spinding og vævning. In M. Ravn, L. Gebauer Thomsen, H. Lyngstrøm & E. Andersson Strand (eds.), *Vikingetidens Sejl, 77–95*. Arkæologiske Skrifter. Copenhagen & Roskilde.

Odgaard, B. V. 1990: Vestdanske lyngheders oprindelse og fortidige udnyttelse, *Bebyggelseshistorisk Tidsskrift* 19, 117–129.

Odgaard, B. V. 1994: *The Holocene vegetation history of northern West Jutland, Denmark.* Opera Botanica 123. Copenhagen.

Odgaard, B.V. 2000: Fra skov til hede: vegetationens historie i Ulfborg herred. In K. Dalsgaard, P. Eriksen, J.V. Jensen & J.R. Rømer (eds.): *Mellem Hav og Hede. Landskab og bebyggelse i Ulfborg herred indtil 1700*, 28–35. Aarhus.

Odgaard, B.V. & Nielsen, A.B. 2009: Udvikling i arealdækning i perioden 0–1850. Pollen og landskabshistorie. In B. Odgaard & J.R. Rømer (ed.): *Danske landbrugslandskaber gennem 2000 år. Fra digevoldinger til støtteordninger*, 41–58. Aarhus.

Olsen, B. 1997: *Fra ting til tekst. Teoretiske perspektiv i arkeologisk forskning.* Oslo.

Olsen, O. & Crumlin-Pedersen, O. 1969: *Fem vikingeskibe fra Roskilde Fjord.* Roskilde.

Olsson, I. 1972: Snäck-namn på Gotland. *Fornvännen* 67, 180–208.

Oppermann, A. 1922: *Skovfyr I Midt- og Vestjylland. Spredte Studier.* Det Forstlige Forsøgsvæsen i Danmark. Udgivet ved Den Forstlige Forsøgskommission, Sjette Bind, Hlæfte 2. Copenhagen.

Orning, H.J. 2008: *Unpredictability and Presence. Norwegian Kingship in the High Middle Ages.* Leiden & Boston.

Ossowski, W. 2010: *Przemiany w szkutnictwie rzecznym w Polsce.* Gdansk.

O'Sullivan, A. 1994: Trees, woodland and woodsmanship in early medieval Ireland. In J.H. Dickson & R. Mill (eds.): *Plants and people. Economic botany in northern Europe AD 800–1800*, 674–681. Edinburgh.

Pedersen, A. 2014: Skagerrak and Kattegat in the Viking Age – Borders and Connecting Links. In H.C. Gulløv (ed.): *Northern Worlds – landscapes, interactions and dynamics. Research at the National Museum of Denmark.* Proceedings of the Northern Worlds Conference. Copenhagen 28–30 November 2012. Studies in Archaeology & History Vol. 22. Copenhagen.

Pelegrin, J. 1990: Prehistoric lithic technology: some aspects of research. *Archaeological Review from Cambridge* 9 (1), 116–125.

Pentz, P. 2014: De lange skibes tid. *Skalk* 2014 (3), 6–10.

Persson, C. 2013: Hur gjorde vikingarna tågvirke? In H.S. Lyngstrøm & L.G. Thomsen (eds.): *Vikingetid i Danmark. tekster skrevet til Jørgen Poulsen i anledning af den eksperimentelle og formidlende arkæologi, som Vikingelandsbyen i Albertslund har praktiseret og udviklet fra 1992 til 2012*, 145–148. Copenhagen.

Petersen, O. 1957: *Materialelære for træskibs- og bådebyggere.* Odense.

Planke, T. 2006: Lave og brede seil allikevel? – En diskusjon av paradigmer og tolkninger av kildegrunnlaget. In T. Arisholm, K. Paasche & T.L. Wahl (eds.): *Klink og seil – festskrift til Arne Emil Christensen*, 187–204. Oslo.

Poulsen, B. 2003: Middelalderens fødsel – tiden 1000–1340 – samfund og mennesker. In L.S. Madsen & O. Madsen (eds.): *Det Sønderjyske Landbrugs Historie. Jernalder, Vikingetid og middelalder*, 375–433. Haderslev.

Poulsen, J. 2005: *Salshuset – fra drøm til virkelighed.* Albertslund.

Price, N.S. 2002: *The Viking Way. Religion and War in Late Iron Age Scandinavia.* Uppsala.

Rackham, O. 2003: *Ancient Woodland: Its History, Vegetation and Uses in England.* Colvend.

Rahbek, V.A. 1980: *Et julekort fra A/S Dansk Rørindustri og A/S Ribe Jernindustri.*

Randsborg, K. 1980: *The Viking Age in Denmark. The Formation of a State.* London.

Randsborg, K. 1998: Offensive armies and navies. *Acta Archaeologica* 69, 163–174.

Rasmussen, M. 2001: Experiments in Archaeology – A View from Lejre, an "Old" Experimental Centre. *Zetschrift für Schweizerische Archäologie und Kunstgeschichte* 58 (I), 3–10.

Rasmussen, M. 2007: Eksperimental arkæologi. Her og der og alle vegne… *Arkæologisk Forum* 17, 13–18.

Rasmussen, P., Hansen, H.J. & Nielsen, B. 1998: Kulturlandskabets udvikling i et langtidsperspektiv. To sjællandske områder gennem de sidste 6000 år. *Nationalmuseets arbejdsmark* 1998, 101–114.

Ravn, M. 2012a: Maritim læring i vikingetiden. Om praksisfællesskabets marginale deltagere. *Kuml* 2012, 137–149.

Ravn, M. 2012b: Maritime praksisfællesskaber – skabelse af produktionsmåder. I: H.S. Lyngstrøm & M. Ravn (eds): *Produktionen, Smedens Rum 4,* 13–23. Arbejdsrapport fra det fjerde seminar i netværket Smedens Rum 14. marts 2012. Arkæologiske Skrifter 11. Copenhagen.

Ravn, M. 2013: Mellemråberen – kommunikation om bord på vikingetidens langskibe. I: H. Lyngstrøm & L.G. Thomsen (eds.): *Vikingetid i Danmark. Tekster skrevet til Jørgen Poulsen i anledning af den eksperimentelle og formidlende arkæologi, som Vikingelandsbyen i Albertslund har praktiseret og udviklet 1992 til 2012,* 157–160. Copenhagen.

Ravn, M. 2014: *Bygning og brug af skibe til krigsførelse i 1000-tallets danske rige.* Ph.d.-afhandling. Saxo-Instituttet, Copenhagens Universitet & Vikingeskibsmuseet i Roskilde. Copenhagen.

Ravn, M. 2015a: Begrebsparret emisk og etisk – en refleksiv brug af betegnelser. *Arkæologisk Forum* 32, 22–26.

Ravn, M. 2015b: Tradition as process. Reflections on Viking Age shipbuilding. In the proceedings from the international conference: The Baltic Sea a Mediterranean of North Europe. In the Light of Geographical, Archaeological, Historical and Natural Science Research. From Ancient to Early Medieval Times, 63–68. Gdańsk.

Ravn, M. 2016: Om bord på vikingetidens mandskabsskibe – en eksperimentalarkæologisk analyse af besætningsorganisation og kommunikation. *Kuml* 2016, 131–152.

Ravn, M. 2017: Building War Fleets: Investigating resource management in Late Viking Age Denmark. *International Symposium on Boat and Ship Archaeology 14. Baltic and beyond. Change and continuity in shipbuilding,* 237-242. Gdansk.

Ravn, M., Bischoff, V., Englert, A. & Nielsen, S. 2011: Recent Advances in Post-Excavation Documentation, Reconstruction, and Experimental Maritime Archaeology. In A. Catsambis, B. Ford & D.L. Hamilton (eds.): *The Oxford Handbook of Maritime Archaeology,* 232–249. New York.

Ravn, M., Gebauer Thomsen, L., Lyngstrøm, H. & Andersson Strand, E. (eds.) 2016: *Vikingetidens Sejl.* Arkæologiske Skrifter. Copenhagen & Roskilde

Rectitudines singularum personarum. Oversat til dansk af Niels Lund i 2015a. In T. Christensen 2015: *Lejre bag myten – de arkæologiske udgravninger,* 239–241. Højbjerg.

Remarque, E.M. [1928] 2014: *Intet nyt fra Vestfronten.* Copenhagen.

Reynolds, S. 1977: *An Introduction to the History of English Medieval Towns.* Oxford.

Reynolds, S. 1994: *Fiefs and Vassals. The Medieval Evidence Reinterpreted.* Oxford.

Rieck, F. 2004: The anchor from Sct. Nicolaigade in Ribe. In M. Bencard, A. Kann Rasmussen & H. Brinch Madsen (eds.): *Ribe Excavations 1970–76, Vol. 5,* 173–182. Jutland Archaeological Society publications 46. Højbjerg.

Robertsson, A.-M. 1973: *Late-Glacial and Pre-Boreal pollen and diatom diagrams from Skurup, southern Scania.* Series C: Avhandlingar och uppsatser – Sweden, Geologiska Undersökningen. Uppsala.

Rodger, N.A.M. 1995: Cnut's Geld and the Size of Danish Ships. *The English Historical Review* 110 (436), 392–403.

Roesdahl, E. 1987: *Vikingernes verden. Vikingerne hjemme og ude.* Copenhagen.

Roesdahl, E. 1999: Vikingetid og trosskifte (800–1050). In P. Ingesman, U. Kjær, P.K. Madsen & J. Vellev (eds.): *Middelalderens Danmark. Kultur og samfund fra trosskifte til reformation,* 16–27. Copenhagen.

Roesdahl, E., Sindbæk, S. M. & Pedersen, A. (eds.) 2014: *Aggersborg i vikingetiden. Bebyggelsen og borgen.* Højbjerg.

Rogers, P.W. 1997: *Textile Production at 16–22 Coppergate.* The Archaeology of York. Volume 17: The Small Finds. York.

Rosborn, S. 2004: *Den skånska historien. Vikingar.* Foteviken.

Rose, S. 2002: *Medieval Naval Warfare 1000–1500.* London & New York.

Rothe, T., J. 1781: *Nordens Staetsforfatning før Lehnstiden, og da Odelskab med Folke-friehed i Lehnstiden og da Birkerettighed, Hoverie, Livegenskab med Aristokratie. 1. Deel.* Copenhagen.

Rothe, T.J. 1782: *Nordens Staetsforfatning før Lehnstiden, og da Odelskab med Folkefriehed i Lehnstiden og da Birkerettighed, Hoverie, Livegenskab med Aristokratie. 2. Deel.* Copenhagen.

Rud, M. 2008: *Bayeux-tapetet og slaget ved Hastings 1066.* Copenhagen.

Rundberget, B. 2012: Østnorsk jernutvinning i sen vikingtid og middelalder – særegen metode og kontrollert overskudd. In H.S. Lyngstrøm & M. Ravn (eds.): *Produktionen, Smedens Rum 4,* 55–69. Arbejdsrapport fra det fjerde seminar i netværket Smedens Rum 14. marts 2012. Arkæologiske Skrifter 11. Copenhagen.

Rundberget, B. 2015: Sørskandinavisk jernutvinning I vikingetiden – lokal produksjon eller handelsprodukt? In A. Pedersen & S. M. Sindbæk (eds.): *Et fælles hav – Skagerrak og Kattegat i vikingetiden,* 168–187. Seminar på Nationalmuseet, Copenhagen, 19.–20. September 2012. Copenhagen.

Ryder, M.L. 1983: The primitive breeds of domestic sheep of Europe. In M. Kubasiewicz (ed.): *Proceedings of the 3rd International Archaeozoological Conference, Poland 1978,* 533–558. Szczecin.

Sands, R. 1997: *Prehistoric Woodworking. The Analysis and Interpretation of Bronze and Iron Age Toolmarks.* London.

Sawyer, P.H. 1962 [1971]: *The Age of the Vikings.* London.

Sawyer, P.H. 2002: *Da Danmark blev Danmark. Fra ca. år 750 til ca. år 1050. Politiken & Gyldendals Danmarkshistorie* 3. Copenhagen.

Saxo Grammaticus, *Gesta Danorum. Danmarkshistorien:* Latinsk tekst udgivet af Karsten Friis-Jensen. Dansk oversættelse ved Peter Zeeberg. Copenhagen 2005.

Schmidt, H. 1993: Reconstruction of the Lejre Hall. *Journal of Danish Archaeology* 10, 186–190.

Schjødt, J. P. 1995: The Ship in Old Norse Mythology and Religion. In O. Crumlin-Pedersen & B. M. Thye (eds.): *The Ship as Symbol in Prehistoric and Medieval Scnadinavia,* 20–24. Copenhagen.

Schjødt, P. J. 2003: War, state and society. In L. Jørgensen, B. Storgaard & L.G. Thomsen (eds.): *The spoils of victory. The North in the shadow of the Roman Empire,* 90–102. Copenhagen.

Schou Jørgensen, M. 1997: Vikingetidsbroen i Ravning Enge – nye undersøgelser. *Nationalmuseets Arbejdsmark* 1997, 74–87.

Shetelig, H. 1917: Skibet. Skibets tilstand – optagelse og transport. Restaurering. In A.W. Brøgger, H. Falk & Haa. Shetelig (eds.): *Osebergfundet* 1, 283–366. Kristiania.

Shetelig, H. 1929: Karakteristikk av fundet. Andre myrfund av fartøier. In Haa. Shetelig & F. Johannessen: *Kvalsundfundet og andre norske myrfund av fartøier*, 34–56. Bergen.

Sehested, N.F.B. 1884: Archæologiske Undersøgelser 1878–1881. Copenhagen.

Sigurðsson, J. V. 2003: Viken og fullføringen av rikssamlingen. In J. Viðar Sigurðsson & P.G. Norseng (eds.): *Over grenser. Østfold og Viken i yngre jernalder og middelalder*, 7–29. Skriftserie nr. 5. Oslo.

Sigurðsson, J. V. 2005: Høvdingene, storkirkene og den litterære aktiviten på Island fram til ca. 1300. In S. Imsen (ed.): *Den kirkehistoriske Utfordring*, 181–196. Trondheim.

Sindbæk, S. M. 2008: Kulturelle forskelle, sociale netværk og regionalitet i vikingtidens arkæologi. *Hikuin* 35, 63–84.

Skamby Madsen, J. 1984: Et skibsværft fra sen vikingetid/tidlig middelalder ved Fribrødreå på Falster. *Hikuin* 10, 261–274.

Skamby Madsen, J. 1995: Leding. *Skalk* 1995 (4), 5–11.

Skamby Madsen, J. 2010: Archaeological investigations along the Fribrødre River, 1982–93. In J. Skamby Madsen & L. Klassen: *Fribrødre Å. A late 11th century ship-handling site on Falster*, 13–22. Højbjerg.

Skamby Madsen, J. & Klassen, L. 2010: *Fribrødre Å. A late 11th century ship-handling site on Falster*. Højbjerg.

Skamby Madsen, J. & Vinner, M. 2005: Skibe, navigation og havne & Søvejen til Aros. In A. Damm (ed.): *Vikingernes Aros*, 80–105. Højbjerg.

Skre, D. 2007: Towns and Markets, Kings and Central Places in South-western Scandinavia. In D. Skre (ed.): *Kaupang in Skiringssal. Kaupang Excavation Project. Publication Series, Volume 1*, 445–469. Aarhus/Oslo.

Sköld, E. 2006: *Kulturlandskapets förändringar inom röjningsröseområdet Yttra Berg, Halland – en pollenanalytisk undersökning av de senaste 5000 åren*. Unpublished student report in geology at Lunds Universitet, 196. Lund.

Snorre Sturluson: *Heimskringla. Olav Tryggvasons saga*. In F. Hødnebø & H. Magerøy 1979a (eds.): Norge konge sagaer, bind 1. Oslo.

Snorre Sturluson: *Heimskringla. Olav den helliges saga (Annen del)*. In F. Hødnebø & H. Magerøy (eds.) 1979b: Norge konge sagaer, bind 2. Oslo.

Sorokin, P. 2015: The medieval vessels in the northwest Russia on written and archaeological sources. Paper presented at the symposium: *International Symposium on Boat and Ship Archaeology 14. Baltic and beyond. Change and continuity in shipbuilding*. National Maritime Museum in Gdansk, Polen, 21–25 September.

Steensberg, A. 1979: *Draved. An Experiment in Stone Age Agriculture. Burning, Sowing and Harvesting*. Copenhagen.

Stefánsson, H. 1997: Medieval Icelandic Churches. In L. Árnadóttir & K. Kiran (eds.): *Church and Art. The medieval church in Norway and Iceland*, 25–41. Reykjavik.

Stenholm, L. 1986: *Ränderna går aldrig ur – en bebyggelsehistorisk studie av Blekinges dansktid*. Lund Studies in Medieval Archaeology 2. Lund.

Steuer, H. 2006: Warrior Bands, War Lords, and the Birth of Tribes and States in the First Millennium AD in Middle Europe. In T. Otto, H. Thrane & H. Vandkilde (eds.): *Warfare and society. Archaeological and Social Anthropological Perspectives*, 227–236. Aarhus.

Stilke, H. 2001: Grauware des 8. bis 11. Jahrhunderts. In H. Lüdtke & K. Schietzel (eds.): *Handbuch zur mittelalterlichen Keramik in Nordeuropa, Band 1: Text*, 23–82. Neumünster.

Stoklund, B. 1998: Bønder og binæringer. *Bol og By, landbohistorisk tidsskrift* 1998 (2), 8–40.

Suenson, E. 1922: *Byggematerialer. Metaller, Træ, Natursten, lervarer, Mørtler, Beton, Kunststen, Glas. Fremstilling, Egenskaber, Anvendelse, Prøvning*. 2. Bind: Træ, Plantestoffer, Varme- og Lydisolering. Copenhagen.

Sugita, S. 1994: Pollen representation of vegetation in Quaternary sediments: theory and method in patchy vegetation. *Jounal of Ecology* 82, 881–897.

Surminski, J. 1997: Ancient Methods of Wood Tar and Birch Tar Production. In W. Brzezinski & W. Piotrowski (eds.): *Proceedings of the First International Symposium on Wood Tar and Pitch*, 117–121. Warsaw.

Svabo, J. [1781–1782] 1959: *Indberetninger Fra en reise i Færøe. Om baade*. Copenhagen.

Svanberg, F. 2003: *Death Rituals in South-East Scandinavia AD 800–1000. Decolonizing the Viking Age 2*. Acta Archaeologica Lundensia Series in 4, No. 24. Lund.

Svanberg, F. & Söderberg, B. 2000: Arkeologiska lämningar och historiska förhållanden. In F. Svanberg, B. Söderberg (eds.): *Porten till Skåne. Löddeköpinge under järnålder och medeltid*, 310–320. Malmö.

Sverris Saga. Tilrettelagt og udgivet af þorleifur Hauksson i 2007. In J. Kristjánsson & þ. I. Gudjónsson (eds.): Íslenzk Fornri XXX. Reykjavík.

Sørensen, A. C. 2001: *Ladby. A Danish Ship-Grave from the Viking Age*. Ships and Boats of the North 3. Roskilde.

Sørensen, T., Krogh-Nielsen, M., Broen, M., Tavs Ravn, S. and Dael, M. forthcoming: The Gislinge Boat Open Source Project: an old boat and a new idea. *EXARC journal*.

Sørensen, T.F. 2015: Sømløse sammenvævninger? Rekonstruktionens realitet og virkelighed. I: H. Lyngstrøm (ed.): *Stof til eftertanke – rekonstruktion af vikingetidens* dragt, 13–16. Copenhagen.

Tauber, H. 1965: *Differential pollen dispersion and the interpretation of pollen diagrams. With a contribution to the interpretation of the elm fall*. Danmarks Geologiske Undersøgelser, serie II, 89. Copenhagen.

Thestrup, C.S. 1756: *Danmarks og Norges Krigs-Armatur i de ældste, mellemste og sidste Tider*. Kiøbenhavn.

Thier, K. 2002: *Altenglische Terminologie für Schiffe und Schiffsteile. Archäologie und Sprachgeschichte 500–1100*. BAR. International Series. Oxford.

Thirslund, S. & Poulsen, H. 1986: Jens Kusk Jensens praktiske forsøg og rekonstruktioner. *Handels- og Søfartsmuseets årbog* 1986, 99–134.

Thorvildsen, K. 1957: *Ladby-Skibet*. Copenhagen.

Tullberg, J. 2010: Var Danmark nogen sinde et stammesamfund? *Tidskrift for historie 1066* 40 (3): 23–31.

Turney-High, H. [1949]1991: *Primitive War. Its Practice and Concepts*. Columbia, USA.

Ulriksen, J. 1998: *Anløbspladser. Besejling og bebyggelse I Danmark mellem 200 og 1100 e. Kr.* Roskilde.

Vadstrup, S. 1984: *Referat af møde i ROAR's styringsgruppe, fredag den 26. oktober 1984 kl. 10.* Skrevet af Søren Vadstrup den 11. november 1984. Unpublished. Roskilde.

Vadstrup, S. 1991: *Projekt Helge. Byggedagbog. 1990–1991.* Unpublished. Roskilde.

Vadstrup, S. 1993a: *I vikingernes kølvand. Erfaringer og forsøg med danske, svenske og norske kopier af vikingeskibe 1892–1992.* Roskilde.

Vadstrup, S. 1993b: *Rapport over rekonstruktion og bygning af Skuldelev 5-kopien Helge Ask for Vikingeskibshallen i Roskilde oktober 1990 til august 1991. Skroget 1. del. Baggrund, rekonstruktions-grundlag og rekonstruktion, træ- og jernteknologi samt erfaringer og litteratur.* Unpublished report. Roskilde.

Vadstrup, S. 1993c: *Rapport over rekonstruktion og bygning af Skuldelev 5-kopien Helge Ask for Vikingeskibshallen i Roskilde oktober 1990 til august 1991. Skroget 2. del. Arbejdsbeskrivelse A. Arbejdsbeskrivelser og arbejdstegninger til: Køl, stævne, bordplanker, bordlægning, overfladebehandling og farver.* Unpublished report. Roskilde.

Vadstrup, S. 1993d: *Rapport over rekonstruktion og bygning af Skuldelev 5-kopien Helge Ask for Vikingeskibshallen i Roskilde oktober 1990 til august 1991. Skroget 3. del. Arbejdsbeskrivelse B. Arbejdsbeskrivelser og arbejdstegninger til skrogets indvendige dele samt ror, årer, skjolde, anker, dragehoved og -hale.* Unpublished report. Roskilde.

Vadstrup, S. 1995: *Rapport over rekonstruktion og bygning af Skuldelev 5-kopien Helge Ask for Vikingeskibshallen i Roskilde oktober 1990 til august 1991. Skroget 4. del. Værktøj til vikingeskibsbygning.* Unpublished report. Roskilde.

Vadstrup, S. 1997a: Kapitel 2. Materialerne. In E. Andersen, O. Crumlin-Pedersen, S. Vadstrup & M. Vinner: *Roar Ege. Skuldelev 3 skibet som arkæologisk eksperiment*, 35–48. Roskilde.

Vadstrup, S. 1997b: Kapitel 4. Bygning af skroget. In E. Andersen, O. Crumlin-Pedersen, S. Vadstrup & M. Vinner: *Roar Ege. Skuldelev 3 skibet som arkæologisk eksperiment*, 75–139. Roskilde.

Valentin Eriksen, B. 2000: Chaîne opératoire – den operative proces og kunsten at tænke som en flinthugger. In B. Valentin Eriksen (ed.): *Flintstudier. En håndbog i systematiske analyser af flintinventarer*, 75–100. Århus.

Valtavuo-Pfeifer, R. 1989: Interessanta namn på åländska hamnar. In L. Peterson (ed.): *Studia onomastica. Festskrift till Thorstein Andersson, 23.2.1989*, 405–413. Stockholm.

Varenius, B. 1998: *han ägde bo och skeppslid. Om rumslighet och relationer i vikingatid och medeltid.* Studia Archaeologica Universitatis Umensis 10. Umeå.

Varenius, B. 2002: Maritime warfare as an organizing principle in Scandinavian society 1000–1300 AD. In A. Nørgård Jørgensen, J. Pind, L. Jørgensen & B. Clausen (eds.): *Maritime Warfare in Northern Europe. Technology, organization, logistics and administration 500 BC–1500 AD. Papers from an International Research Seminar at the Danish national museum, Copenhagen, 3–5 May 2000*, 249–256. Publications from the National Museum. Studies in Archaeology & History 6. Copenhagen.

Vellev, J. 2004: Om Sorø Klosters Gavebog – og om produktion af jern og salt i Halland. *Hikuin* 31, 37–66.

Villumsen, J. D. & Raben, J. 2010: *Duelighedsbogen.* Copenhagen.

Vinner, M. 1997a: Grundlag for prøvesejladser. In E. Andersen, O. Crumlin-Pedersen, S. Vadstrup & M. Vinner: *Roar Ege. Skuldelev 3 skibet som arkæologisk eksperiment*, 233–244. Roskilde.

Vinner, M. 1997b: Erfaringer fra sejladsforsøg. In E. Andersen, O. Crumlin-Pedersen, S. Vadstrup & M. Vinner: *Roar Ege. Skuldelev 3 skibet som arkæologisk eksperiment*, 259–271. Roskilde.

Voss, O. 1986: Jernudvindingsanlæg i Danmark fra forhistorisk og historisk tid. *Arkæologiske Udgravninger i Danmark* 1985, 25–30.

Voss, O. 1993a: Jernudvinding. In S. Hvass & B. Storgaard (eds.): *Da klinger i muld… 25 års arkæologi i Danmark*, 206–209. Århus.

Voss, O. 1993b: Snorup. Et jernudvindingsområde i Sydvestjylland. *Nationalmuseets Arbejdsmark* 1993, 97–111.

Voss, O. 1995: Arkæologiske spor efter middelalderens jernudvinding i det nuværende Danmark. In S.-O. Olsson (ed.): *Medeltida danskt järn. framsställning av och handel med järn i Skåneland och Småland under medeltiden*, 27–35. Halmstad.

Voss, O. 2002: Jernproduktionen i Danmark i oldtid og middelalder – status og fremtid. In J. Pind, A. Nørgaard Jørgensen, L. Jørgensen, B. Storgaard, P.O. Rindel & J. Ilkjær (eds.): *Drik – og du vil leve skønt. Festskrift til Ulla Lund Hansen på 60-årsdagen*, 139–148. Publications from the National Museum. Studies in Archaeology & History 7. Copenhagen.

Wagner, P. 1986: Wood Species in Viking Age Shipbuilding. In O. Crumlin-Pedersen & M. Vinner (eds.): *Sailing into the Past. Proceedings of the International Seminar on Replicas of Ancient and medieval Vessels, Roskilde, 1984*, 130–137. Roskilde.

Wahl, T. L. 1999: *Kan ankerfunn spille en rolle i en marinarkæologisk funnkontekst? Et fokus på ankerets utvikling og dets arkeologiske potensiale.* Unpublished kandidat-dissertation. Institut for Arkæologi og Etnologi, Københavns Universitet. København.

Wamers, E. 1995: The Symbolic Significance of the Ship-graves at Haiðaby and Ladby. In O. Crumlin-Pedersen & B.M. Thye (eds.): *The Ship as Symbol in Prehistoric and Medieval Scandinavia*, 149–159. Copenhagen.

Warburg, L. 1974: *Spindebog.* Copenhagen.

Wendrich, W. (ed.) 2012: *Archaeology and Apprenticeship. Body Knowledge, Identity and Communities of Practice.* Tucson.

Wenger, E. 1998: *Communities of practice. Learning, meaning, and identity.* Cambridge.

Westerdahl, C. 1989: *Norrlandsleden I. Källor till det maritime kulturlandskapet. En handbok i marinarkeologisk inventering.* Härnösand.

Westerdahl, C. 2002: The cognitive landscape of naval warfare and defence. Toponymic and archaeological aspects. In A. Nørgård Jørgensen, J. Pind, L. Jørgensen & B. Clausen (eds.): *Maritime Warfare in Northern Europe. Technology, organization, logistics and administration 500 BC–1500 AD. Papers from an International Research Seminar at the Danish national museum, Copenhagen, 3–5 May 2000*, 169–190. Publications from the National Museum. Studies in Archaeology & History 6. Copenhagen.

Westphal, F. 2006: *Die Holzfunde von Haithabu.* Die Ausgrabungen in Haithabu, Elfter Band. Neumünster.

White, L. 2012: A Sticky Business. Characterizing Non-Wooden Shipbuilding Materials Using Intensive Analytical Techniques. Paper presented 9th October 2012 during the 13th International Symposium on Boat and Ship Archaeology, Dutch Maritime Museum, Amsterdam, October 8–12.

Wild, J. P. 1988: *Textiles in archaeology.* Aylesbury.

Williams, G. 2002: Ship-levies in the Viking Age. The methodology of studying military institutions in a semi-historical society. In A. Nørgård Jørgensen, J. Pind, L. Jørgensen & B. Clausen (eds.): *Maritime Warfare in Northern Europe. Technology, organization, logistics and administration 500 BC–1500 AD. Papers from an International Research Seminar at the Danish national museum, Copenhagen, 3–5 May 2000,* 293–308. Publications from the National Museum. Studies in Archaeology & History 6. Copenhagen.

Williams, G. 2008: Raiding and warfare. In S. Brink & N. Price (eds.): *The Viking World,* 193–203. London & New York.

Wimmer, L.F.A. (ed) 1908: *De Danske Runemindesmærker* IV. Copenhagen.

Winther Olesen, M. 2011: Hvornår starter dansk jernudvinding? Kulstof–14 dateringer af midtjyske jernovne fra ældre jernalder. *Museum Midtjylland. Midtjyske fortællinger* 2010, 83–92.

Wright, Q. 1965: *A Study of War. Second Edition, with a Commentary on War since 1942.* Chicago and London.

Zinck, L.H.O. 1893: *Nordisk Archæologi, Stenalderstudier, II.* Copenhagen.

Ödman, A. 2000: Kolonisation och järnskatt i norra Skåne med Vittsjö socken som exempel. In A. Ödman (ed.): *Järn. Wittsjöskog-konferensen 1999,* 7–28. Institute of Archaeology. Report Series No. 75. Lund.

Østergård, E. 2003: *Som syet til jorden. Tekstilfund fra det norrøne Grønland.* Århus.

Aaby, B. 1990: Pollen og jordstøv fortæller om fortidens landbrug. *Nationalmuseets Arbejdsmark* 1990, 130–140.

Aaby, B. 1992: Sjællands kulturlandskaber i jernalderen. In U. Lund Hansen & S. Nielsen (eds.), *Sjællands jernalder. Beretning fra et symposium 24. IV.1990 i København,* 209–236. Copenhagen.

Aaby, B., Robinson, D. & Bloch Jørgensen, A. 1994: En gård fra førromersk jernalder og dens omgivende landskab. *Kuml* 1991–92, 71–103.

Åkerlund, H. 1948: *Rekonstruktion av Äskekärrsskeppet.* Gothenburg.

Catalogue:
11th-century ship finds in Danish waters

The ship finds and parts of ships from the area investigated whose datings make it likely that they were among the operational ships of the 11th century are analysed below. The Äskekärr 1 ship is also analysed, although its find location is not within the primary investigation area of the book. However, since the ship was probably built within the area of investigation, it is included in the catalogue. The terms used in the catalogue are defined in the terminology list. Unless otherwise stated, it is the greatest reconstructed, length, breadth etc., that is listed.

The following abbreviations are used:
- K: Keel.
- S: Stem components.
- Ks&M: Keelson & Mast-fish.
- P: Planks.
- F&I: Frame components & other Internal elements
- Tn: Treenails.
- W: Wedges.
- P&P: Between the Planks.
- P&F: Between Planks & Frame components.
- K&P: Between the Keel & the Planking of the first strake.

Fotevik 1

Find region and location:
Skanør-Falsterbo, Foteviken.
Felling date (construction):
[14]C (Lu-2213, Lu-2214, Lu-2215, K3728 & Lu-2001): 1040-1190. Dendro: ca 1023.
Timber provenance (construction):
Building technique and woods used make it likely that the ship was built in southern Scandinavia.
Felling date (repairs): –
Timber provenance (repairs): –
Length: 10.3 m.
Beam: 2.36 m.
Draught: 0.5 m.

Displacement: Theoretical calculation: 3.1 t.
Cargo or crew capacity:
Ship type: Boat or small cargo ship.
Shipbuilding technology: Nordic.
Woods used: K: oak; P: oak; F&I: oak; Tn: willow and pomaceous fruit.
Fastening: P&P: rivets and roves; P&F: treenails and wedges; K&P: rivets and roves, and spikes.
Propulsion: Both sail and oars.
References: Crumlin-Pedersen 1984: 27-60; Bill 1997: 167-168; Jensen 1999: B36-B37; Crumlin-Pedersen & Olsen 2002: 241; Rosborn 2004: 198.

Fotevik 2

Find region and location:
Skanør-Falsterbo, Foteviken.
Felling date (construction):
[14]C (Lu-2213, Lu-2214, Lu-2215, K3728 & Lu-2001): 1040-1190.
Timber provenance (construction):
Building technique and woods used make it likely that the ship was built in southern Scandinavia.
Felling date (repairs): –
Timber provenance (repairs): –
Length: ca 10 m.
Beam: ca 2 m.
Draught: –
Displacement: –
Cargo or crew capacity: –

Ship type: Boat or small cargo ship.
Shipbuilding technology: Nordic.
Woods used: P: oak; F&I: oak.
Fastening: P&P: Rivets and roves;
P&F: treenails and wedges.
Propulsion: Both sail and oars.
References: Crumlin-Pedersen 1984:
27–60; Bill 1997: 167–168.

Fotevik 3

Find region and location:
Skanør-Falsterbo, Foteviken.
Felling date (construction):
[14]C (Lu-2213, Lu-2214, Lu-2215, K3728
& Lu-2001): 1040-1190.
Timber provenance (construction):
Building technique and woods
used make it likely that the ship
was built in southern Scandinavia.
Felling date (repairs):
Timber provenance (repairs):
Length: More than 20 m.
Beam: –
Draught: –
Displacement: –
Crew capacity: Estimated number
of oars: 30. Theoretical calculation
of maximum crew size: 40.
Ship type: Large personnel carrier.
Shipbuilding technology: Nordic.
Woods used: P: oak; F&I: oak.
Fastening: P&P: rivets and roves;
P&F: treenails and wedges.
Propulsion: Both sail and oars.
References: Crumlin-Pedersen 1984:
27–60; Bill 1997: 167–168.

Fotevik 4

Find region and location:
Skanør-Falsterbo, Foteviken.
Felling date (construction):
[14]C (Lu-2213, Lu-2214, Lu-2215, K3728
& Lu-2001): 1040-1190.
Timber provenance (construction):
Building technique and woods used
make it probable that the ship was
built in southern Scandinavia.

Felling date (repairs): –
Timber provenance (repairs): –
Length: –
Beam: –
Draught: –
Displacement: –
Cargo or crew capacity: –
Ship type: –
Shipbuilding technology: Nordic.
Wood species used: P: oak.
Fastening: P&P: rivets and roves;
P&F: treenails and wedges.
Propulsion: –
References: Crumlin-Pedersen 1984:
27–60; Bill 1997: 167–168.

Fotevik 5

Find region and location:
Skanør-Falsterbo, Foteviken.
Felling date (construction):
[14]C (Lu-2213, Lu-2214, Lu-2215, K3728
& Lu-2001): 1040-1190.
Timber provenance (construction):
Building technique and woods
used make it likely that the ship
was built in southern Scandinavia.
Felling date (repairs): –
Timber provenance (repairs): –
Length: more than 20 m.
Beam: –
Draught: –
Displacement: –
Crew capacity: Estimated number
of oars: 30. Theoretical calculation
of maximum crew size: 40.
Ship type: Large personnel carrier.
Shipbuilding technology: Nordic
Woods used: P: oak; F&I: oak.
Fastening: P&P: rivets and roves;
P&F: treenails and wedges.
Propulsion: Both sail and oars.
References: Crumlin-Pedersen 1984:
27–60; Bill 1997: 167–168.

Fribrødre Å

Find region and location:
Northern Falster, Maglebrænde.
Felling date (construction):
Dendro: 1040-1085. Period
of ship-related activities on site:
1050–1100.
Timber provenance (construction):
Timbers most likely from Denmark,
Scania, Schleswig-Holstein, the southern
Baltic region, the southern and western
regions of Norway and western Sweden
Felling date (repairs):
Timber provenance (repairs):
Length: Minimum ten personnel carriers:
four between 14 and 20 m and six more
than 20 m. Minimum seven cargo ships:
three between 10 and 14 m, two between
14 and 20 m and two more than 20 m.
Minimum two boats less than 10 m.
Beam: –
Draught: –
Displacement: –
Cargo or crew capacity: –
Ship type: Minimum five boats or
small cargo ships, two medium-sized
cargo ships, and two large cargo ships.
Plus a minimum of four medium-
sized personnel carriers and six large
personnel carriers.
Shipbuilding technology: Mixed
technologies (both Slavic and Nordic).
Woods used: K: oak; S: oak; P: oak, beech
& red alder; F&I: oak, red alder, ash,
beech & hazel; Tn: hazel, ash, willow,
hawthorn, elder, buckthorn, maple, oak
& lime; W: oak, willow, beech & red
alder.
Fastening: P&P: rivets and roves, and
treenails and wedges; P&F: treenails
and wedges; K&P: treenails and wedges,
and rivets and roves.
Propulsion: Vessels propelled primarily
by the wind (sail) and vessels propelled
both by sail and oars.
References: Bonde 1984; Skamby Madsen
1984; Skamby Madsen & Klassen 2010.

Hasnæs 2

Find region and location: Djursland, Hasnæs.

Felling date (construction): [14]C (K1097): 1000-1225. Sample from a treenail.

Timber provenance (construction): –

Felling date (repairs): –

Timber provenance (repairs): –

Length: Less than 20 m.

Beam: –

Draught: –

Displacement: –

Crew capacity: Estimated number of oars: 30. Theoretical calculation of maximum crew size: 40.

Ship type: Medium-sized personnel carrier.

Shipbuilding technology: Nordic.

Woods used: Ks&M: oak; P: oak; F&I: oak; Tn: willow.

Fastening: P&P: rivets and roves; P&F: treenails and wedges.

Propulsion: Both sail and oars.

References: The Danish National Maritime Archaeological Archives (Det Marine Arkiv) No. 168; Bill 1997: 174–175.

Hedeby 1

Find region and location: Schleswig-Holstein, in the harbour of Hedeby.

Felling date (construction): Dendro: ca 985.

Timber provenance (construction): Dendro: Schleswig-Holstein

Felling date (repairs): –

Timber provenance (repairs): –

Length: 30 m.

Beam: 2.2 m.

Draught: 0.75 m.

Displacement: Theoretical calculation: 18 t.

Crew capacity: Number of oars: ca 60. Theoretical calculation of maximum crew size: 70.

Ship type: Large personnel carrier.

Shipbuilding technology: Nordic.

Woods used: K: oak; S: oak; Ks&M: oak; P: oak; F&I: oak, ash, red alder & maple; Tn: willow; W: oak.

Fastening: P&P: rivets and roves; P&F: treenails and wedges; K&P: rivets and roves, and spikes.

Propulsion: Both sail and oars.

References: Crumlin-Pedersen 1997b: 81-95, 179-186 & 224-236 & 2010: 83–85; Jensen 1999: B22–B23.

Hedeby 2

Find region and location: Schleswig-Holstein, in the harbour of Hedeby.

Felling date (construction): Dendro: ca 970.

Timber provenance (construction): Dendro: Schleswig-Holstein (not the pine planking)

Felling date (repairs): –

Timber provenance (repairs): –

Length: 9-12 m.

Beam: –

Draught: –

Displacement: –

Cargo or crew capacity: –

Ship type: Boat or small cargo ship.

Shipbuilding technology: Mixed technologies (both Slavic and Nordic).

Woods used: Ks&M: oak; P: oak, pine & beech; F&I: oak; Tn: juniper.

Fastening: P&P: rivets and roves, and treenails and wedges; P&F: treenails and wedges.

Propulsion: Relying primarily on the wind (sail) for propulsion.

References: Crumlin-Pedersen 1997b: 96–99, 179–186 & 236–241.

Hedeby 3

Find region and location: Schleswig-Holstein, in the harbour of Hedeby.

Felling date (construction): Dendro: ca 1025.

Timber provenance (construction): Dendro: Schleswig-Holstein.

Felling date (repairs): –

Timber provenance (repairs): –

Length: ca 22 m.

Beam: ca 6.3 m.

Draught: ca 1.5 m.

Displacement: Theoretical calculation: ca 75 t.

Cargo capacity: Theoretical calculation: ca 60 t.

Ship type: Large cargo ship.

Shipbuilding technology: Nordic.

Woods used: Ks&M: oak; P: oak; F&I: oak, ash, red alder & maple; Tn: willow; W: oak.

Fastening: P&P: rivets and roves; P&F: treenails and wedges; K&P: rivets and roves and spikes.

Propulsion: Relying primarily on wind (sail) for propulsion.

References: Bill 1997: 175–176; Crumlin-Pedersen 1997b: 99–104, 179–186 & 242–251; Jensen 1999: B24–B25; Englert 2015: 326.

Roskilde 3

Find region and location: Zealand, in the harbour of Roskilde.

Felling date (construction): Dendro: ca 1055-1065.

Timber provenance (construction): Dendro: Jutland or Schleswig-Holstein.

Felling date (repairs): –

Timber provenance (repairs): –

Length: ca 20 m.

Beam: ca 4.4 m.

Draught: ca 1 m.

Displacement: –

Cargo capacity: Theoretical calculation: 11 t.

Ship type: Large cargo ship.

Shipbuilding technology: Nordic.

Woods used: K: oak; P: oak; F&I: oak; Tn: conifer; W: oak.

Fastening: P&P: rivets and roves; P&F: treenails and wedges; K&P: spikes.

Propulsion: Relying primarily on the wind (sail).

References: Daly 1999: 2–5; Bill *et al.* 2000: 229–231; Englert 2015: 327; Bill 2006b: 3–35.

Roskilde 6

Find region and location: Zealand, in the harbour of Roskilde.

Felling date (construction): Dendro: ca 1015-1025.

Timber provenance (construction): Dendro: Oslo Fjord region, Norway.

Felling date (repairs): Dendro: after 1039.

Timber provenance (repairs): Dendro: Baltic Sea region.

Length: ca 37 m.

Beam: ca 4 m.

Draught: ca 0.82 m.

Displacement: Theoretical calculation: ca 29 t.

Crew capacity: Number of oars: ca78. Theoretical calculation of maximum crew size: 90.

Ship type: Large personnel carrier.

Shipbuilding technology: Nordic.

Woods used: K: oak; P: oak & beech (rep.); F&I: oak; Tn: conifer.

Fastening: P&P: rivets and roves; P&F: treenails and wedges; K&P: rivets and roves, and spikes.

Propulsion: Both sail and oars.

References: Bill et al. 2000: 217–220; Bill 2007b: Bonde 2010: 2–9; Bonde & Stylegar 2011: 247–249; Gøthche 2012: pers. comm.

Schleswig (Schild, S1)

Find region and location: Schleswig-Holstein, in the city of Schleswig.

Date: Stratigraphy: 11th century.

Timber provenance (construction): –

Felling date (repairs): –

Timber provenance (repairs): –

Length: 12–18 m.

Beam: –

Draught: –

Displacement: –

Cargo or crew capacity: –

Ship type: Boat or small cargo ship.

Shipbuilding technology:

Woods used: Ks&M: oak.

Fastening: –

Propulsion: Relying primarily on wind (sail) for propulsion.

References: Bill 1997:191; Crumlin-Pedersen 1997b: 119 & 261-263.

Schleswig (Plessenstraße, S10)

Find region and location: Schleswig-Holstein, in the city of Schleswig.

Date: Stratigraphy: late 11th century or 12th century.

Timber provenance (construction): –

Felling date (repairs): –

Timber provenance (repairs): –

Length: 10-14 m.

Beam: –

Draught: –

Displacement: –

Cargo or crew capacity: –

Ship type: Boat or small cargo ship.

Shipbuilding technology: –

Woods used: S: oak.

Fastening: –

Propulsion: –

References: Bill 1997:191; Crumlin-Pedersen 1997b: 113 & 265.

Schleswig (Plessenstraße, S21-S31)

Find region and location: Schleswig-Holstein, in the city of Schleswig.

Felling date (construction): Dendro: ca 1095.

Timber provenance (construction): –

Felling date (repairs): –

Timber provenance (repairs): –

Length: 14-20 m.

Beam: –

Draught: –

Displacement: –

Cargo or crew capacity: –

Ship type: Medium-sized cargo ship.

Shipbuilding technology: Nordic.

Woods used: P: oak; F&I: oak.

Fastening: P&P: rivets and roves; P&F: treenails and wedges.

Propulsion: –

References: Bill 1997:191; Crumlin-Pedersen 1997b: 266–268.

Schleswig (Hafenstraße, S40-42, S43-46 & S54-60)

Find region and location: Schleswig-Holstein, in the city of Schleswig.

Date: Stratigraphy: second half of the 11th century.

Timber provenance (construction): –

Felling date (repairs): –

Timber provenance (repairs): –

Length: –

Beam: –

Draught: –

Displacement: –

Cargo or crew capacity: –

Ship type: –

Shipbuilding technology: Nordic.

Woods used: P: oak; F&I: oak; Tn: willow.

Fastening: –

Propulsion: –

References: Bill 1997:192; Crumlin-Pedersen 1997b:115 & 269–273.

Skuldelev 1

Find region and location: Zealand, Roskilde Fjord, 4 km south of Frederikssund.

Felling date (construction): Dendro: ca 1025.

Timber provenance (construction): Dendro: Western Norway, possibly from the Sognefjord region.

Felling date (repairs): Dendro: first phase after ca 1045; second phase after ca 1059.

Timber provenance (repairs): Dendro: first phase: Oslo Fjord region; second phase: eastern Denmark, Scania, Småland or Västergötland.

Length: ca 16 m.

Beam: ca 4.8 m.

Draught: ca 1.28 m.

Displacement: Theoretical calculation: ca 36 t.

Cargo capacity: Theoretical calculation: ca 28 t.

Ship type: Medium-sized cargo ship.

Shipbuilding technology: Nordic.

Woods used: K: oak; S: oak & pine; P: pine & oak;

F&I: pine, oak & lime; Tn: willow; W: pine.

Fastening: P&P: rivets and roves, between the 11th and 12th strakes: treenails and wedges; P&F: treenails and wedges; K&P: spikes. .

Propulsion: Relying primarily on the wind for propulsion (by sail).

References: Olsen & Crumlin-Pedersen 1969: 131; Bartholin 1998; Jensen 1999: B28–B29; Englert 2015: 328; Crumlin-Pedersen & Olsen 2002: 65–66 & 97–140; Crumlin-Pedersen 2010: 109–110.

Skuldelev 2

Find region and location: Zealand, Roskilde Fjord, 4 km south of Frederikssund.

Felling date (construction): Dendro: ca 1042.

Timber provenance (construction): Dendro: Ireland, possibly from the Dublin and Waterford region.

Felling date (repairs): Dendro: 1059–1095.

Timber provenance (repairs): Dendro: England.

Length: 29.2–31.2 m.

Beam: ca 3.74 m.

Draught: ca 0.88 m.

Displacement: Theoretical calculation: ca 21.4 t.

Crew capacity: Number of oars: ca 60. Theoretical calculation of maximum crew size: 70.

Ship type: Large personnel carrier.

Shipbuilding technology: Nordic.

Woods used: K: oak; S: oak; Ks&M: oak; P: oak; F&I: oak and willow; Tn: willow; W: pine & oak.

Fastening: P&P: rivets and roves; P&F: treenails and wedges; K&P: spikes.

Propulsion: Both sail and oars.

References: Bonde 1999; Jensen 1999: B34–B35; Crumlin-Pedersen & Olsen 2002: 66–67 & 141–194.

Skuldelev 3

Find region and location: Zealand, Roskilde Fjord, 4 km south of Frederikssund.

Felling date (construction): Dendro: 1030-1039.

Timber provenance (construction): Dendro: Western Denmark.

Felling date (repairs): Dendro: after 1035.

Timber provenance (repairs): –

Length: ca 14 m.

Beam: ca 3.3 m.

Draught: ca 0.90 m.

Displacement: ca 9.6 t.

Cargo capacity: Theoretical calculation: ca 4.6 t.

Ship type: Medium-sized cargo ship.

Shipbuilding technology: Nordic.

Woods used: K: oak; S: oak; Ks&M: oak; P: oak; F&I: oak and beech; Tn: willow; W: oak & willow.

Fastening: P&P: rivets and roves; P&F: treenails and wedges; K&P: rivets and roves, and spikes.

Propulsion: Relying primarily on wind (sail) for propulsion.

References: Bonde 1998; Jensen 1999: B30-B31; Englert 2015: 330; Crumlin-Pedersen & Olsen 2002: 67 & 195–243; Crumlin-Pedersen 2010: 110.

Skuldelev 5

Find region and location: Zealand, Roskilde Fjord, 4 km south of Frederikssund.

Felling date (construction): Dendro: after 1024, probably between 1030 and 1049.

Timber provenance (construction): Dendro: Jutland, Schleswig-Holstein or Scania.

Felling date (repairs): Dendro: after 1055, probably between 1060 and 1079.

Timber provenance (repairs): –

Length: ca 17.3 m.

Beam: ca 2.47 m.

Draught: ca 0.54 m.

Displacement: Theoretical calculation: ca 6.1 t.

Crew capacity: Number of oars: ca 26. Theoretical calculation of maximum crew size: 40.

Ship type: Medium-sized personnel carrier.

Shipbuilding technology: Nordic.

Woods used: K: oak; S: oak; Ks&M: oak; P: oak, pine, ash & red alder; F&I: oak; pine & red alder; Tn: willow; W: oak.

Fastening: P&P: rivets and roves; P&F: treenails and wedges; K&P: rivets and roves, and spikes.

Propulsion: Both sail and oars.

References: Olsen & Crumlin-Pedersen 1969: 131; Jensen 1999: B26-B27; Crumlin-Pedersen & Olsen 2002: 67-68 & 245-278; Crumlin-Pedersen 2010: 86-87.

Skuldelev 6 (the rebuilt version)

Find region and location: Zealand, Roskilde Fjord, 4 km south of Frederikssund.

Felling date (construction): Dendro: after 1026, probably between 1030 and 1049.

Timber provenance (construction): Dendro: Western Norway, possibly from the Sognefjord region.

Felling date (repairs): –

Timber provenance (repairs): –

Length: ca 11.2 m.

Beam: ca 2.15 m.

Draught: ca 0.63 m.

Displacement: Theoretical calculation: ca 4.6 t.

Cargo capacity: Theoretical calculation: ca 3 t.

Ship type: Boat or small cargo ship.

Shipbuilding technology: Nordic.

Woods used: K: oak; S: Pine?; P: pine & oak; F&I: red alder, beech, birch, pine & oak; Tn: pine; W: pine.

Fastening: P&P: rivets and roves; P&F: treenails and wedges; K&P: rivets and roves, and spikes.

Propulsion: Both sail and oars.
References: Olsen & Crumlin-Pedersen 1969: 131; Jensen 1999: B32-B33; Crumlin-Pedersen & Olsen 2002: 68 & 279–304.

Äskekärr 1

Find region and location: Västergötland, Götä Älv valley, ca 25 km upriver from Gothenburg.

Felling date (construction):
  Dendro: ca 1000.
Timber provenance (construction):
  Dendro: Götä Älv valley.
Felling date (repairs): –
Timber provenance (repairs): –
Length: ca 15.8
Beam: ca 4.5
Draught: ca 1.17
Displacement: Theoretical calculation: ca 29 t.
Cargo capacity: Theoretical calculation: ca 20 t.

Ship type: Medium-sized cargo ship.
Shipbuilding technology: Nordic.
Woods used: K: oak; S: oak; Ks&M: oak; P: oak; F&I: oak; Tn: juniper; W: pine;
Fastening: P&P: rivets and roves; P&F: treenails and wedges.
Propulsion: Relying primarily on wind (sail) for propulsion.
References: Humbla 1934: 1-21; Åkerlund 1948; Bråthen 1998: 13-15; Borg **et al**. 2000; Englert 2015: 325; Jakobsson 2003.

Appendix 1:
Analyses of 11th-century ship finds in Danish waters

Appendix 1 contains an analysis of the 59 ship finds that make up the primary empirical material of the book. In the following, the dating and provenance of the ship finds, the ship dimensions and ship types, and the hydrostatic data and methods of propulsion for the ships are analysed.

Dating and provenance

The datings of the ship finds are based partly on the methods of natural science,[1] partly on archaeological methods.[2] Five ships[3] have been dated exclusively using ^{14}C analysis; 12 ships[4] and the Fribrødre Å complex have been dated using dendrochronological analyses. Three ships[5] have been dated using stratigraphical analysis, and finally, one ship[6] has been dated by combining ^{14}C analysis and dendrochronological analysis (fig. 1).

Attempts have been made to identify the approximate construction date and the construction site for the ship finds as well as the date and place of repairs. In this connection, it should be remarked that dendrochronological and ^{14}C analyses date the period during which the tree from which the ship's timber was made was felled. If a log or a plank was stored before it was used for the actual building, the construction period may be inaccurate.

In five cases it has been possible to demonstrate a dating period for the subsequent repair of a ship (fig. 1), which among other things makes an approximate assessment of its useful life possible.[7] All these datings are based on dendrochronological analyses, which, furthermore, in three cases enabled the identification of a probable area where the repair was carried out (fig. 2).

The Fotevik ships have not been provenanced by means of tree-ring analysis, but the raw materials used and the building technology suggest that the ships were built in southern Scandinavia (fig. 2).

Dimensions

In 12 cases both the length and breadth of the ship could be determined. All lengths and breadths are stated as the length and breadth of reconstructions of operational ships. For the ship finds Fotevik 2, 3 and 5, neither length nor breadth could be reconstructed because of the character of the preserved find material; hence the dimensions stated are only estimated measurements. The lengths of the ship finds from Hasnæs 2, Hedeby 2, Fribrødre Å and Schleswig Schild S1, as well as Plessenstraße S10 and S21-S31 could only be estimated and the breadths of the ships could not be determined. The ships and ship parts from Fotevik 4, as well as Schleswig Hafenstraße S40–42, S43–46 and S54–60 could not provide a basis for a reconstruction of length and breadth (fig. 3).

In 11 cases it has been possible to reconstruct the draught. In these cases the point of departure is a fully loaded or equipped ship (fig. 3).

1. [14]C and dendrochronological analyses.
2. Typologies and stratigraphic observations.
3. Fotevik 2–5 & Hasnæs 2.
4. Hedeby 1–3; Roskilde 3 & 6; Skuldelev 1–6; Schleswig: Plessenstraße S21-S31.
5. Schleswig: Schild 1, Plessenstraße S10 & Hafenstraße S40–42, S43–46 & S54–60.
6. Fotevik 1.
7. See chapter III, section: Building and maintaining war fleets, for a more detailed account.

Fig. 1. Dating of building phase and repair phases. Based on data from the catalogue. Table: The author, Viking Ship Museum in Roskilde.

Ship finds	Number of ships	Date (AD.): Building phase	Date (AD.): Repairs
Fotevik 1	1	^{14}C: 1040-1190 Dendro: Ca 1023	
Fotevik 2	1	^{14}C: 1040-1190	
Fotevik 3	1	^{14}C: 1040-1190	
Fotevik 4	1	^{14}C: 1040-1190	
Fotevik 5	1	^{14}C: 1040-1190	
Fribrødre Å	Minimum 38	Dendro: 1040-1085. Period of ship related activities on site: 1050-1100.	
Hasnæs 2	1	^{14}C: 1000-1225	
Hedeby 1	1	Dendro: Ca 985	
Hedeby 2	1	Dendro: Ca 970	
Hedeby 3	1	Dendro: Ca 1025	
Roskilde 3	1	Dendro: Ca 1055-1065	
Roskilde 6	1	Dendro: Ca 1015-1025	Dendro: After 1039
Schleswig (Schild, S1)	1	Stratigraphic: 11th-century	
Schleswig (Plessenstraße, S10)	1	Stratigraphic: After 1095	
Schleswig (Hafenstraße, S40-42, S43-46 & S54-60)	1	Stratigraphic: 1050-1100	
Skuldelev 1	1	Dendro: Ca 1025	Dendro: First phase: After ca 1045 Second phase: After ca 1059
Skuldelev 2	1	Dendro: Ca 1042	Dendro: 1059-1095
Skuldelev 3	1	Dendro: 1030-1039	Dendro: After 1035
Skuldelev 5	1	Dendro: After 1024, probably between 1030-1049	Dendro: After 1055, probably between 1060-1079
Skuldelev 6 (the rebuilt version)	1	Dendro: After 1026, probably between 1030-1049	
Äskekärr 1	1	Dendro: Ca 1000	

Fig. 2. Timber provenance, building phase and repair phases. Based on data from the catalogue. Table: The author, Viking Ship Museum in Roskilde.

Ship finds	Timber provenance: Building phase	Timber provenance: Repairs
Fotevik 1	Building technique and applied tree species make it probable that the ship was built in southern Scandinavia	
Fotevik 2	Building technique and applied tree species make it probable that the ship was built in southern Scandinavia	
Fotevik 3	Building technique and applied tree species make it probable that the ship was built in southern Scandinavia	
Fotevik 4	Building technique and applied tree species make it probable that the ship was built in southern Scandinavia	
Fotevik 5	Building technique and applied tree species make it probable that the ship was built in southern Scandinavia	
Fribrødre Å	Timbers most likely from both Denmark, Scania, Schleswig-Holstein, the southern Baltic Sea region, the southern and western regions of Norway and the western Sweden	
Hasnæs 2		
Hedeby 1	Dendro: Schleswig-Holstein	
Hedeby 2	Dendro: Schleswig-Holstein (not the pine planking)	
Hedeby 3	Dendro: Schleswig-Holstein	
Roskilde 3	Dendro: Jutland or Schleswig-Holstein	
Roskilde 6	Dendro: The Oslo Fjord region, Norway	Dendro: The Baltic Sea region
Schleswig (Schild, S1)		
Schleswig (Plessenstraße, S10)		
Schleswig (Plessenstraße, S21-S31)		
Schleswig (Hafenstraße, S40-42, S43-46 & S54-60)		
Skuldelev 1	Dendro: Western Norway, possibly from the Sognefjord region	Dendro: First phase: Oslo Fjord region Second phase: Eastern Denmark, Scania, Småland or West Gothland (Västergötland)
Skuldelev 2	Dendro: Ireland, possibly from the Dublin and Waterford region	Dendro: England
Skuldelev 3	Dendro: Western Denmark	
Skuldelev 5	Dendro: Jutland, Schleswig-Holstein or Scania	
Skuldelev 6 (the rebuilt version)	Dendro: Western Norway, possibly from the Sognefjord region	
Äskekärr 1	Dendro: Götä Älv valley	

Appendix 1: Analyses of 11th-century ship finds in Danish waters

Fig. 3. Reconstructed length, beam and draught. Based on data from the catalogue. Table: The author, Viking Ship Museum in Roskilde.

Ship finds	Length (m)	Beam (m)	Draught (m)
Fotevik 1	Ca 10.3	Ca 2.36	Ca 0.5
Fotevik 2	Ca 10	Ca 2	
Fotevik 3	More than 20		
Fotevik 4			
Fotevik 5	More than 20		
Fribrødre Å	Minimum ten personnel carriers: Four between 14-20 & six more than 20; Minimum seven cargo ships: Three between 10-14, two between14-20 & two more than 20; Minimum two boats less than 10		
Hasnæs 2	Less than 20		
Hedeby 1	Ca 30	Ca 2.2	Ca 0.75
Hedeby 2	9-12		
Hedeby 3	Ca 22	Ca 6.3	Ca 1.5
Roskilde 3	Ca 20	Ca 4.4	Ca 1
Roskilde 6	Ca 37	Ca 4	Ca 0.82
Schleswig (Schild, S1)	12-18		
Schleswig (Plessenstraße, S10)	10-14		
Schleswig (Plessenstraße, S21-S31)	14-20		
Schleswig (Hafenstraße, S40-42, S43-46 & S54-60)			
Skuldelev 1	Ca 16	Ca 4.8	Ca 1.28
Skuldelev 2	29.2-31.2	Ca 3.74	Ca 0.88
Skuldelev 3	Ca 14	Ca 3.3	Ca 0.90
Skuldelev 5	Ca 17.3	Ca 2.47	Ca 0.54
Skuldelev 6 (the rebuilt version)	Ca 11.2	Ca 2.15	Ca 0.63
Äskekärr 1	Ca 15.8	Ca 4.5	Ca 1.17

Displacement, and cargo and crew capacity

Displacement is understood as the estimated maximum weight of a fully equipped or loaded vessel. Cargo capacity is understood as the estimated maximum cargo, measured by weight, that a vessel can load and still remain seaworthy.[8]

It is possible to reconstruct the displacement for ten ships by theoretical calculations, and it is further possible to propose a theoretical reconstructed cargo-carrying capacity for five of these ten. In addition to this, Roskilde 3's cargo capacity could be reconstructed theoretically, but the displacement for this ship has not yet been estimated (fig. 4).

Traditionally, only the cargo capacity of cargo ships is stated. The capacity of the personnel carriers is described in terms of the estimated maximum number of crew members that the ship in question can carry and the maximum number of oars that can be manned (figs. 5 & 6).

Aboard the cargo ships, the size of the crew can be kept to the number necessary to handle the ship during sailing so that the volume of cargo can be as large as possible. If the intention was to transport as many warriors as possible by sea, cargo ships were probably also used. In that case the warriors must have been regarded as passengers rather than part of the crew, and it would thus still be desirable that the number of crew was small so that the number of warriors could be maximised.[9]

8. See Terminology for a detailed explanation of the two terms.
9. Crumlin-Pedersen & Olsen 2002: 137.

Ship finds	Displacement (t)	Cargo capacity (t)
Fotevik 1	Ca 3.1	
Hedeby 1	Ca 18	
Hedeby 3	Ca 75	Ca 60
Roskilde 3		Ca 11
Roskilde 6	Ca 29	
Skuldelev 1	Ca 36	Ca 28
Skuldelev 2	Ca 21.4	
Skuldelev 3	Ca 9.6	Ca 4.6
Skuldelev 5	Ca 6.1	
Skuldelev 6 (the rebuilt version)	Ca 4.7	Ca 3
Äskekärr 1	Ca 29	Ca 20

Fig. 4. Displacement and cargo capacity. Based on data from the catalogue. Table: The author, Viking Ship Museum in Roskilde.

Appendix 1: Analyses of 11th-century ship finds in Danish waters

Fig. 5. Number of oars on board the personnel carriers. Based on data from the catalogue. Table: The author, Viking Ship Museum in Roskilde.

Ship finds	Number of oars
Fotevik 3	Est. 30
Fotevik 5	Est. 30
Hasnæs 2	Est. 30
Hedeby 1	Ca 60
Roskilde 6	Ca 78
Skuldelev 2	Ca 60
Skuldelev 5	Ca 26

Fig. 6. Crew capacity on board the personnel carriers. Based on data from the catalogue. Table: The author, Viking Ship Museum in Roskilde.

Ship finds	Theoretical calculation of maximum crew size	Best functioning crew size (based on trial voyages)
Fotevik 3	40	
Fotevik 5	40	
Hasnæs 2	40	
Hedeby 1	70	
Roskilde 6	90	
Skuldelev 2	70	60
Skuldelev 5	40	30

Propulsion

The propulsion of a vessel through the water is affected on the one hand actively, with the crew of the vessel performing actions, on the other passively by letting current and wind propel the vessel. The passive propulsion can be exploited actively when the currents in the waters are known, and the wind can also be exploited actively for propulsion by setting a sail. In the following, it is the active propulsion that is analysed.

The degree of preservation of the ship parts from Fotevik 4 and Schleswig Plessenstraße, S10 and S21-S31, and of Schleswig Hafenstraße, S40–42, S43–46 and S54–60, does not permit the procurement of useful data on how these ships were propelled (fig. 7).

Ten ships were propelled by a combination of oars and sail. This group of ships can be subdivided into personnel carriers (Fotevik 3, Fotevik 5, Hasnæs 2, Hedeby 1, Roskilde 6, Skuldelev 2 and Skuldelev 5) and small or medium-sized cargo ships (Fotevik 1, Fotevik 2 and Skuldelev 6).

In the case of seven ships (Hedeby 2, Hedeby 3, Roskilde 3, Skuldelev 1, Skuldelev 3, Schleswig Schild S1 and Äskekärr 1) the sail was used as the primary propulsion method, while for harbour manoeuvres or other special manoeuvres oars and poles might have been used. This group consists entirely of cargo ships: two large[10] and four medium-sized.[11] Finally, the Fribrødre Å site ship components were excavated on the one hand from ships primarily propelled by sail, and on the other hand from ships where the propulsion was based on both sail and oars (fig. 7).

10. Hedeby 3 and Roskilde 3.
11. Schild S1, Skuldelev 1, Skuldelev 3 and Äskekärr 1.

Fig. 7. Propulsion. A: Vessels propelled by both sail and oars. B: Vessels relying primarily on wind (sail) for propulsion. Manoeuvres may have been conducted with oars or poles. Table: The author, Viking Ship Museum in Roskilde.

	A	B
Fotevik 1	×	
Fotevik 2	×	
Fotevik 3	×	
Fotevik 4		
Fotevik 5	×	
Fribrødre Å	×	
Hasnæs 2	×	
Hedeby 1	×	
Hedeby 2		×
Hedeby 3		×
Roskilde 3		×
Roskilde 6	×	
Schleswig (Schild, S1)		×
Schleswig (Plessenstraße, S10)		
Schleswig (Plessenstraße, S21-S31)		
Schleswig (Hafenstraße, S40-42, S43-46 & S54-60)		
Skuldelev 1		×
Skuldelev 2	×	
Skuldelev 3		×
Skuldelev 5	×	
Skuldelev 6 (the rebuilt version)	×	
Äskekärr 1		×

Ship find complexes and individual ship finds

The ship finds can be divided into two categories: one consisting of complexes of ship parts, where the archaeological material is so fragmentary, primarily consisting of stray finds of ship parts, that it renders a detailed analysis of the individual ship find impossible; and one consisting of the ship finds whose character and state of preservation permit an analysis of each ship.

Fribrødre Å is described as a complex of vessel parts (fig. 8). The Fribrødre Å site has been interpreted as a place where ships were repaired and fitted out, primarily with re-used ship parts,[12] and as a place where new ships were built, mainly with re-used ship parts.[13] The most recent, highly comprehensive analysis and presentation of the find[14] shows that primary products for ship parts[15] are absent, and that the percentage of newly manufactured ship parts is very small. In addition the topographical fea-

tures at the site indicate that true newbuilding of ships would have been difficult – because of the lack of space for building and launching new, large ships.[16] In summary, it is less likely that new ships were built at the site, but it cannot be wholly precluded. The number of ships that were repaired or fitted out can be interpreted as at least 22, probably closer to 50. Since only a small part of the site has been excavated, Lutz Klassen states that the number of vessels that were repaired and fitted out was probably several hundred. However, the archaeological material only permits the identification of a minimum of 19 vessels: six large personnel carriers, four medium-sized personnel carriers, two large cargo ships, two medium-sized cargo ships, and three small cargo ships, as well as two boats; and a maximum of 38 vessels: 11 large personnel carriers, 11 medium-sized personnel carriers, three large cargo ships, three medium-sized cargo ships and eight small cargo ships, as well as two boats.[17]

12. Skamby Madsen 1984; Klassen 2010: 302–305.
13. Crumlin-Pedersen 1997b: 77; Indruszewski *et al.* 2006: 183.
14. Skamby Madsen & Klassen 2010.
15. Processed raw materials.
10. Klassen 2010: 302–304.
17. Klassen 2010: 116–121.

Fig. 8. Identified ship types from the Fribrødre Å ship-find complex. Based on data from Klassen 2010: 119. Table: The author, Viking Ship Museum in Roskilde.

	Fribrødre Å Minimum identified	Maximum identified
Boats or small cargo ships	2	2
Small cargo ships	3	8
Medium-sized cargo ships	2	3
Largo cargo ships	2	3
Medium-sized personnel carriers	4	11
Large personnel carriers	6	11
Sum	19	38

The 21 vessel finds whose state of preservation permits a more detailed analysis can be divided into five different vessel types and sizes. Five vessels are interpreted as either boats or small cargo ships. Five medium-sized cargo ships and two large cargo ships can be identi-fied, and the personnel carriers can be divided in size into two medium-sized and five large ships. Neither Fotevik 4 nor the ship components from Hafenstraße in Schleswig – S40–42, S43–46 and S54–60 – can be typed (fig. 9).

Fig. 9. Ship finds and ship types. Based on data from the catalogue. Table: The author, Viking Ship Museum in Roskilde.

Ship finds	Boats or small cargo ships	Medium-sized cargo ships	Large cargo ships	Medium-sized personnel carriers	Large personnel carriers
Fotevik 1	✕				
Fotevik 2	✕				
Fotevik 3					✕
Fotevik 4					
Fotevik 5					✕
Hasnæs 2				✕	
Hedeby 1					✕
Hedeby 2	✕				
Hedeby 3			✕		
Roskilde 3			✕		
Roskilde 6					✕
Schleswig (Schild, S1)		✕			
Schleswig (Plessenstraße, S10)	✕				
Schleswig (Plessen-straße, S21-S31)		✕			
Schleswig (Hafenstraße, S40-42, S43-46 & S54-60)					
Skuldelev 1		✕			
Skuldelev 2					✕
Skuldelev 3		✕			
Skuldelev 5				✕	
Skuldelev 6 (the rebuilt version)	✕				
Äskekärr 1		✕			
Sum	5	5	2	2	5

Appendix 2:

Speed analysis of the Skuldelev 5 reconstruction *Helge Ask*

The analysis below is based on the Viking Ship Museum's sailing database. The data has been interpreted in collaboration between Anton Englert and the author. Due to light wind, the stretches marked with darker blue shading have been interpreted as sailed in unfavourable conditions.

Area and date	Route	Duration of voyage	DMG (measured in nm)	Theoretical daily average (measured in nm)	Wind force and direction
Kattegat					
3 July 2003	Als Odde – Odden Harbour	11 h, 10 min	59.6	127	Gentle breeze, NE-NW winds
24 July 2008	Ramsjö – Gilleleje	11 h, 07 min	20.3	44	Light breeze, NW winds
12 July 2009	Lynæs – Anholt	16 h, 33 min	49.6	72	Light/gentle breeze, W-SSW winds
14 July 2009	Anholt – Læsø	16 h, 43 min	41.1	59	Light/gentle breeze, S winds
21 July 2010	Hallands Väderö – Anholt	12 h, 47 min	39.7	75	Light/gentle breeze, SE-SSE winds
17 – 18 July 2011	Rørvig – Anholt	9 h, 44 min	48.5	120	Gentle/moderate breeze, S winds
20 – 21 July 2011	Anholt – Grenå	14 h, 30 min	27.3	45	Light/gentle breeze, SW-N winds
28 July 2011	Hjelm – Lynæs	9 h, 30 min	39.8	101	Gentle breeze, NNW winds

(DMG: *Distance Made Good*, the shortest navigable route between harbours)